KU-436-192

'The Trouble with Kids Today'

Youth and crime in post-war Britain

John Muncie

Lecturer in Social Policy at the Open University

Hutchinson

London Melbourne Sydney Auckland Johannesburg

Hutchinson & Co. (Publishers) Ltd

An imprint of the Hutchinson Publishing Group

17-21 Conway Street, London W1P 6JD
and 51 Washington Street, Dover, NH 03820, USA

Hutchinson Publishing Group (Australia) Pty Ltd
PO Box 496, 16-22 Church Street, Hawthorne, Melbourne,
Victoria 3122

Hutchinson Group (NZ) Ltd
32-34 View Road, PO Box 40-086, Glenfield, Auckland 10

Hutchinson Group (SA) (Pty) Ltd
PO Box 337, Bergvlei 2012, South Africa

First published 1984

© John Muncie 1984

Printed and bound in Great Britain by
Anchor Brendon Ltd,
Tiptree, Essex

British Library Cataloguing in Publication Data

Muncie, John
    The trouble with kids today.
    1. Juvenile delinquency — Great Britain
    I. Title
    364.3'6'0941   HV9146.A5

Library of Congress Cataloguing in Publication Data

Muncie, John.
    The trouble with kids today.

    Bibliography: P.
    Includes index.
    1. Juvenile delinquency — Great Britain. 2. Youth —
Great Britain — social conditions. 3. Juvenile justice,
administration of — Great Britain. 1. Title.
HV9145.A5M86 1984   364.3'6'0941   84-4581

ISBN 0   09   155051   3

KING ALFRED'S COLLEGE
WINCHESTER·

364·36   83056
MUN

Contents

Conclusion: youth in the 1980s 179

Acknowledgements

The author and publishers would like to thank the copyright holders below for their kind permission to reproduce the following material:

Figure 1 the front page of the *Daily Mirror*, 24 February 1982, by permission of Syndication International Ltd.

Figure 2 from *Criminal Statistics of England and Wales* (1981), by permission of the Controller of Her Majesty's Stationery Office.

Introduction

Young people have probably attracted more public criticism in Britain since the Second World War than almost any other social group. Both academic and popular analyses of their behaviour, life-styles and leisure pursuits have resulted in their definition as a major social problem. The very category of 'youth' seems to attract adult censure and moral outrage. In the 1950s these fears centred around the image of a teenager who had no respect for authority and lived in a world unpenetrated by adult interests. Teddy boys were Britain's first post-war teenage 'folk devils' popularized as ruthless, violent, depraved and sex-crazed. In the 1960s student unrest, the increased use of drugs, from pep-pills to LSD, mods and rockers, sexual permissiveness, football hooliganism, vandalism, truanting, skinheads and rock festivals all combined to amplify public concern over 'troublesome kids'. In the 1970s black youth, mugging, the blank generation, punks, violence in schools and groups of 'vicious young criminals' were the most potent symbols of the 'youth condition', while in the 1980s, the sight of thousands of young people rioting on the streets completely mystified adult sensibilities. The youth of contemporary Britain continue to be a source of anxiety and despair for adults. 'Hooligan', 'teenager', 'criminal' and 'delinquent' have become almost synonymous terms in describing young people's deviant patterns of behaviour. The major response of the state, despite the 'liberal' intentions of the Children and Young Persons Act of 1969, has been characteristically punitive. In the 1980s more young people are being arrested and placed in custody than ever before.

The increasing attention drawn to youthful 'delinquency' has been largely responsible for the resurgence of British sociology's interest in criminology over the past three decades. Coupled with a growing body of interest in cultural studies, social policy research and socio-legal studies, sociological criminology has now overturned psychology's traditional dominance in studies of delinquency.

This book offers a critical overview of this research. It also provides an analysis of how the *media* looks at youth today, how youth has been treated historically and it finishes with an examination of the contemporary *practice* of youth control. Chapter 1 examines how the daily press informs the general public about youth in contemporary society. It focuses on the processes by which the press has presented youth as a major social problem. Using various forms of analysis derived from media studies, the chapter provides a critical analysis of popular images of youth, crime and deviance. Youth has not always been seen as a distinct social problem. Chapter 2 traces the origins of moral panics about youth dating from the early nineteenth century and examines the implications of the use of such categories as 'childhood', 'juvenile delinquency' and 'adolescence'. It identifies key shifts in the analysis of youth and situates various theories which have attempted to explain the causes of youth's delinquency in their specific historical settings. The chapter thus provides both a 'history of the theory', and also, in its organization, a 'theory of the history' of 'youth as a social problem'. Chapter 3 brings this history and theory up to date. It illustrates how theory has been, or can be, applied to contemporary cases of youthful criminality. It concentrates on five specific forms of crime – theft, criminal damage, robbery with violence, riotous assembly and public order offences. Chapter 4 shifts the focus away from those youth legally defined as criminal to those youth socially defined as deviant. It provides a critical analysis of British subcultural studies of youth. The relationships between deviance, leisure pursuits and subcultural style are examined, as well as the processes whereby particular aspects of subcultural action have been subject to criminalization. Chapters 5 and 6 shift attention away from subcultural and ethnographic studies of youth, to questions of social reaction and institutional control. Chapter 5 looks at how the general parameters of youth control are contained within the processes of schooling, work, unemployment and policing. Chapter 6 examines in detail the more 'exceptional' interventions applied through the juvenile justice system which have to date found their most practical expression in the use of detention and youth custody centres. The book concludes by discussing how the 'problem of youth' has been addressed, and responded to, in the 1980s.

It is, however, important to emphasize at the outset that these sociologies of youth, crime and deviancy also have serious weaknesses. First, the most studied youth were also those most publicly identified as deviant or criminal. There is, as a result, an almost complete hiatus of research into youthful conformity. Second, sociological research has almost exclusively focused on white, male and working-class forms of deviancy. Feminist researchers have pointed to the significant absence of any consideration of girl delinquency. Youth culture theory has only in the past few years acknowledged this serious omission. Another startling absence, until the late 1970s, was any discussion of ethnic divisions and the existence of black youth subcultures. Thus while the sociologies of youth, crime and deviancy have generally operated under the global banner of *youth* studies, it is important to recognize that it is only *particular* elements of youth behaviour and *particular* sections of youth which have received anything like a sustained analysis.

This book should not be seen as an attempt to overcome these weaknesses. Rather its purpose is to amalgamate and draw together the many and diverse areas of research that have already been established. This is important because analyses of youth have, and continue to be, tied to particular disciplines and sub-disciplines. For example, studies of youth subcultures have been generally restricted to sociology, analyses of leisure pursuits to cultural studies, juvenile courts to socio-legal studies, youth offender rates to criminology, youth unemployment to social policy and so on. This book is an attempt to draw these disparate areas together for the first time.

The needs of the undergraduate student have remained firmly in mind. Although some familiarity with sociological concepts is assumed, the book attempts to provide an exposition of criminological theory that is not only accessible, but that also suggests ways in which it can be responded to critically. As always, there is no real substitute for reading the original texts. I can only hope to have offered a flavour of these here. For this reason each chapter concludes with recommendations for further reading.

In many ways this book is the outcome of some of the work I have been engaged in during the past four years at the Open University. The teaching texts prepared for courses on social work, popular culture and crime have provided a firm basis for this book. In this respect I am indebted to Tony Bennett, John Clarke,

Mike Fitzgerald and Stuart Hall at the Open University for their helpful criticisms and suggestions. In addition I would like to thank Gordon Hughes, Robert Mears and John Williams for their continual encouragement, Claire L'Enfant at Hutchinson, Carol Johns who did the typing, and particularly Carole Jasilek without whose patience and support none of this would have been possible.

John Muncie
Leicester
July 1983

1 Media images of youth

The majority of us rely on the mass media, particularly television and the popular press, for our information about the social world and the role and position of youth within it. Indeed a chief characteristic of living within large urban societies is that we depend on the media to learn not only of events occurring outside the nation, but also those happening closer to home. Without the social knowledge provided by the media we would in fact remain ignorant of current affairs and of the life-styles of social groups other than those in which we participate. The media thus play a major role in our perception and construction of the social world. Notwithstanding the problems of assessing public opinion and how it is informed, it can be safely argued that one of the major institutions that informs the public about 'youth as a social problem' is the national daily press.

'NEW PUNK CRAZE SHOCKS PARENTS'[1]*
'BANK PLOT KIDS ARE BUSTED'[2]
'230 YOUTHS ARRESTED IN SEASIDE GANG FIGHTS'[3]
'SCHOOLBOYS IN £42,000 SNATCH'[4]
'TEENAGE GANG ATTACKS LONE P.C.'[5]

Such headlines are as familiar as they are frequent. 'Teenagers', 'kids' and 'youths' are readily associated with a lack of discipline, violence and crime. Patricia Morgan, for example, has recently warned of a delinquent syndrome of 'new barbarism' in which youth seems to delight in crudity, cruelty and violence so that a 'frightening ugliness and hostility' pervades all human inter-action.[6] It is as if youth's very age automatically renders its behaviour newsworthy. The press seems continually concerned to report youthful behaviour in terms of its more bizarre and

---

* Superior figures refer to the References beginning on p. 185.

sensational aspects. This process is reinforced when seemingly unconnected events are clustered together to form an overall picture. On the August bank holiday weekend of 1982 *The Sunday Times* chose to place the following three stories together in a front page News Brief and report them in a similar vein:

The mods – 3,000 of them, with scooters – packed the ferries for a 'friendly invasion' of the Isle of Wight. Police called for reinforcements in case some were not so friendly.

The first soccer hooliganism was reported from Cleethorpes, where Leeds United fans smashed shop windows and damaged a hotel and a pub hours before the start of the second division game with Grimsby Town. Fourteen were arrested and kept in custody.

At Reading rock festival, police had made about 50 arrests, mainly for drug offences, by mid-afternoon. One fan was taken to hospital after being stabbed and more than 160 were being treated for minor injuries.[7]

Such selective reporting has serious social consequences. Between 1965 and 1979 national opinion polls discovered that juvenile crime was considered to be one of the most serious social problems faced by Britain. Respondents were asked whether they thought that crimes of violence, juvenile crime, drug-taking, organized crime, rape, drunkenness and prostitution were very serious social problems. The category of juvenile crime was consistently evoked more than organized crime, rape, drunkenness or prostitution. It never failed to produce less than a 50 per cent 'yes' response rate and was only considered slightly less serious than crimes of violence.[8]

Against this background there has been lamentably little research in Britain which details how youth is in fact reported in the press. To date our only available informatioin is supplied by Bradford University's Social Work Research Unit which scanned eight national daily newspapers and two local (Yorkshire) papers during June 1979.[9]

Any article which involved people between 11 and 19 years was analysed. The articles were categorized according to size, location and content, and each assigned an evaluation category (positive, negative, neutral) based on the researchers' assessment of the general feeling about adolescents which each article might arouse in the 'average' reader.

A total of 913 articles were analysed. The local *Bradford Telegraph and Argus* contained most stories (15 per cent of total) followed by the popular dailies, (between 10 per cent and 12 per cent of total), the serious dailies (between 7 per cent and 9 per cent of total) and the *Morning Star* (2 per cent of total). Their content analysis revealed that sporting stories accounted for 11.4 per cent of the total content, education 6.7 per cent, but most notably 34.9 per cent of all reports were related to crime in one form or another. Of these the most frequent category were crimes such as burglary, theft, vandalism and breach of the peace (9.2 per cent), murder (5.1 per cent), and sex crimes (2.3 per cent). Reporting was also found to be frequent where adolescents were the victims of such crimes as assault. The authors concluded that:

according to our daily press a typical adolescent is a sporting youngster, criminally inclined, likely to be murdered or injured in an accident.[10]

However, their evaluation variable was symmetrically distributed. 52 per cent of the articles were evaluated neutrally, 24 per cent positively and 24 per cent negatively, indicating that the press do not present a totally negative picture of youthful behaviour. However there are many aspects of young people's lives which the press never mention. The researchers found hardly any discussion of education or (un)employment issues. Only 2 per cent of the articles discussed youth employment, despite the fact that the numbers of unemployed youth were growing rapidly. In 1979 over 20 per cent of under-18s were without a job. Stories concerned with education only amounted to 6.7 per cent of the total (almost half of these appearing in the *Guardian*'s weekly feature 'Education Guardian').

Their report suggests, therefore, that a degree of imbalance exists in reporting. The most newsworthy aspects of young people would appear to be their involvement in crime – perhaps over-represented than its occurrence in real life would warrant.

Moreover, although some of the positive achievements of youth are given coverage, this is accounted for by a small number of media and sporting personalities.

Entertainers, sports stars and the children of the aristocracy and the famous 'tend to commandeer the limelight in a stereotyped presentation of the "good life"'.[11] Those youth occupying a different social position tend only to be presented as subversive or criminal.

This simple dichotomy of the young offender or troublemaker

(negative images of youth) set against the young media star (positive images of youth) tends to dominate how the media inform us about youth.

A good example of this process in action was supplied by the *Daily Mirror* in February 1982. Its front page was shared equally between a report of children rioting in St Saviour's junior school in Toxteth, Liverpool, and a full-length picture of Toyah Willcox voted Best Female Singer in the British Rock and Pop Awards. Their respective headlines – 'Girl 10, Led School Terror Gangs' and 'Toyah's the pop queen' – told their own stories.[12] Interestingly, both had claims to newsworthiness because they both presented images of deviancy within youth. The girl in the Toxteth school was depicted as uncontrollable and violent, while Toyah Willcox was seen as deserving of media attention because of her flamboyant and outrageous use of fashion and subcultural style (see Figure 1). Both of these images of youth contained elements considered to be extraordinary and were therefore newsworthy. The essential difference between them, of course, lies in one image being available for commercial popularization, whereas the other supports a general and popular mobilization of concern for lack of control in our schools. Such a juxtaposition of images increases the tendency of the press to inflate the criminal propensities of some youth. For example, the girl rioter described in the *Daily Mirror* as an extortionist gang leader, arsonist, tearaway and vandal, was four days later the subject of a *Sunday Times* in-depth analysis which gave a completely different view of the girl's character and performance in school. This article described her as 'bright, highly imaginative, good at games' and discovered that her last two school reports were generous with praise of her academic abilities.[13] Such investigative reporting however only occurred after the terms of reference – 'mini mafia leader', 'mini mobster' – had been firmly established by the popular press. Such images as those supplied by the *Daily Star*, which described her as 'big, black and really nasty', arguably had the most lasting impact, even when their accuracy was in question.[14]

But why are such images of youth constructed by the press? How are they maintained? What are their social consequences?

To answer these questions we need to broaden our range of inquiry to examine more generally the relationship between youth crime and the press, via the three interrelated concepts of 'news values', 'media definitions' and 'moral panics'.

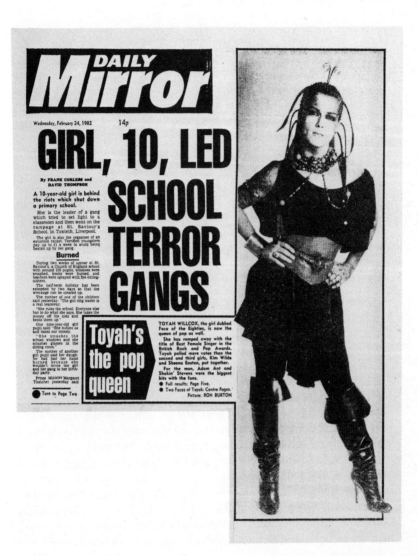

The newspaper clipping reads:

DAILY Mirror

Wednesday, February 24, 1982   14p

GIRL, 10, LED SCHOOL TERROR GANGS

By FRANK CORLESS and DAVID THOMPSON

A 10-year-old girl is behind the riots which shut down a primary school.

She is the leader of a gang which tried to set light to a classroom and then went on the rampage at St. Saviour's School, in Toxteth, Liverpool.

The girl is also the organiser of an extortion racket. Terrified youngsters pay up to £1 a week to avoid being beaten up by her gang.

Burned

During two weeks of uproar at St. Saviour's, a Church of England school with around 120 pupils, windows were smashed, books were burned, and teachers were sprayed with fire extinguishers.

The half-term holiday has been extended by two days so that the wreckage can be cleared up.

The mother of one of the children said yesterday: 'The girl ring leader is a real tearaway.

"She rules the school. Everyone else has to do what she says. She takes the money off the kids and beats them up."

One nine-year-old girl pupil said: "She bullies us and takes our money.

"She smashes the school windows and she smashes glasses in the dining room."

The mother of another girl pupil said her daughter had had her hand burned because she wouldn't invite the girl and her gang to her birthday party.

Prime Minister Margaret Thatcher yesterday said

● Turn to Page Two

Toyah's the pop queen

TOYAH WILLCOX, the girl dubbed Face of the Eighties, is now the queen of pop as well.

She has romped away with the title of Best Female Singer in the British Rock and Pop Awards. Toyah polled more votes than the second and third girls, Kim Wilde and Sheena Easton, put together.

For the men, Adam Ant and Shakin' Stevens were the biggest hits with the fans.

● Full results: Page Five.

● Two Faces of Toyah: Centre Pages.
Picture: RON BURTON

Source: Daily Mirror, 24 February 1982, p. 1

Figure 1   *Two faces of youth*

News values and newsworthiness

There is a powerful common-sense view that the press presents a more or less perfect mirror-reflection of what is happening in the world. It is assumed that there is first a problem – riots, hooliganism, vandalism, muggings – and that newspapers simply provide factual reports of the problem. Crime occurs, police apprehend criminals, the courts punish them: this is news and gets reported as accurate information in the press. Such a view, however, oversimplifies the complex relationship between events and press reports, for at least two primary reasons. First, press reports cannot be simply a straight reflection of real events because there always intervenes a whole process of *selection* –which events to report, which to leave out, which aspects of an event to report, which to omit. Second, the impact of press reports are affected by their *presentation* – choosing what sort of headline, language, imagery, photograph and typography to use. In a study of popular crime journalism, Chibnall noted five sets of informal rules of relevancy which govern this selection and presentation process.[15] These were

1   visible and spectacular acts;
2   political or sexual connotations;
3   graphic presentation;
4   individual pathology;
5   deterrence and repression.

These five rules can clearly be seen to operate in reporting youth crime. Consider again the *Daily Mirror* report of the 'riots' at St Saviour's School. Certainly it stressed the relevance of visible and spectacular violence involving smashing of windows, burning of books and the threatening of teachers and pupils. As Chibnall argues, the violence most likely to receive coverage in the press is indeed that which involves sudden physical injury to innocent others, especially in public places. Concern with such violence has typified newspaper accounts throughout the post-war years and has been bolstered by such media labels as 'cosh boys', 'bully boy skinheads', 'vandals', 'muggers', and 'football hooligans'. This time it was the turn of 'terror gangs' and 'mini-mobsters'. The concentration on these forms has, however, reinforced a limited concept of violence and other forms have been unduly neglected. Woman and baby battering, unsafe working conditions, pollution of the environment and the 'mental' violence involved in boring and repetitive jobs are listed by Chibnall as phenomena that have caused as much human suffering but receive little press consideration because they do not conform to the criteria of spectacular newsworthiness.[16]

Second, the report contained something of a 'sexual angle' in that the person identified was a girl. Media representations of women are characteristically informed by sexual stereotypes in which women are portrayed as naturally passive and submissive. In contrast the 'aggressive' female is automatically viewed as abnormal and thus worthy of front-page news.

Third, the graphic presentation of events plays its part in constructing a particular image of crime and criminality. The headlines of catch-all phrases and the use of particular labels combine to sensitize us to certain types of crime. The *Daily Express* of 8 April 1980 devoted half of its front page to a picture of skinheads attacking another youth at Southend.[17] The accompanying headline declared 'The Boot Goes In'. In this way a photograph of one incident was used to depict a whole event. And the related report describing the youths as 'thugs' engaged in an 'orgy of terror' and 'lusting for blood' appeared to substantiate the 'facts' from the photograph. But as Hall has argued, the choices of photograph and of a particular moment in an event are governed by an ideological procedure.[18] By appearing literally to reproduce the event as it really happened, news photos suppress their underlying selective, interpretive and ideological function. They give a story more weight but also reinforce its ideological message. Certainly the presence of a 'supporting photograph' helps to make a particular event front-page news. The drama similarly depends on the easy identification of opposing factions: skinheads versus innocent youth, hooligans versus police, black people versus white, young people versus old. In this way crimes are depicted in terms of a basic confrontation between the symbolic forces of good and evil. This collapsing of events into simplistic questions of right and wrong also tends to force the reader to side with one or other of the positions offered. The intricate history and consequences of an event necessary to provide a fuller and more complex picture are rarely provided, or are only provided at a later date when the terms of debate have already been firmly set.

Fourth, if one person can be singled out as the ringleader in a gang then the dramatic stage takes on another dimension. Crime becomes viewed solely as a matter of individual pathology – a few bad apples in an otherwise healthy barrel. Any social context relevant to criminal activity is ignored or, if noted, rarely followed through. To do so would necessitate the questioning of some fundamental characteristics of society: the unequal distribution of housing, low levels of pay, the nature of welfare benefits, the rise in unemployment and so on. And such questions, of course, do not usually conform to the imperatives of newsworthiness.

The combination of these themes leads to the inescapable conclusion that programmes of deterrence and incarceration are far more suitable for dealing with offenders than any measure of social reform or reorganization. Indeed the Prime Minister's reaction to the St Saviour's School troubles (as reported in the same issue of the *Daily Mirror*) was that law and order must be upheld at all costs and that she would fight strenuously against any reduction in police services in the area. Since crime breaches our 'normal' expectations of the world, the public rely on such sources as the police, MPs and subsequently the press to define, place and 'make sense of' the illegal and abnormal.

The press thus plays an active and constructing role, not merely a passive and reflecting one. This is not to argue that the press make up stories and that without their intervention the problem, of pupils attacking teachers for example, would suddenly disappear. However the major responsibility that does lie with the press is their exaggeration and sensationalization of particular problems, and their tendency to isolate violent and sensational acts from their proper social context. The key to this process is 'news values'.

News values are a code, formally and informally learned. They represent a collective sense among journalists of what is the most significant; what is the most unusual or unexpected or *new* thing about the world which appears to threaten the status quo. As Hall argues:

we can gather up all the separate news values into two, closely related, general news values. They are *change* and the tendency of things to *change for the worse*. It's as if newspapers set out each day with the unspoken assumption that things in the world will be exactly as they left them yesterday. Then against this flat background they etch, in order of significance, all the things that have changed or altered. Naturally the bigger, the more unexpected, the more violent the change the bigger the story. These big, dramatic, unexpected violent shifts in the world are what is new about it – the news.[19]

There is indeed a striking convergence between crime as a topic and the structure of news values. Crime stands out against a background of a taken-for-granted conformity in the social world. Thus, although crime is forever present in society, it is always reported as unpredictable, disruptive and therefore dramatic and sensational. Youth crime occupies this position to an even greater extent because of the ever present fear that 'kids will grow up to be criminal' and that their presumed 'natural' innocence and naïvety are at stake. The crimes of youth are, it seems, automatically considered more serious and dangerous for the stability of the social order.

A number of consequences follow from this aspect of news-making. For while the press is driven to find and report the most startling stories to fill its papers, it must also reassure readers that despite these continual violent shifts in the world, an essential core of unity and order always remains. Thus, if there are elements of youthful behaviour that can be safely popularized then these will be drawn out too. The press can then play a dual role by condemning youth's violent behaviour while attempting to incorporate other aspects of youth's behaviour as natural and healthy exuberance. As Hebdige noted, the emergence of specta-cular youth subcultures (such as punk in 1976) is invariably accompanied by a wave of hysteria in the press.[20] But the hysteria is ambivalent, fluctuating between condemnation and fascination, alarm and amusement. In December 1976 the *Daily Mirror* ran a series of alarmist centre spreads on the newly emergent punk subculture. One of these contained two reports. One headlined 'They're obnoxious, arrogant and outrageous' discussed the presumed anarchy and violence surrounding the focal concerns of punk, largely through using a photograph of 'weapons' taken from fans at a London concert. The other attempted to soften this image by interviewing the mother of a young punk under the headline 'Roger's mum gives her blessing'.[21] As Hall has argued, the press not only sensitize us to the new and the violent, they also 'situate it within the dominant framework of meanings'.[22] Thus subcultural youth are depicted as outrageous outsiders but, at the same time, are returned to an appropriate place – in the family, up-to-date, modern – which does not upset the social order.

Official, media and public definitions

The nature of the news we receive about youth crime is further affected by the way in which such crime is defined. These definitions are also socially constructed – they exist as social interpretations rather than as facts – and are produced by a distinctive social and institutional process. The news media have little direct access to crime as such. The majority of crime stories come to them via the police, the courts and the Home Office. Thus, agencies of crime control occupy the position of being the primary source and definers of crime news. The credibility of their definitions is in turn enhanced by their 'official' and 'institutional' standing. Their regular access to media reportage is both open and 'acceptable'. As they stand in the front lines of crime control and have an assumed knowledge of the extent of crime, it appears quite 'natural' that they should be the main source of the news about crime. It is, however, important to recognize police and court reports as both privileged and particular versions of social reality. The tone of any later review of particular cases in the press is significantly tempered by the initial definitions gleaned from official sources. Thus, although journalists are not incapable of presenting alternative views to those offered by politicians and police, in the vast majority of cases their accounts are grounded in the interpretations provided by these primary sources. These sources are in turn dependent largely on the rate of reported crime, the focused and organized police response to certain crimes, and the reports of Home Office statisticians reliant on eventual rates of conviction. Thus the primary definers can in themselves only offer a partial definition of crime which reflects their own institutional constraints. The partiality of our knowledge about crime is further exacerbated because the media not only relay and reproduce these official definitions, but they transform and translate them into their own selective patterns of crime-as-a-news-event.[23] The shaping power of news values and the practices of news presentation are of course central to this.

This translation often involves selectivity and the use of dramatic and sensational language, but also works to transform partial information about events and incidents into finished news items. Indeed, most crime news is not about an event but about a court case. Many of the most vivid headlines are taken directly from a judge's summing up or reflection on the state of society as a result of a particular crime. Stan Cohen's study of media reaction to the mods and rockers' conflicts on south and east coast beaches in 1964 illustrated clearly this process of transformation from official to media pronouncements.[24] In one case, the Margate magistrate, Dr George Simpson, referred to the arrested youths as 'Sawdust Caesars' who 'seem to find courage, like rats, by hunting only in packs'.

Virtually every court report quoted Dr. Simpson's 'Sawdust Caesars' speech in full and his terminology significantly influenced the mass media symbolisation and the process of spurious attribution. His phrases were widely used as headlines: ' "Sawdust Caesars hunt in pack" says magistrate', ' "A Vicious Virus" says MP'. ' "Town Hits back on Rat Pack Hooligans" '.[25]

In this way the language of an official source becomes public and is used within the language of popular journalistic rhetoric. However this process of redefinition and mediation of 'news' does not end here. By appearing to assume 'the public voice', newspapers can begin actively to shape public opinion on issues of crime. At such times the press openly takes the role of guardians of a presumed 'moral concensus'. And the success of this process rests initially on the media's use of 'informed' and 'credible' institutional sources. ⁓

The media do not then simply reflect social reality but define it in a particular way, subsequently affecting the quality of public opinions. To illustrate this Hall *et al.* replace the simple equation, crime = apprehension = news about crime, with a more complex model which takes account of the shaping power of the intervening institutions.[26] First, they recognize that we know little of the actual volume and incidence of crime as much remains unreported, undetected and thus not represented within the official statistics. In its most raw form, 'crime' exists initially through its institutional definition by the crime control agencies of police, courts and the Home Office. However, we only hear of crime when it becomes news. At this stage the practices of 'newsmaking' – selectivity, news values, notions of newsworthiness – have intervened, so that we are provided with an even more partial picture. In this sense, popular images of crime are only 'popular' in so far as they are the consequences of information provided by official sources with a vested interest in crime control, and media sources with a vested interest in maintaining news values.

Moral panics and deviancy amplification

The media not only play a part in constructing youth crime into a social issue, they also play a role in the orchestration of the concern which they have helped to create. Sections of the press frequently use these causes of concern as the basis for stimulating the public into a moral panic, or for organizing a public crusade and expressing public, moral indignation.

The tendency to create moral panics is related directly to the aspects of newsmaking we have so far discussed. First, the professional requirements of journalists and the competitive requirements of the press always necessitate the search for the most sensational, unexpected and dramatic aspects of youthful behaviour. Through the repeated use of such dismissive labels as 'thugs', 'vandals' and 'hooligans', aspects of their behaviour are readily stereotyped and become easily recognizable. This stereotypical distorted image is then contrasted against the hypothetical conformity of the 'man-in-the-street'. In Jock Young's phrase, the media 'select events which are *atypical*, present them in a *stereotypical* fashion and contrast them against a backcloth of normality which is *overtypical*'.[27] From this, simple moral directives are produced demanding that something be done. For example, at the time of the hippie squat in London's Piccadilly in 1969, the *Sunday People* ran the following headline:

HIPPIE THUGS – THE SORDID TRUTH: Drugtaking, couples making love while others look on, rule by a heavy mob armed with iron bars, foul language, filth and stench that is the scene inside the hippies' fortress in London's Piccadilly. These are not rumours but facts – sordid facts which will shock ordinary decent family loving people.[28]

Here the atypical, the stereotypical and the overtypical are fused into two sentences. As such the tendency to sensationalize the news also carries with it a tendency to amplify the phenomenon being reported. Such amplification can also lead to the impression that a phenomenon is occurring more often, or affecting more people than it actually is. For once a dramatic social problem has been identified and labelled, the attention of journalists and readers tends to be directed to finding more examples of the same problem. For example, following the release of the 1981 official criminal statistics, the *Daily Mirror* devoted eight of its thirty-two pages (including front page and centre spread) to an analysis of

'Our Violent Cities'.[29] In each of the reports, from eight urban areas, youth were implicated in the stories of gang fights, pub brawls, muggings and violent attacks. Such reporting is rarely related to an actual increase in such violent incidents at any particular time, but for a short moment, public attention is sensitized to these kinds of incidents. By clustering a number of unrelated events under a single headline the press can indeed create a trend, a trend which then becomes newsworthy in its own right.

The first systematic empirical study of such media amplification was Stan Cohen's research of the 'mods and rockers' panic of 1964.[30] Groups of working-class youth arrived in the seaside resort of Clacton over the Easter bank holiday. It was cold and wet and the facilities and amusements for young people were strictly limited. Eventually windows were broken and beach huts wrecked. Those on scooters and bikes roared up and down the promenade. The next day these incidents were given front page treatment in the national press:

'DAY OF TERROR BY SCOOTER GROUPS'[31]
'YOUNGSTERS BEAT UP TOWN'[32]
'WILD ONES INVADE SEASIDE'[33]

They were presented as confrontations between easily recognizable rival gangs. Identikit images of these youths, and ready-made explanations of their behaviour, followed. This act of labelling, Cohen argues, had several consequences. First it instigated a moral panic, which obliged the police to step up their surveillance of the two groups. The result was more frequent arrests which appeared to confirm the initial panic. Second, by emphasizing the antagonism between the groups, and their stylistic differences, the youths were inadvertently encouraged to place themselves in one of the opposing camps. This polarization cemented the original image and produced more clashes on subsequent bank holidays. These in turn attracted renewed news coverage and increased police activity and further moral panic. However, as Cohen argued, the media's singling out of such deviant groups also resulted in an amplification of their deviance, both in real and perceived terms. The effects of media reaction and social control may then result in deviant youth identifying with the label attached to themselves and thus perceiving themselves as being *more* separate and deviant from the rest of society. This has been termed a *deviancy amplification spiral*.[34] In certain crucial respects, then, the media can create social problems. They can stir up public indignation and engineer moral panics about certain types of deviancy. Indeed, it has been argued that there is an *institutionalized* need in the media to create moral panics which will seize the imagination of the public.[35]

In such situations de-amplification can only be achieved by deterring potential and existing deviants with more punitive control measures. Cohen ends on the pessimistic note that:

More moral panics will be generated and other as yet nameless folk devils will be created. This is not because such developments have an inexorable inner logic, but because our society as presently structured will continue to generate problems for some of its members like working class adolescents and then condemn whatever solution these groups find.[36]

In this way the media construct moral panics about certain sections of society and bolster the position of those advocating more control. The core of Cohen's argument is that the media do not simply reflect social reality, but are able to define it in a particular way. Thus in times of rapid social change, such as the mid 1960s when traditional values were being disturbed by the rise of affluence and increased working-class aspirations, the ensuing public disquiet was resolved by identifying certain social groups as scapegoats or folk devils. They became the visual symbols of what was wrong with society. Meanwhile, the more intractable and structural problems to do with restricted opportunities were overlooked and ignored.

During the 1970s youth were to play a central part in this diversionary process. In 1978 Hall *et al.* reused the concept by identifying a series of moral panics to do with permissiveness, vandals, drug abusers, student radicals and so on which characterized the 1960s and 1970s, culminating in 1972-3 with the moral panic of 'mugging'.[37] They show how the news media, working with images from the New York ghetto, defined the incidence of street robberies by youth in Britain's inner-city areas as an outbreak of a new and dangerous kind of violent crime. They trace the way this definition was employed to justify punitive sentencing and how it reinforced and justified a gathering moral panic about a generalized breakdown of law and order in society. Also, as the panic developed, mugging became defined almost exclusively as a problem with black youth – they became the primary folk devils of our society. As Cohen had concluded, Hall *et al.* noted how such problems were publicly defined as ones solely of lawlessness, rather than social deprivation and class and racial inequality. The notion of 'moral panic' is central to both studies in explaining how particular sections of youth (working class/black) become identified as worthy of police and judicial attention. The implications of such identification however are extended by Hall *et al.* in their analysis. A moral panic is the first link in a spiral of events leading to the maintenance of law in society by legitimized coercion and the general exercise of authority. Thus, while sections of youth may be in the front line, the response to their amplified deviance has implications for the whole of society. It is indeed worth recalling that the Conservative government was returned to power both in 1979 and 1983 while supporting a strong 'return to the rule of law' lobby. And in certain crucial respects the press have played, and continue to play, their part in the maintenance of our present 'law 'n' order' and authoritarian society.

As a result there is an increasing tendency in our society:

to deal with any problem, first by *simplifying* its causes, second by *stigmatising* those involved, third by whipping up public feeling into a *panic* about it and fourth by *stamping hard on it from above*.[38]

The role and consequences of media moral panics was again clearly seen in operation in the 1982 World Cup football finals in Spain. Months before the event the press consistently warned English supporters to keep out of trouble and harked back to incidents of crowd disorder in Switzerland the previous year. The Spanish authorities were thus suitably forewarned and sensitized to the media's view of the English soccer fan as a potential troublemaker. As a result the most serious outbreaks of violence were to be instigated not by the travelling fans, but by the Spanish police. In one instance a group of English supporters were cleared from a bar and beaten by the police for no apparent reason, other than that they were English and thus automatically carried with them an image of being 'violent and unruly hooligans'.

Present-day fears and anxieties about 'unruly' youth are further exacerbated by what Pearson has identified as a 'twenty year rule' in press announcements.[39] He notes how contemporary incidents of youthful disorder are always reported and responded to as unprecedented events: as continual signs that things are becoming progressively worse than they were say, 'some twenty years ago'. In a sequence of backward glances through English social history,

Pearson shows how this image of a more peaceful, orderly and harmonious past (against which the present can be unfavourably compared) fails to stand up to close scrutiny. Twenty years before the moral outrage surrounding soccer violence in the 1980s, similar fears centred on the 'lawlessness' of the Teddy boys. In the inter-war years the main targets for criticism were again football rowdyism and the demoralizing influence of the Hollywood cinema. Victorian England was similarly 'plagued' by the 'un-English' hooligan of the 1890s, the garotters of the 1860s and lawless gangs of street urchins in the 1840s. The propensity of the press and other 'informed sources' to deny this history not only raises contemporary levels of anxiety about youthful behaviour, but also, in glorifying a mythical past, enables the forces of reaction to come to the fore.[40]

Through these three devices – 'news values', 'media definitions' and 'moral panics' – the press plays a significant role in distorting the public's view of youth in society. Their propensity to commit crimes is overstressed, while their only salvation lies in the few successful individuals who have 'made it good'. The situation is indeed serious, for sections of youth are all too readily defined as deviant or criminal and thus are continually feared on the streets and in the schools. This is not to argue that the activities of youth receive a more extensive press coverage than other sections of society, but when it does occur it is sufficiently weighted to sensationalizing their more spectacular, deviant and criminal practices. In this sense, there is as much 'trouble' created for the youth of today through the processes of media and public reaction as youth itself may create for its critics.

Suggested reading

The only quantitive study of how youth in general is reported in the press is Porteous and Colston (1980), though particular forms of youth behaviour have attracted more attention. Of note are Stan Cohen's (1973) work on mods and rockers, Hall's (1978) analysis of football hooliganism and Hall *et al.*'s (1978) research on mugging. The relationship between the media and crime in general is addressed in detail by Chibnall (1977) and Hall (1975).

2 Studies in the history and theory of youth

Youth have not always been seen as a distinct social problem. Until the early nineteenth century 'childhood' was considered a brief and relatively unimportant stage of life. Children were introduced into the responsibilities of adult life as quickly as possible. As a result the now well established categories of 'juvenile delinquent', 'adolescent' and 'young offender' did not exist. Thus adolescence and childhood are not natural and universal stages in human development. Rather they are as much social constructs as are the contemporary media labels of 'vandals', 'hooligans' and 'muggers'. This chapter will examine the origins of 'youth as a social problem' and trace successive stages in the development of related efforts to explain and control their behaviour. It attempts to answer the question of why youth in general, and youth (mis)behaviour in particular, have come to occupy a central position in contemporary discussions of crime and social order.

The invention of childhood

In pre-industrial society the forms of differentiation by age that we now take for granted did not exist for much of the population. Beyond a period of infancy, characterized by the physical dependency of child on mother or other adults, there was no understanding of 'childhood'. From infancy children were directly absorbed into the world of adults. Age was thus considered in terms of degrees of adulthood, and children and youth were considered as no more than 'small adults'. This lack of age differentiation was duly reflected in all spheres of the social and economic life of pre-industrial societies. Children mingled with adults in work, leisure and sport. They did not occupy a different social position, dress differently or adhere to different habits and codes of morality. So children were quite naturally involved in dancing, gambling, drinking alcohol and engaged in work activities that we would now describe as adult.

This absence of a conception of childhood was directly related to the structure of a pre-industrial rural economy. Children were a vital source of family income and were placed in work as soon as they could be economically active. The most prevalent form of child labour was in the home or within the family economy. Children from the ages of 4 or 5 worked through the hours of daylight in all weathers in the fields and in the cottages, preparing the raw materials for domestic industry.[1] Child labour was universal and an economic necessity. Coupled with such economic demands was the precarious nature of infancy itself. The high infant mortality rate militated against attributing any distinctiveness to childhood. Even by 1831, 50 per cent of children born in that year died before they reached the age of 5.

While Aries has argued that some conception of childhood was developing by the sixteenth and seventeenth centuries,[2] this was contained solely within the prosperous middle and aristocratic strata of society. It was first manifested in an attitude towards children as playthings: as objects of affection and amusement for adults. Children began to be seen as young innocents unpolluted by adult knowledge. Even so, 'childhood' rarely lasted beyond the age of 5 or 7. The emergence of childhood was also linked at this time to a belief in the need for a period of training between infancy and adulthood, in which the child could be prepared for the expanding range of knowledge in theology and science. As Aries points out, childhood lengthened faster for boys than for girls, for it was they who were expected to benefit most from an extended period of education in their future work roles.[3] However the children of the labouring poor continued to work, from necessity, to supplement the family income from the first moment they were physically able. Not until the 1870s and the instigation of compulsory education did the bourgeois notion of childhood have much bearing on their lives.

There was, as Thane argues, a 'clear correspondence' between the emergence of European capitalism and modern age groups.[4] Those who had access to wealth and property strove to maintain their control over it by handing it to their children. Similarly, as adult life became more demanding, a prolonged period of education was required to learn relevant work skills. It was not surprising that the emerging bourgeoisie began to devote more attention to tightening their control over their children and training them into the habits of work discipline. In this way the invention of childhood was conditioned by economic, rather than biological, changes. As a social construct, childhood simply did not exist for a majority of the labouring poor, not just in pre-industrial society but until late in the nineteenth century.

In the first stages of industrialization, the major forms of factory employment, such as spinning and weaving, encouraged families to stay together. Children worked with their parents, as they had at home, collecting waste and minding machines. Discipline was imposed on children largely by their own parents. If physically fit and active, children, from the age of 4, were treated very much as adults. If parents worked a fifteen hour day then so did their children. Children were also used extensively in mining to work the narrower mines and passages. In the early nineteenth century birth and death rates were high and as a result 40 per cent of the population were under the age of 5.[5] Children were thus an essential part of the workforce. Gillis estimated that in the first decades of the nineteenth century 80 per cent of the workers in English cotton mills were children.[6] The use of child labour remained unquestioned, not only by families who relied on their income, but also by factory owners who were keenly aware of this ever-increasing source of cheap labour. The treatment of children as small adults, however, did not mean that they achieved adult status. Children were legally the property of parents and were used by them as family assets. Thus among the poor the labour of children was exploited, among the rich their marriages were contrived, all to the economic advantage of parents.[7] Before the 1830s the main pressure for imposing a minimum age for work came only from such external 'interested' parties as landowners wishing to control the advance of manufacturers' power; adult trade unionists wanting their own limitation on working hours; and middle-class intellectuals and humanitarians.[8] When heavier machinery was introduced into the factories, the kinship relationships of labour began to break down. For example when the automatic mules were brought into the cotton mills in 1824, each adult worker needed as many as nine young assistants, rather than two or three. Accordingly, standards of daily work-discipline began to be imposed by foremen and managers, and the loci of control over children shifted from parents into the impersonal hands of factory owners.

The crime of the factory system was to inherit the worst features of the domestic system in a context which had none of the domestic compensations. In the home the child's conditions will have varied according to the temper of parents or of master and to some degree his work will have been scaled according to his ability. In the mill the machinery dictated environment, discipline, speed and regularity of work and working hours, for the delicate and strong alike.[9]

Successive commissions for children's employment set up in the early nineteenth century recorded how children apprenticed to employers were regularly beaten, inadequately clothed and rarely paid for their labour. Others were abandoned by parents if work could not be found: boys were sold to chimney-sweeps as climbing boys, girls to brothel keepers or traded to beggars to attract pity from passers-by. Such indifference was indeed sanctioned, not just by employers and parents, but also by the church and the law. For example, John Wesley revived the extreme Calvinist belief that emphasized the depravity rather than the innocence of infancy and argued that children were doomed to sin and evil unless their play was controlled and restrained by parents, schooling or work. Those children without work were duly viewed as lacking in moral and social discipline. Indeed, this new 'problem population' was to be extended after 1833 when the Factory Acts tried to control the extent of child labour. The Acts stipulated that no child under the age of 9 was to be employed in cotton mills or factories and hours were to be limited to eight per day for those under 13 and twelve hours for those under 18. They also stated that factory owners should provide some elementary schooling (for example, bible reading, for two hours a day) for their juvenile employees. Although in subsequent years factory owners and parents deliberately contravened these laws, when the law was upheld it meant that more and more youth were effectively unemployed.

While both parents were at work, children were left to their own devices or neglected. A growing number were thrown on to the streets to become vagrants or to engage in petty criminality. This complacency was matched by the law. Children were deemed to be adult if above the age of 7 and were therefore held responsible for any misdemeanour. Those aged 7 to 14 were presumed incapable of crime, but it was open to the prosecution to prove that such children knew their conduct was wrong and in most cases the child would be prosecuted. There was no special public provision for young offenders. To spare the child from the penalties of the law merely on account of age would have undermined the prevailing classicist principles of the law that all individuals acted with free will, should be treated equally and that punishment should act as a deterrence. Accordingly, children accused of crimes were treated as adults at both trial and sentencing stages and many were consequently executed, transported to the colonies or imprisoned.

On one day alone in February 1814 at the Old Bailey sessions, five children were condemned to death: Fowler aged 12 and Wolfe aged 12 for burglary in a dwelling; Morris aged eight, Solomons aged nine and Burrell aged 11, for burglary and stealing a pair of shoes.[10]

Between 1812 and 1817, 916 youths under the age of 21 were transported to Australia. Even by 1834 a 14-year-old boy was sentenced to transportation for seven years for stealing a silk handkerchief.[11] The crimes of youth were mainly petty theft. The usual first step in incarceration was being sent to the hulks – old ships lying in the Thames, the Medway and at Portsmouth, which served as overflows for the prisons after the American War of Independence. Lack of sanitation and overcrowding caused many juvenile deaths and was in part the impetus behind many of the efforts of voluntary societies in the early nineteenth century to try and provide alternative methods of containment for children. But normally the punishment for juveniles was likely to be imprisonment. In 1835 nearly 7000 young people between 10 and 20 were in prison, increasing to 12,000 in 1853.[12] Despite criticisms voiced by voluntary societies and various commissions of inquiry, the state's primary concern remained to punish rather than to reform.

Many of these harsh conditions of employment and punishment for children were largely tolerated for the very reason that childhood was not viewed as a particularly important stage of life in the eyes of parents, employers and the law, except as a source of industrial wealth.

During the nineteenth century, however, children were gradually singled out from adults as a distinctive category in relation to both criminal behaviour and legal control. But as May reveals:

Any consideration of the problem of protecting juveniles was incidental. The swelling prison population however stimulated efforts at reform and in the process the problem of the young offender was revealed.[13]

The discovery of juvenile delinquency

The interpretation of youthful misbehaviour and law-breaking as a serious threat to the social order can be traced to the moral panic about juvenile gangs in the early nineteenth century. As a result of abandonment, unemployment and the excitement of the city, an increasing number of children spent much of their time on the streets. There, they played, gambled and earned some living through the sale of small commodity items (necklaces, matches, boxes of dominoes), fruit and vegetables. Mayhew's vivid descriptions of the 'rookeries' in the East End of London catalogued the activities of such young 'precocious' traders, 'daring' thieves and 'loutish' vagabonds.[14] Children attracted to the streets as a result of the 'brute' tyranny of parents, association with costermongers, orphanhood or destitution, necessarily lived on the edge of crime. There was no clear demarcation between honest work and illegal trading for those existing on a subsistence level in the streets. It was in such conditions that bands of young pickpockets, footpads and other 'artful dodgers' thrived. As Gillis argued:

The street gang was in some sense the school of the poor, bringing together young people from early teens to mid-twenties in a comprehensive learning situation. It was through the peer group that the young person gained a sense of place and a measure of individual worth.[15]

Such 'measures of individual worth' were, however, rarely shared by the police, who were trying to secure their own authority on the streets, and the growing number of middle-class observers and journalists. The camaraderie of the gangs was more frequently interpreted as debauchery and observed only through the eyes of moral outrage and indignation. Such observers carried with them their own conception of childhood – peculiar to the upper classes – as a period of dependency and vulnerability, and stressed the importance of the family and educational institutions to care for and discipline children prior to adulthood. It was such concern over the apparent lack of parental and institutional control that instigated the first moral panic about juvenile delinquency. The Society for Investigating the Causes of the Alarming Increase of Juvenile Delinquency in the Metropolis published its report in 1816. Whether or not the rate of juvenile crime was increasing at this time remains unknown because the report contained no statistical evidence. But it is clear that it was contemporary conviction that the crime rate was rising and that juveniles should be protected not only from themselves but from contamination by those adults already engaged in criminal 'careers'. The Society's evidence was taken largely from interviewing children already incarcerated in prisons and concluded that the main causes of delinquency were the improper conduct of parents, the want of education, unemployment and the violation of the Sabbath. Interestingly, the report also referred to such auxiliary causes as the severity of the criminal code (200 offences were liable to capital punishment) and corruption within the police.[16] It was such beliefs that helped to encourage more voluntary effort in providing institutions whose aim would be to reform, and not merely punish, youth convicted of crimes.

Pressure was also building up from such would-be prison reformers as John Howard, who brought to public attention the overcrowding and insanitary conditions endured by prison inmates. The very size of the prison population in the 1820s forced several prison authorities to introduce a categorization and segregation system in order to secure a greater control of inmates. Within this process a separate convict hulk was introduced for juveniles in 1823, a boys' penal colony at Point Puer was set up in 1837, and a separate prison at Parkhurst, Isle of Wight, was established in 1838 for offenders under the age of 18. As such, young offenders were gradually to be granted the status of deserving a different form of punishment to that endured by adults. Prisons began to be criticized not merely as institutions which aided the corruption of all inmates, but as significant agencies in the corruption of the young. The high recidivism rate, too, tended to suggest that imprisonment only strengthened the criminal habits of the young:

Imprisonment scarred the young with a life-long stigma which prevented respectable, honest employment and forced children back into criminal life. Children treated as adult criminals reacted accordingly. 'Branded as prison birds' they played their role for the admiration of their peers; for a boy once labelled as criminal regards himself as belonging to the criminal class.[17]

At the same time prison inspectors began to report that the isolation of children and adults in prison cells had revealed their essential mental and physical differences and that 'so marked is the distinction in the feeling and habit of manhood and youth that it is quite impractical to engraft any beneficial plan for the lengthened confinement of boys upon a system adapted to adults'.[18] Thus, it was the experiences of imprisonment, rather than the behaviour of the juveniles themselves, that first allowed the apparently unique needs of the young to be recognized. For the first time the earlier bourgeois conception of childhood as a special and separate stage of development began to have implications for the lives of the children of the labouring and 'criminal' classes. An influential body of opinion from lawyers, magistrates, ministers of religion and prison administrators argued that children could not be held fully responsible for their misconduct and that their criminality could be accounted for more by a lack of moral and religious education than by any innate propensities for evil. However, in no sense was there a unified reform movement. As Platt notes, there were various strands and motivations underlying the child savers' ideology:

From the medical profession they borrowed the imagery of pathology, infection, immunisation, and treatment; from the tenets of social Darwinism, they derived their pessimistic views about the intractability of human nature and innate moral defects of the lower classes; finally their ideas about the biological and environmental origins of crime can be attributed to the positivist tradition in European criminology and anti-urban sentiments associated with the Protestant, rural ethic.[19]

Such evaluations of criminality clearly influenced Mary Carpenter and were forcibly expressed in her books *Reformatory Schools for the Children of the Perishing and Dangerous Classes and for Juvenile Offenders*[20] and *Juvenile Delinquents, Their Condition and Treatment*.[21] She staunchly criticized the prison regime at Parkhurst, arguing that because it was based on harsh punishment and strict control 'it attempted to fashion children into machines through iron discipline, instead of self acting beings'.[22] Parkhurst was also condemned for enforcing the use of leg-irons and a distinctive prison dress, and because it provided an inadequate diet for its young inmates. While the use of leg-irons ended in 1840, the prison was not closed until 1884. Carpenter's work remained influential however in advocating alternatives to prison through the establishment of educational and home-like reformatories. The central characteristic of all wayward children, she argued, was not poverty or physical destitution but moral destitution resulting from parental neglect. Delinquent children needed to be returned to the bosom of the family in order to achieve their reformation. Preventing the contamination of youth and restoring their moral guardianship in the family served as the principles for 'humanitarian' reform.

The child must be placed where the prevailing principle will be, as far as practicable carried out – where he will be gradually restored to the true position of childhood. . . . He must perceive by manifestations which he cannot mistake that this power whilst controlling him, is guided by interest and love; he must have his own affections called forth by the obvious personal interest felt in his own individual well being by those around him; he must, in short, be placed in a family.[23]

Implicit in this understanding of childhood is the dependency of children on parents. The exposure of children to the street by working-class parents was thus believed to precipitate the child from its position of innocence and dependency into an *unnatural* knowledge and premature worldliness.[24]

The latter [the delinquent] is a little stunted man already – he knows too much and a great deal too much of what is called life – he can take care of his own immediate interests. He is self-reliant, he has so long directed or mis-directed his own actions and has so little trust in those about him, that he submits to no control and asks for no protection. He has consequently much to unlearn – he has to be turned again into a child.[25]

Similarly, the commander of the reformatory ship, Akbar, had little doubt about where the problems of reform had to begin:

the first great change which has to be affected when they are received on board in their vagrant state is to make them 'boys'. They are too old, too knowing, too sharp, too much up in the ways of the world.[26]

In this way working-class standards of child-rearing were denounced and the conduct of street children universally condemned. This occurred precisely because the conditions of existence, the independence and worldly knowledge of the young offender violated the images of childhood held by the social investigators and philanthropists. The disjuncture between the realities of slum childhood and her own sense of a protected childhood is implicit in Carpenter's work. Indeed Carpenter, in accordance with the prevailing concern for categorization, distinguished between two classes of problem children: the 'dangerous classes' of young offenders and the 'perishing classes' of potential delinquents. As a result she recommended the setting up of reformatory schools for the former and industrial schools for the latter. Each were to provide adequate conditions for the exercise of a sound moral and religious influence, discipline, the inculcation of industrious habits and the creation of a position of dependence which would effectively return the delinquent and pre-delinquent to a true position of childhood.

As reformatories achieved state acceptance through the Youthful Offenders Act of 1854, methods of rehabilitation based on bourgeois principles of child-rearing remained alien to the delinquent and destitute child. The reformatories essentially aimed to remove children from the moral topography of their own class and train them in different ways through which the 'value of labour' could be learned. Concern was thus not only expressed towards delinquent children, but also began to encompass orphans, the illegitimate and abandoned children. Because crime was believed to be generated from the conditions of working-class family life, these sections of youth were seen within a continuum of delinquency as pre-delinquent or near-delinquent. It was no longer necessary to have a criminal act to justify intervention and control. It was the failure of working-class socialization to nurture and discipline the child that was the root cause of what was seen as 'the progressive career of the delinquent child'. The extent of adult crime was also explained in these terms: as a failure in the early family life of the offender.

By 1858 over fifty reformatory schools had been established mainly through voluntary effort. State support for the schools was not won without opposition. A strong lobby persisted in arguing that all individuals should take responsibility for their actions and should remain equal, no matter what age, in the eyes of the law. As a result younger offenders who were committed to reformatories had to serve a sentence of imprisonment, of not less than fourteen days, prior to their entrance. Reformatories were thus used not as an alternative to prison but rather as a supplement to it. Punishment by imprisonment as a precedent for reformatory school treatment indeed persisted until 1899.[27] Within the reformatories the nature of rehabilitation also remained dubious. As Carlebach argues, an excessive use of hard labour in brickmaking and woodchopping was exercised in many of these institutions:

Since it was considered to be a measure of an institution's worth to run it as cheaply as possible and since it was necessary to convince those who subscribed funds towards the management of institutions that their money was being well spent, a number of undesirable factors became deeply entrenched. . . . A number of institutions eventually confined themselves to industries which were not only useless in a training sense but which were often very harmful to the children, in order to achieve a maximum profit from the labour force which the children represented.[28]

Equally, the government's system of paying a per capita allowance for each child led many institutions to admit more children than they could properly cater for, and to retain the services of the most economically productive even when the criteria for their release had been met. The impact of the schools in offering an alternative to prison was slight. A majority of young offenders were still sent directly to prison. It was not until the 1908 Children Act that children under the age of 14 could no longer be sent to prison.

Despite their failures, the reform movements of the mid nineteenth century remain important in that they constituted the first major assault on the classical views of crime, law and punishment. And central to this was their discovery of 'juvenile delinquency'.

The establishment of separate institutions gave the juvenile delinquent a new legal status. The operation of the English penal and educational systems and the perceptions of social investigators had resulted in new distinctions between the child and adult. The acceptance of Mary Carpenter's belief that children should not be dealt with as men, but as children, was a seminal point in the evolution of the modern child.[29]

In arguing that age, parental neglect and depraving circumstances should be taken into account when summoning the law to provide justice for children, the reformers were also influenced by the rise of a positivist criminology in nineteenth-century Europe. Notions of determinism replaced free will as the major perceived cause of crime. The search for factors to explain criminal behaviour shifted away from material explanations (poverty, deprivation and so on) to notions that the major predisposition to crime was situated within the individual. The factors which caused crime were seen to be treatable and curable. Persons without choice, it was argued, could not be seen as responsible for their behaviour and so should be treated rather than punished. As Clarke notes, it was from the success of instituting separate methods of treatment and punishment for children that the pervading classical principles of law came to be questioned.[30]

Nevertheless, even though, by the end of the nineteenth century, delinquent children were no longer seen as 'small adults' and fully responsible for their crimes, they still remained subject to similar deprivations and punishments as those endured by adults. In practice the ideal philosophies of the reformers were never implemented in their pure form but were accommodated within already existing sets of social relations and beliefs concerning crime and punishment.

In essence the birth of the concept of 'juvenile delinquency' did not so much engender a greater humanitarian attitude towards young offenders, as justify an increased surveillance and regulation of both themselves and their working-class families.

The creation of adolescence

During the latter half of the nineteenth century the visibility of youth as a social problem appears to have declined. It may be that the advances in youth reform were thought to be sufficient, and that a significant reduction in the juvenile crime rate had been achieved.

Perhaps of most significance are the number of arguments which claim that, from the 1850s, social relations in Victorian society had become more stable and orderly. 'New model' trade unions, the rise of an aristocracy of labour, the diminished political stridency of the proletariat, more systematic and professional policing and increased popular confidence in the legal system have all been cited as important elements in establishing a mid Victorian 'concensus'.[31] However, between 1890 and 1910, with the publication of more accurate national statistics of juvenile crime, youth once more became the object of adult concern. Using figures based on police court records in Oxford, Gillis argues that the juvenile crime rate was rising from a decennial average of 29.6 offences per year in the 1880s to 99.2 in the first decade of the twentieth century.[32] However, much of this rise was accounted for by such non-indictable crimes as drunkenness, gambling, malicious mischief, loitering, begging and dangerous play. This evidence suggests that the 'increase in crime' was due largely to increased efforts on the part of the police and the courts to control working-class youth leisure pursuits, particularly gambling and the playing of games in the streets. Forms of activity that had been formerly ignored increasingly came to be perceived as indicative of a new social problem. Central to the identification of this new delinquency was the discovery of 'adolescence'.

'Adolescence', like 'childhood', was originally a 'discovery' of the professional middle classes. From the 1860s onwards 14- to 18-year-olds found their independence undermined by an extension of their period of education. Youth were becoming increasingly subject to parental and other institutional controls. With a drop in the rate of child mortality the affluent middle classes began to limit the size of their families. Their investment in a long and expensive education for their children was now carefully planned and protected. The instigation of compulsory education to the age of 13 by the 1870 Education Act, with all but the poorest of parents obliged to pay school fees, no doubt accelerated such notions of dependency and spread them to those families lower in the social hierarchy. But it was in the years of secondary schooling (14 to 18) that a period of adolescence was constructed. What were historically evolved social norms of a particular class became 'enshrined in medical and psychological literature as the "natural" attributes of adolescence'.[33]

By the turn of the century, youngsters of all classes were viewed as sharing certain characteristics solely because of their age. The social construct 'adolescence' had come to replace the social reality of class inequality as a major determinant in all youthful behaviour. However, while a stage of life untainted by adult pleasures was seen as desirable, it was also believed to expose the young to idleness and depravity. Thus, by 1900 juvenile delinquency was being explained in terms of adolescent waywardness. Although originally related to the adult desire to regulate the increased leisure and period of dependency of middle-class youth, the equation of deviancy with a particular period of life enabled all youthful behaviour to be subject to adult scrutiny and suspicion. Every child was thus seen as in need of firm supervision and control during these years of maturation. In 1904 the American child psychologist G. Stanley Hall published his influential work *Adolescence: its psychology and its relation to physiology, anthropology, sociology, sex, crime, religion and education*. Influenced by Darwinism, he argued that individual development passes through stages comparable to those that occurred during the evolution of the human species. Thus each individual re-lived the development of the human race from animal-like primitivism (childhood) through periods of savagery (adolescence) to finally achieve civilized ways of life (adulthood). Within such a psycho-biological framework he thus argued that 'adolescence is pre-eminently the criminal age',[34] and that 'criminals are like overgrown children'.[35]

Youthful delinquency was also explained in a cluster of converging theories rooted in a Freudian view of the fundamental egoistic and individualistic nature of man. Crime was defined in terms of a psycho-pathology which achieved its most acute form within the inner turmoil, uncertainty and 'storm and stress' of adolescence. Such concepts were dutifully applied to explain crime among working-class youth. It was claimed that a general laxity of morals within working-class families produced children who were inadequately socialized or 'civilized'. Such families were believed to have little control over their children's instinctually savage and animalistic behaviour. However, as with the earlier concept of childhood, this notion of adolescence had little or no connection with the actual conditions of existence of the poorer classes. Children of the working classes were needed in the factories as soon as compulsory schooling was completed and the experience of secondary education which gave birth to 'adolescence' was rarely able to reach them. Rather the notion of 'adolescence' was displaced on to them and served to exaggerate their deviancy. Such developments were all the more anachronistic because even by 1909 only 1.5 per cent of 15- to 18-year-olds were from families who could afford secondary education.

It was against this background that various youth movements and organizations, such as the Boys Brigade and the Boy Scouts, were formed by adults to preserve the idealism of youth and redirect their wayward tendencies.

The model adolescent therefore became the organised youth dependent but secure from temptation while the independent and precocious young were stigmatised as delinquent.[36]

Thus changing perceptions of youth, and the power of such groups as moralistic middle-class teachers and 'child-savers' to place their definitions into the public arena, led to a 'crime wave' even though the behaviour of working-class youth had not really altered at all. The move towards organizing working-class youth necessarily involved curtailing such traditional leisure activities as street football, 'promenading' and public bathing, and redirecting them towards military drill and school games. As this became the new mission of middle-class reformers, anxieties about delinquency increased and expanded. However, as Blanch notes, although the principles of organized youth were to apply to all, they were most popular with those who were already 'organized' – middle-class youth and children of skilled workers. A majority of youth were excluded from youth clubs and organizations because membership fees could not be met, or more pertinently because the principle of being organized was alien to their cultural background.[37] Thus the end result of the move to organizing youth was only to highlight divisions within youth and make its 'delinquent' element more highly visible and detectable:

The spread of secondary schools and youth organisations helped establish in the public mind what seemed to be a moral distinction between rough and respectable youth, for the school and athletic uniforms of the model adolescent produced their antithesis in the wide leather belts and bell bottomed fustian trousers which were becoming the costume of many working youths at the turn of the century. Boys in short trousers were exposed to savage mockery by working lads who proudly modified adult dress as a suitable symbol of their independence and maturity. The contrasts between the military style of the Brigades and Scouts on the one hand and the costuming of corner boys and girls on the other served only to create in the public mind an awareness of differences within the youth population which, because they no longer followed class boundaries in an obvious manner, could be interpreted as moral in nature.[38]

Gangs of working-class youths known as 'peaky blinders', 'sloggers', 'hooligans' or 'scuttlers' that existed at this time were increasingly viewed as violent and criminal. As Blanch argues, their behaviour and dress represented their rejection of 'expected' standards of behaviour and the attempts of adults to organize them.[39] Their differences were to become all the more visible and alarming with the emergence of a popular nationalism, based on the military exploits and imperialist ideology of the Boer and First World Wars, and fostered by the Scouts and Boys Brigades. These images of the innocent adolescent and the dangerous delinquent continued to form an 'historical dialectic' during the twentieth century. Both images originated in the same period as projections of the hopes and fears of the middle classes. In order to keep the dream of adolescent innocence alive, they imposed on the young a conformity and dependence that was an anathema to large sections of the population. Instead of accepting the independence and nonconformity of the poor as a product of economic conditions, they inflated their own fears by treating the 'legitimate traditions of youth as punishable delinquencies'.[40]

In this way the 'youth problem' significantly shifted from the nineteenth to the twentieth century. Prior to the 1890s, juvenile crime was a problem of 'childhood', more or less linked to class-based poverty and deprivation. By the twentieth century it had become a problem of 'natural adolescence' – a concept that made all individual youths potential delinquents. What began as an effort to allow the young to live by the rules of this constructed 'nature', ended in chaining them to a new conformity sanctioned by positivist social science and 'welfare' interventions. As such, both those youth legally defined as 'criminal' and those socially defined as 'deviant' became 'legitimate' targets for adult concern and control.

The establishment of special prisons, courts and welfare agencies for juveniles in the twentieth century all became part of this process of offering a unique status to those who were no longer children, but not yet deemed to be fully adult. In 1908 the principle was established that young offenders should be dealt with separately from adults by way of juvenile courts. These were courts of summary jurisdiction empowered to act both in criminal cases and for those children found begging, vagrant, in association with known thieves or whose parents were considered to be unworthy. As such, Carpenter's classification of children into separate categories of 'delinquent' and 'destitute' became conflated. The juvenile courts remained essentially criminal courts despite their 'welfare' responsibilities. The idea that the child was a wrongdoer prevailed and the procedures for dealing with adults were usually thought to be the most appropriate.[41] While imprisonment for children under 14 was ended, later in the same year the Crime Prevention Act enabled the establishment of specialized detention centres where rigid discipline and work training were provided in a secure environment. The first of these was at Borstal in Kent. The juvenile courts did, however, provide magistrates with more personal discretion in the definition and treatment of delinquent behaviour, by offering a range of sentences from fine, discharge and probation to whipping and imprisonment. The concept of adolescent crime, and its analysis in terms of individual psychopathology, no doubt played its part in supporting this discretionary process. Delinquency, it was argued, could be best treated on the merits of each individual case.

The 1933 Children and Young Persons Act, while raising the age of criminal responsibility from 7 to 8, directed magistrates to take primary account of the welfare of the child. They were to 'treat as well as punish'. In order to determine the most appropriate course of action, the courts were to have full access to a juvenile's history, home surroundings, personal circumstances, school career and medical reports. In effect the court became a site for adjudicating on matters of family socialization and parental behaviour even when no 'crime' as such had been committed. When families were found to be 'at fault' the court acted *in loco parentis*. The concept of punishment was extended to include such 'humanitarian' and 'treatment' options offered by children's homes, child guidance clinics and the committal of children to the care of 'fit persons'.

The defining of delinquency as a personality problem associated with a troublesome adolescence and a lack of parental guidance secured the portrayal of juvenile crime in terms of a fundamental weakness of character. This form of analysis dominated criminological thought through to the 1950s. Cyril Burt's claim that 85 per cent of the juvenile offenders he studied in the 1920s were emotionally impaired[42] was one of many studies that concluded that delinquency was essentially a response to personality problems associated with the primitivism of adolescence.

The commoner delinquencies committed by the young are apparently either the direct expression of a few primitive, and universal impulses which seem to have been handed down to us as part of our instinctive equipment or else modified reactions elaborated out of, but still ultimately springing from, these cruder modes of emotional response.[43]

the delinquent is to be approached more as an animal than as a hedonist ... he is liable always to be spurred fatally onward by some natural force – a force which closely resembles those vital springs that animate the humbler brutes.[44]

The concentration of juvenile crime among the working class was attributed primarily to defective family discipline. Burt's image of the 'normal' family against which the 'abnormal' was juxtaposed, was typically idealized and class specific.

The ordinary child in an ordinary home is the member of a small and self-contained society, cared for by the united efforts of both father and mother, and possessing at least one other relative of his own age and outlook to play with him and so to some extent to regulate his ways, or at least to report on any serious fault. The delinquent child is devoid of all such benefits. He leads an existence warped, onesided, incomplete.[45]

Similar images of the 'normal' and the 'delinquent' appear to be at work in the many attempts of psychologists to 'discover' the distinguishing features of adolescence. 'Identity confusion', 'schizoid characteristics', 'ego experimentation', 'psychological disequilibrium', 'a second period of negativism' and 'ideological instability' are just a few of the bewildering array of concepts that have been invented to pin down new and disturbing aspects of this stage of life.[46]

However, oral histories (i.e. personal recollections) of the early twentieth century have increasingly come to challenge the relevance of adolescent psychological pathology as an adequate explanation of crime. Humphries's study of juvenile property theft from 1890 to 1940 illustrates that petty theft was viewed by both working-class parent and child as a customary right and essential for the subsistence of the family domestic economy.[47] He prefers to describe the traditional, though illegal, activities of the working class – 'scrumping' apples, 'scrounging' coal, 'poaching' rabbits and so on – as '*social crimes*'.

social crime offers a class based alternative to the derogatory labels of delinquency and psychopathology which have been favoured by a long tradition of criminologists, who with few exceptions, have accepted a bourgeois perspective in condemning all juvenile working class crime as evidence of ignorance and immorality.[48]

In this way petty larceny can be seen as an elementary form of working-class resistance to the prevailing property laws of the privileged. Moreover, rather than suggesting that working-class families were always on the point of self destruction, juvenile delinquency can now be seen as inspired by motives of family duty. Such forms of delinquency were also legitimated by the working class because:

From the 1900's onwards the imposition of successive prohibitive legislation which regulated street trading, together with the extension of compulsory state education to the age of fourteen led to the virtual extinction of the street children's culture by the mid 1930's. However, there was a direct relationship between the criminalisation of their practices and the upward trend in petty crime amongst city children during the 1920's and 30's for they were forced to turn to other illegal activities to compensate for their dispossessed earnings, the loss of which placed an intolerable financial burden on the poorest families.[49]

The significance of poverty, inequality and class conflict as important factors in the production of crime was, however, largely overlooked by studies of delinquency until the 1950s. In the first half of the twentieth century the notion of adolescence helped to provide interpretations of delinquency which were based primarily in a biological and psychological tradition. The concept of delinquents as less than complete human beings and the acceptance of a rehabilitative ideal, presupposing that delinquents should be treated like irresponsible sick patients, were the hallmarks of this period.

The emergence of a sociology of delinquency

This section draws together a number of formative sociological studies of delinquency dating from the work of the 'Chicago School' in America in the 1920s and 1930s. Sociologists have been eager to dissociate themselves from the limited focus of the individualistic approaches of psychological and biological determinism and have directed attention more to the social context in which the delinquent was situated. In stressing the importance of social factors as causes of delinquency, sociologists have attempted to explain both the existence of delinquency and its distribution in society. Much of this work has been developed in America. In contrast British criminology has been, until comparatively recently, dominated by psychological studies locating the seeds of delinquency in early childhood experiences and 'adolescence'. British sociologists appear to have been disinterested in the subject prior to the 1950s.

our reliance upon theories developed in other countries and particularly in the United States is sometimes so pronounced in the teaching context that students gain the impression of an almost complete hiatus in British research. Erroneous as such an impression may be, the fact remains that the heavy traffic in ideas about delinquency has tended to flow almost exclusively in one direction. As a result we have reached the point where a working knowledge of the American literature becomes a pre-requisite to making sense of most British investigations.[50]

While the study of delinquency can be traced back to the observational work of Mayhew in the mid nineteenth century, a more 'scientific' approach did not emerge until the 1920s when a group of sociologists and criminologists in Chicago began researching juvenile crime. Guided by an ex-journalist, Robert Park, their research was initially based on elements of urban sociology and social ecology. In particular they examined various aspects in the development of urban life, including delinquency, in terms of the changing physical characteristics of the city. In particular Shaw and McKay discovered that there were marked variations in the rates of school truancy and juvenile delinquency in different areas of Chicago.[51] These rates tended to vary inversely in proportion to their distance from the city centre: the nearer to the centre, the higher the rates of delinquency and crime. These areas were also marked by significant population changes, dominated by the influx of European immigrants. The consequential problems of social change and culture conflict were visible and acute. Delinquency was thus believed to be inevitable and inherent in those communities where children were presented with a variety of contradictory standards of behaviour. By reviewing the records of offenders in the juvenile court, Shaw and McKay noted that relatively high rates of delinquency persisted in these areas even though the composition of their population changed over time. The key to explaining delinquency was found in the identification of areas of 'social disorganization' which were subject to physical deterioration and rapid shifts in population. These were areas undergoing the process of transition from residential to industrial use. Such elements, they argued, had undermined traditional social solidarities and modes of social control. When industry invaded a community, resistance to deviance decreased and delinquency became progressively more tolerated. At any moment in time it was the structure of the city which determined the life chances of the individual. Individuals lived in clearly demarcated communities which carried their own neighbourhood reputation and structure of opportunities. The existence of delinquency, therefore, was largely determined by geographica location. Delinquency was considered to be a disorganized but 'natural' response to the tensions of urban development. Such theoretical premises were shared by Thrasher in his survey of over a thousand street gangs in Chicago:

The central tripartite area of the gang occupies what is often called the 'Poverty belt' – a region characterised by deteriorating neighbourhoods, shifting populations and the mobility and disorganisation of the slum. Abandoned by those seeking homes in the better residential districts, encroached upon by industry, this zone is a distinctly interstitial phase of the city's growth. As better residential districts recede before encroachments of business and industry, the gang develops as one manifestation of the economic, moral and cultural frontier which marks the interstice.[52]

Thrasher had also traced the career of urban, working-class male gangs, showing how spontaneous playgroups of early childhood developed into structured adolescent gangs with their own traditions, sense of loyalty and territorial allegiance. Delinquency, therefore, was not only 'natural' in certain areas but was also an activity *learned* in association with others. These conclusions were later to be substantiated by Shaw and McKay. They noted that over 80 per cent of official delinquents committed their delinquencies in the company of other boys of the same age.

A series of ethnographic and 'appreciative' studies of delinquent indeed directed Shaw's attention away from the spatial organization of the city towards the interpersonal relationships of known delinquents.[53] This led to the analysis of how delinquent attitudes and values were learnt and transmitted from one generation to the next. 'Cultural transmission' theory proposed that in the most socially disorganized city areas particular forms of crime had become the cultural norm. Successful criminals became a model for youth and subsequently criminal behaviour became normative to the area and accepted by its inhabitants. Thus the focus of the Chicago School shifted away from exclusively ecological factors to cultural ones. Herein lies a fundamental ambiguity in its work. We are presented with two different images of delinquency: one as random and uncontrolled behaviour caused by disorganization, the other as a relatively well organized group activity which is controlled by older offenders.

However, both the ecological and cultural processes were regarded as one-directional and inevitable. A considerable degree of determinism remained implicit in the Chicago studies. Delinquents were viewed as having little free will and were propelled into a life of crime by factors outside their control. In this way 'social disorganization' theory retained some of the positivist assumptions that underlay those earlier psychological theories of juvenile delinquency. As Taylor remarks:

whilst the Chicago ecologists had considerable sympathy with the deviants they studied, they were not always immune from thinking of them as unfortunate products of a regrettable urban expansion.[54]

Nevertheless, Shaw and McKay had achieved an important breakthrough. They had established that the focus for sociological research should no longer be the search for the causes of 'some nebulous behavioural entity called delinquency, but of describing and accounting for certain distinctive patterns of group behaviour'.[55]

Additionally their research findings provided a forceful criticism of official responses to delinquency, and suggested that the most appropriate interventions were compensatory housing programmes, improved work conditions and forms of community engineering, rather than criminal convictions and incarceration.

Despite the fact that Shaw and McKay relied on evidence, both statistical and observational, of *convicted* delinquents, their investigations remained dominant until the 1950s. The post Second World War era in America, however, brought the problems of low social status youth to a head. A massive disjuncture was increasingly apparent between the ideal of the American Dream – that anyone, regardless of class origin, religion or race, could achieve material wealth – and the closed opportunity structure by which American society was in reality constrained. It was by reference to this wider social context that Albert Cohen attempted to explain the rising number of gangs in American inner-city ghettos.[56] Cohen pointed out that previous research had focused on the processes through which individual boys had adopted delinquent values, but had not examined the nature of delinquent gangs or *subcultures* sufficiently. The typical delinquent, as Shaw and McKay conceived him, had been a thief. Now this view of the delinquent was modified in order to take account of the diversity of illegal activities of youth in inner-city areas. Cohen stressed the compensatory function of the juvenile gang. Working-class youth, he argued, used a delinquent subculture as a way of reacting against a dominant middle-class society that indirectly discriminated against them because of their working-class position. Those youth who under-achieved at school joined gangs in their leisure time in order to develop alternative sources of self-esteem. He developed this thesis by arguing that working-class youths were socialized into a different value system, while remaining exposed to middle-class aspirations and judgements which they then could not fulfil. Their 'status frustration' manifested itself in negativistic forms of delinquency involving hedonism, defiance of authority and the search for 'kicks', whereby the middle-class ethics of ambition, tangible achievement and respect for property were overturned. In contrast to the conclusions of social disorganization theory, Cohen argued that delinquency is rarely motivated by financial gain. Gang delinquents steal 'for the hell of it' and take pride in reputations for being tough and 'hard'. In the gang the norms of the larger society are reversed, so that non-utilitarian deviant behaviour becomes a legitimate activity.

Similarly Cloward and Ohlin explained working-class juvenile delinquency as a collective rather than an individual solution.[57] They argued that criminal behaviour was learned from association with a social milieu in which the codes of such behaviour were widely available and highly esteemed. Delinquent subcultures originated from marked discrepancies between culturally induced aspirations among lower-class youth and the possibilities of achieving them by legitimate means.

One of the paradoxes of social life is that the processes by which society seeks to ensure order sometimes result in disorder. If a cultural emphasis on unlimited success-goals tends to solve some problems in the industrial society, it also creates new ones. A pervasive feeling of position discontent leads men to compete for higher status and so contributes to the survival of the industrial order, but it also produces acute pressure for deviant behaviour.[58]

This imbalance between expectation and reality resulted in a collective alienation which enabled those youths most at risk to develop in the delinquent gang a counter authority to that of the state. The gang thus provided an opportunity system for working-class youths to achieve conventional goals of self-esteem and financial gain but through the illegitimate means available in the organized slum. Cloward and Ohlin developed their argument by proposing a typology of differential responses via a criminal subculture which was devoted largely to securing an income through theft and organized crime; a conflict gang subculture where participation in acts of violence became an important means of securing status; and a retreatist subculture occupied by those who had failed to take advantage of both the illegitimate and legitimate means of securing wealth and social status. With the formulation of Cloward and Ohlin's theory, subcultural studies of delinquency became the centre of an increasing controversy concerned with delinquency prevention. Their association of delinquency with opportunity was partly based on their contact with a lower East Side 'Settlement House' project in New York designed as a delinquency prevention programme. This in turn developed into a far larger project: 'Mobilisation for Youth'. As the project was based on the assumed link between delinquency and thwarted aspiration, the main aim was to expand job and educational opportunities for youth. This soon involved strategies which led the project workers into conflict with established power structures and, as a compromise, the emphasis moved to preventing delinquency through training programmes and the employment of detached youth workers.

Cohen and Cloward and Ohlin's theories also raised consider- able academic debate. Both of these subcultural studies built on the notion first presented in Merton's theory of anomie, that deviance was particularly likely to be engendered in societies such as the United States in which all citizens are urged to strive for success, but many (according to Merton the vast majority) are cut off from opportunities to gain this success because of structural inequalities of power and privilege.[59] Thus crime and delinquency arise from the discrepancy or '*strain*' between culturally induced aspirations and realistic opportunities. The appeal of such an approach in the 1950s was undoubtedly related to the concurrent concern of American sociology to insist that there was a basic concensus of values in society which outweighed any conflicts of value and interest. The dysfunctions and delinquencies caused by anomie were viewed as peripheral, rather than basic, to the social structure. The central argument of this variety of positivism was that individual behaviour is determined by the existence of consensual norms. Thus both 'ordinary' and 'deviant' members of society have no option but to conform to the opportunities facing them. The deviant does not choose an alternative way of life, but is propelled by factors outside his control. Such argument was influential because it located delinquency within the wider social structure and granted its study an objective and scientific basis.

However the basic premises of such positivism have come under increasing criticism. Lemert, for example, has argued that American society was more accurately characterized by value diversity and value pluralism than by concensus.[60] Thus regional and subcultural groups were characterized by different value systems rather than by an allegiance to some hypothesized set of unified values. If this was the case then it was futile trying to account for deviancy simply as behaviour that did not conform to an assumed, but non-existent, cultural norm.

Strain theory was also faced with a series of other problems. Matza and Sykes questioned the degree to which the delinquency of boys was determined by their socialization, and suggested that the commitment to delinquent norms was only partial and temporary.[61] They proposed that the so-called delinquent shares many values with the middle-class citizen. Rather than forming a subculture which stands in antithesis to the dominant order, they argued that such deviants adapt such acceptable values as masculinity, material aspiration and physical courage but translate these into behaviour 'that the majority are usually too timid to express'.[62] While strain theory relied on principles of structural determinism, Matza's framework was derived from naturalism – that is, being true to the phenomenon under study. His major objection to subcultural theory was that its causative factors were too far removed from the world which the deviants themselves recognized. Rather than deviants inverting conventional values, as Cohen had argued, Matza proposed that they are committed to aspects of conventional morality but seek to neutralize its moral bind. Thus delinquents use 'techniques of neutralization' which attempt to justify their own deviance. He listed these as denial of responsibility (I didn't mean it); denial of injury (I didn't really harm him); denial of victim (he deserved it); condemnation of control agencies (they always pick on us); and appeals to higher loyalties (you've got to help your mates).[63] In this way Matza suggested that delinquents were not an immoral species apart, but rational human beings. Instead of viewing normative morality as a unitary system, he argued that the conventional was complex enough to include such subterranean values as bohemianism, radicalism and delinquency. Youth 'drift' into, and out of, such subterranean traditions in periods of boredom and frustration and exist in a limbo between convention and delinquency in which commitment and decision can be postponed or evaded.

In 1958 Walter Miller advanced another explanation of gang behaviour which was also at variance with the anomie theorists.[64] He underlined the similarities between juvenile gang and working-class culture, arguing that many of the values of the deviant group merely reiterated, in a distorted form, the 'focal concerns' of the adult working-class population. Toughness, smartness, excitement, fate and autonomy combine in several ways to produce criminality. Such long established traditions of working-class life placed the individual in a situation that contained a variety of direct influences towards delinquent conduct. Implicit in Miller's formulation is a critique of the notion that delinquency originates as a response to lack of status or thwarted aspirations. Instead, what is alleged to be their delinquency is more a way of life – a response to the micro social realities of their lives. While both Matza and Miller attempted to advance their theories from the perspectives of the delinquents themselves, Miller was not concerned with the influence of their interpersonal relationships. In congruence with positivist principles, Miller stressed the importance of a structural determinism, while in Matza's theory the relationships between delinquency norms, behaviour and social situation are more complex and problematic.

Like the Chicago School, strain theory and the subcultural studies were also based on a determinate view of human nature. Neither seemed to recognize a central paradox in their work. In cataloguing the various activities of delinquent gangs, they adopted a determinist theoretical position which denied human *action* and rendered people passive. By the 1960s the study of delinquency thus moved away from structural theories involving anomie and strain, to interactionism and an examination of the delinquent as a person and the nature of his relations with both other delinquents and the wider society.

In the two main strands of sociological theory of delinquency we have so far discussed, deviants were seen either as the victims of urbanization, or as the products of an unequal distribution of opportunity. Little attention was paid to questions of the nature or origins of the norms that deviants were thought to be violating. Publicly identified delinquents were presumed to be a representative sample of all nonconformists. For example, neither social disorganization nor subcultural theorists paid much attention to middle-class or girl delinquency. No concern was voiced about the role of law enforcement and judicial agencies in the identification and processing of delinquents. The labelling or social reaction perspective developed in response to such shortcomings. The rise of this new approach has been explained by reference to changes in American society during the 1960s. Finestone has argued that the rise of civil rights, women's and gay movements undermined the functionalist view of society as a cohesive organic whole. An image of America emerged as a mosaic of different groups each with its own separate goals and value systems.

The more complex and differentiated a society and the more sensitive individuals become to their group identifications, the more problematic become the social encounters among individuals of competing groups. Those who work with deviance must ask the questions: Who says a particular act is deviant? Who has the power to make this concept of deviance stick?[65]

In attempting to answer these questions, theories of social structure were replaced by empirical studies focusing on concrete social practices. This in turn renewed interest in the earlier 'ethnographic' studies of the Chicago School. However the new 'appreciative' studies, particularly Becker's study of marijuana smokers,[66] were not concerned with examining the isolation and separation of the deviant from mainstream society, but the interrelationship between the deviant and non-deviant worlds. Such an approach initially owed much to the work of Sutherland.[67] He argued that delinquent behaviour is not a product of a lack of socialization but is learnt in an identical fashion to non-criminal behaviour. The potential to become delinquent is dependent on factors of '*differential association*': that is the frequency, duration, priority and intensity of association with other deviant groups. Sutherland's work paved the way to granting authenticity to deviants' own accounts of their activities by making explicit the importance of their consciousness of, and degree of intention behind, their actions. Labelling theory extended this line of inquiry by shifting the object of criminological attention away from individual motivation towards analysis of the types of social interactions which enable behaviour to be defined as deviant and provoke social reaction and control.

Lemert began his study of juvenile delinquency by noting a

massive increase in the number of youths being dealt with by the juvenile court in the 1950s and 1960s.[68] He traced this rise against the increasing influence of the 'rehabilitative ideal' among agencies of juvenile social control which encouraged a maximum intervention into the lives of those individuals and families thought to be at risk. He argued that under the guise of this ideal, definitions of delinquency had been expanded to include a variety of behaviour outside of the criminal law. With this evidence he presented a theory of deviance which proposed that social control, and not behaviour, was the key to understanding delinquency. The 'delinquent' was seen merely as a product of the courts and penal system. Social control was viewed as a 'cause' rather than an effect of deviance. For Lemert it is not deviance which leads to social control, but social control which leads to deviance. As Becker had argued earlier:

> deviance is not a quality of the act the person commits, but rather a consequence of the application by others of rules and sanctions to an offender. The deviant is one to whom that label has successfully been applied; deviant behaviour is behaviour that people so label.[69]

Becker was interested in labelling in so far as it created deviants through a process of interaction between the labeller and the labelled. Whether an act is considered deviant depends, therefore, partly on the nature of the act and whether or not it violates some rule, and partly on what social reaction it evokes. At this stage the labelling perspective was based on a voluntaristic conception of human nature. Individuals were recognized as being actively engaged in constructing their social world, rather than as being passive objects of a particular social structure. In opposition to positivist principles, human beings were thus viewed as being born free, and only losing their voluntaristic capacity in the structures that society lays down in order to control their behaviour. So in the middle of his analysis Becker shifted his position. Once marijuana smokers have been identified as 'deviant' they no longer play an active part in the process of labelling; they become passive recipients of a stigmatizing label imposed on them from above. He concludes, however, that social reaction rarely discourages deviant behaviour, but reinforces the individual's image of self-as-deviant and thus indirectly promotes prolonged deviation and further social control.

By focusing on such *processes* of criminalization labelling theorists opened up whole new areas of interest in criminology. The wider context of social experience, the definition of crime and deviance, and the subsequent reactions to labelled acts and people, became central problems for criminology. Labelling theory questioned how particular acts came to be defined as criminal or deviant, who did the defining and with what consequences for the people so defined. As such it moved the study of juvenile delinquency into an analysis of power relations, social reaction and social control. It had begun the process of 'radicalizing' criminology.

British delinquency research since the 1950s has above all been influenced by these American sociological innovations. In the following two chapters we will be examining how these new approaches came to fruition in a flood of ethnographic, labelling and subcultural studies of youthful deviance which surfaced in post-war Britain.

Suggested reading

There are few well developed social histories of youth and crime. Gillis (1974) provides a useful introduction to the changes in definitions of, and attitudes to, youth during the eighteenth and nineteenth centuries. The early nineteenth century is given more detailed treatment by May (1973) and the early twentieth century by Gillis (1975). Pearson (1983) explodes the myth of a peaceful and orderly past in England by documenting recurring incidents and fears of youth rowdyism and violence from the seventeenth century to the present day.

A good example of psychological interpretations of delinquency is provided by Burt (1945) and an important alternative view is given by Humphries (1981). A detailed review of early American theories of delinquency, which also places them in their institutional and social context, can be found in Finestone (1976). These theories are more briefly discussed by Heathcote (1981) and Muncie and Fitzgerald (1981).

3 Youth and crime

Juvenile crime is constantly in the news. Hardly a week passes without reports in the press of some serious, and usually violent, act which has been committed by youth. Football hooliganism, vandalism, violence in schools, mugging, gang fights and riots have all hit the headlines and provoked some official pronouncement expressing anxiety about the escalation of crimes of violence. Since the Second World War hardly a year has gone by without the publication of the official criminal statistics being greeted with both alarm and fear of a seemingly ever growing number of 'vicious young criminals' who are making the streets unsafe for law abiding citizens.

Official statistics and the youth 'crime wave'

Some of these fears would appear to be substantiated by the available statistical data for England and Wales. Throughout the 1970-80 decade the highest rate of known offending was among males between the ages of 14 and 17. The peak age for committing offences was 15 years for males and 14 for females. Interestingly, this peak age appears to coincide with the final year of compulsory education. Thereafter, offending rates decline steadily, suggesting that most juvenile offenders become less criminally inclined as they grow older.[1]

In 1981 94,900 boys aged between 14 and 17 were cautioned or found guilty for indictable offences, compared with 18,800 girls. 20 per cent of all indictable offences in 1981 were accounted for by this particular age group. Growing concern over youth crime is further fuelled by the statistical evidence that 54 per cent of all such offences are committed by those between the ages of 10 and 21.[2] However, the seriousness of youth crimes, as widely voiced by the media, is somewhat undermined when these offences are broken down into various categories. The majority of juvenile offenders are involved in theft and in handling stolen goods. In 1981 this accounted for some 53 per cent of 10- to 14-year-old and 51 per cent of 14- to 17-year-old offenders found guilty. In contrast, crimes of violence against the person only accounted for some 4 per cent of 10- to 14-year-old and 8 per cent of 14- to 17-year-old offenders. Statistically the crimes most likely to be committed by juveniles are theft, burglary and criminal damage. Sexual offences, robbery, fraud, forgery and violent offences are more likely to be committed by those over 21 (see Figure 2).

Evidence of a massive increase in juvenile crime during the 1970s and the existence of a 'crime wave' is equally unsubstantiated by government statistics. Crime rates have been rising generally over the last twenty years, but this is by no means just the work of young offenders. There have been similar rises in adult crime and the relationship between adult and juvenile crime rates remained fairly constant in the last decade. Moreover, between 1980 and 1981 the rate of known offending for male juveniles decreased, while for other age groups the rate increased.[3] Similarly, Pitts has noted that convictions of 14- to 17-year-olds for violence, sexual offences, robbery and criminal damage all fell between 1973 and 1977.[4] It would appear that youth crimes are becoming less, rather than more 'dangerous' and 'serious'.

Evidence of a real rise in juvenile crime is in fact greater for the 1950s and 1960s. In the 1970s the appearance from Home Office figures is generally one of a levelling off or slight fall in the crime rate. Nevertheless, the numbers of juveniles sent to secure and penal institutions has increased dramatically in the past decade.[5] This has been largely explained as a result of the police increasingly prosecuting or cautioning youngsters for trivial and minor offences, and a growing tendency on the part of the courts to lock up first offenders.[6]

The extent to which these official figures actually reflect the real incidence of crime remains highly debatable. They can only provide us with partial information about the extent of crime because they are based on convictions, and these may not be a representative sample of those committing such crimes. Similarly a 'crime wave' may reflect a growth in public sensitivity, increased rates of reportage and police vigilance, rather than any real increase in crimes being committed. Re-classification of offences and changes in police recording also distort any historical comparisons.

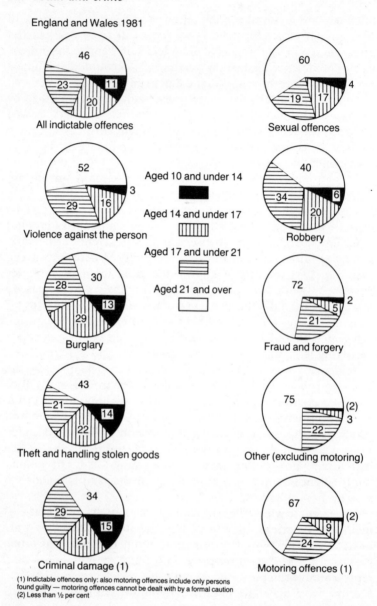

England and Wales 1981

All indictable offences

46
23
20
11

Sexual offences

60
19
17
4

Violence against the person

52
29
16
3

Aged 10 and under 14
■

Aged 14 and under 17
|||||||

Aged 17 and under 21
≡

Aged 21 and over
☐

Robbery

40
34
20
6

Burglary

30
28
29
13

Fraud and forgery

72
21
5
2

Theft and handling stolen goods

43
21
22
14

Other (excluding motoring)

75
22
(2)
3

Criminal damage (1)

34
29
21
15

Motoring offences (1)

67
24
9
(2)

(1) Indictable offences only: also motoring offences include only persons found guilty — motoring offences cannot be dealt with by a formal caution
(2) Less than ½ per cent

Source: Criminal Statistics of England and Wales, HMSO, 1981, p. 85.

Figure 2 *Persons found guilty of, or cautioned for, indictable offences by offence group and age*

Inflation provides a perfect example of one distortion of crime trends. The law is not index-linked and so acts of criminal damage, officially defined as damage exceeding £20 in value, have shot up from 17,000 in 1969 to 124,000 in 1977. Inflation has shifted many thousands of previously trivial incidents of damage into the more serious crime bracket.[7]

In the final analysis we have to admit that there is no reliable measure of either rates of crime or its evaluation as serious. The most accurate answer then to the question, is juvenile crime increasing?, is that we do not know.

As well as being aware of the shaky ground on which the official statistics rest, we must also acknowledge the probable widespread existence of hidden crime in society. For example Radzinowicz has estimated that only 15 per cent of all crimes are officially recorded,[8] while a Home Office crime survey published in 1983 suggested that this 'dark figure' of unrecorded crime is some 75 per cent of all crime.[9] In a self-report study of 1400 London schoolboys, Belson discovered that while 98 per cent admitted having at some time kept something found; 70 per cent having stolen from a shop; and 88 per cent stolen from school, only 13 per cent had been caught by the police (only half of these were subsequently sent to court).[10] Indeed it is probable that all youth qualify for the label of 'juvenile delinquent', having committed some criminal act during their 'childhood' and 'adolescence'. Many crimes remain unreported because they are considered as 'normal' by the observer or too trivial to waste police time. Petty theft, from sweet shops for example, may be regarded as a general childhood 'prank'. Disturbances outside public houses on Saturday nights may be an accepted part of the way in which a particular community lives. Thefts from work may be considered as mere perks of the job.

Nevertheless, as 'facts' the official statistics carry with them a version of truth, even though it is beyond empirical justification. Such statistics remain important because they frequently form the basis for political decision-making and, as we have seen, they also provide the raw data on which many criminological theories are subsequently based.[11]

Juvenile crime: contemporary cases

This section sets out to review critically the main areas of post-war

British research on various aspects of juvenile crime: petty theft, vandalism, football hooliganism, mugging and riot behaviour. Interestingly, although many of these studies aimed to demystify prevailing media images of deviant youth, they took these images as their starting points and have thereby replicated the structure of attention established by the news coverage.[12] As a result, British criminology has tended to follow the news in focusing on the more violent and spectacular aspects of working-class life-styles. It is also significant that, with the exception of theft, the categories of crime that have been explored have been born out of dominant media labels. In legal terms there are in fact no such crimes as 'vandalism', 'hooliganism' and 'mugging'. Rather these emotive labels have served to sensitize us to particular aspects of youth behaviour and, in following such news values, British research may have actually ended up reinforcing their emphases and exclusions.

Juvenile theft

Despite the statistical fact that theft and handling stolen goods account for well over a half of known juvenile offences, this has received very little specific academic attention. However, a number of British studies of juvenile delinquency have implicitly relied on this aspect of law-breaking to illustrate their general argument and to substantiate any subsequent theoretical analysis. The most influential have been Mays (1954),[13] Willmott (1966),[14] Downes (1966)[15] and Parker (1974).[16] Each of these studies was based on empirical research in particular cities – Mays and Parker in Liverpool, Willmott and Downes in London's East End – and accordingly share some similarities with the earlier American 'area' studies in Chicago.

Mays studied eighty boys from the Liverpool University Settlement Project on the basis of unstructured interviews, and produced a vivid picture of an area possessing a cultural background in which shoplifting and petty thieving was considered 'normal' behaviour for adolescents in the 11 to 15 age group. Of the eighty interviewed, he discovered that 42.5 per cent of the boys had been convicted on one or more occasions (forty-one larcenies, ten break-ins, three criminal damage) and 27.5 per cent admitted similar crimes which had been undetected. In all, the total of technically delinquent boys was 78 per cent of the eighty.

Delinquency has become almost a social tradition and it is only a very few youngsters who are able to grow up in these areas without at some time or other committing illegal acts.[17]

He explains the proliferation of petty theft among the boys by reference to adolescent conformity to the particular norms developed within unskilled and slum working-class communities. For Mays, delinquency is not a symptom of maladjustment but of adjustment to a working-class culture which had a significant part to play in the culture of the city as whole. The Liverpool dockside area of his study covered about one quarter of the city but produced over three-quarters of its known delinquents. However, Mays's theoretical approach was closer to that of Miller than to the ecological analyses of Shaw and McKay, despite the fact that Liverpool appeared to reproduce the classic Chicago pattern of 'delinquency areas'. He shares with Miller the view that it is the focal concerns of working-class culture which predispose youth to illegal conduct rather than simply factors of environment or ecology. Such focal concerns as toughness and defiance of authority, however, remain attributed partly to social factors – low status, poverty and unemployment – and partly to ecological factors – slum streets, lack of play facilities. Mays's theory thus presents us with a positivist view of delinquency, in which individuals have little choice but to engage in criminal careers. He thus cannot explain the presence of the non-delinquent within the delinquency area. Similarly, he does not explain how delinquents can give up much of their criminal behaviour in their late teens, if they have been socialized within criminally disposed, 'rough' working-class families.

Some twelve years later, Willmott's study of adolescent boys in Bethnal Green once more emphasized the cultural normality of certain kinds of delinquency, particularly theft. He found that stealing was mainly of a petty kind and accounted for 40 per cent of all known offences for 14- to 16-year-olds. A series of interviews with over a hundred adolescent boys revealed that stealing was a part of their normal behaviour.

An 18 year old said of himself and his friends a few years earlier: 'We used to thieve now and again, same as anyone else, but I don't think we was bad – it was just a normal thing we used to do'. And a 16 year old was probably exaggerating only slightly when he said: 'There's not a boy I know who hasn't knocked something off at some time or another'. A friend who was present commented: 'They're not thieves or anything like that, they're just normal'.[18]

Petty thievery, however, reached a peak at about age 14. Some boys went on stealing though most stopped by about 19 or 20. Juvenile theft was then replaced by the less detectable crimes at work or in industry – pilfering or fiddling from the shop floor.[19] Willmott also recognized a second cycle of juvenile offences mainly associated with joy-riding in stolen cars and some violence, which began at age 15 and lasted until age 19. This second form of delinquency was, however, far less common than the stealing in which a majority indulged when they were younger.

Despite the widespread nature of petty theft, Willmott concludes that 'delinquency was not one of the principal activities of most peer groups'.[20] Most of their offences were relatively trivial and their incidence relatively transitory. Willmott's evidence gives support to some of the American subcultural theories, particularly those of Cohen and Matza. The boys appeared to commit offences out of frustration rather than to acquire wealth, but there was no widespread or continuing sense of resentment among the boys. The applicability of such theories is only partial, however, and Willmott accepts that his study cannot provide a rigorous testing of them. He does not attempt to develop a more comprehensive theoretical account of delinquency. Instead his approach remains eclectic, drawing on whichever aspects of previous theories appear to support his empirical evidence at any particular time.

On the other hand, Downes's study of 'street corner' boys in Stepney and Poplar was specifically designed as a systematic test of the relevance of American theory to the British experience. He argues that dissociation, rather than alienation, is 'the normative response of working-class male adolescents to semi- and unskilled work (and to no work at all) and that this is the primary source of much of the delinquency peculiar to male adolescents'.[21] Downes suggests that the educational system first prepares the less advantaged for routine and unskilled jobs. A majority of working-class boys thus have restricted opportunities, but instead of resenting their position they become relatively fatalistic. Placing a low value on work, they turn to hedonism for relief from the monotony of employment. Leisure rather than delinquency provides their main motivation. However, when the expectation of action via leisure is met with 'nothing going on' then working-class youth may reach a 'delinquent solution by pushing the legitimate values of teenage culture to their logical conclusion'.[22] Like Willmott, Downes discovered that very few boys were committed to deliberate criminality. Groups of boys lacked the systematic organization described by Cloward and Ohlin in their discussion of Chicago gangs. Most offences were trivial, petty and normative. Violent behaviour was minimal. Most of their delinquency stemmed from the illegality of some of their leisure pursuits – rowdyism, joy-riding, vandalism – rather than being born out of 'status frustration', 'alienation' or 'anomie'.

However, to date by far the most detailed research of juvenile theft specifically is Parker's study of unskilled working-class adolescents in an inner-city area of Liverpool. According to official crime statistics, 'Roundhouse' was the most 'delinquent' area of Liverpool. However delinquency was neither a core part of 'the Boys'' activities, nor the aspect of their behaviour which cemented the group together. Instead they were a loose-knit peer group who had experienced the problems associated with having few educational qualifications in an area of high unemployment. Collectively they had turned to a highly instrumental form of delinquency – stealing 'catseyes' (car radios) as a solution to their lack of money. Such theft, however, was important mainly because it provided the resources with which 'the Boys' could participate in and enjoy leisure. Much of this is in congruence with Downes's 'dissociation' thesis, but Parker also extends his analysis to take account of labelling, social reaction, and deviancy amplification theories. Roundhouse was in general a 'condoning community' towards most kinds of delinquency. Thus theft was regarded as acceptable, if it was from people outside the local area. 'The Boys' only 'became delinquent' in the eyes of outsiders, social workers, the police and the courts – the 'Authority Conspiracy':

What is constantly in question is the behaviour of the officials who represent Authority.... Authority for the The Boys has strong connections with conspiracy. Their dislike and distrust of it are centred round an embittered and perhaps occasionally exaggerated sense of injustice.[23]

Although conflict with authority may have sometimes shifted 'the Boys' from 'dissociation' to 'alienation', Parker found little conclusive evidence to support the deviancy amplification thesis. Interaction with authority was to make any amplification peripheral and temporal in relation to its more overall deterrent and coercive effects. The threat of incarceration was then grudgingly taken as a fact of life, but 'the Boys' only partially accepted the 'delinquent' label that had been attached to them.

> In a sense The Boys are the losers, but they only lose battles, not the war; they refuse to be objectified and labelled as 'no good' because their side is still united in the sense that 'they' are 'no better than us'.... Isolated and with little powers The Boys may be, but objects, accepting definitions stamped on them they are not.[24]

Accordingly, 'the Boys' ' commitment to the dominant social order was ambiguous. Moral restraint tended to be community bound, extending beyond only in relation to their fear of authority.

In many ways Parker's participant observation of 'the Boys' over a period of three years led him to suggest that theft and delinquency was not the 'real problem' at all. Rather these were accommodative and rational solutions arrived at by some working-class youth faced with the constraints of a particular social context. Congruent with much contemporary British research into delinquency, Parker remains not so much concerned with identifying the causes of delinquency but with placing it in both its micro- and socio-structural contexts. In a later review of his own work, Parker recognizes some of the problems to be encountered in such an endeavour:

> A micro case study basically appreciative in nature, can only measure the impact of macro structural issues in a fairly impressionistic way by documenting how they impinge on a particular social context and affect the actions of people within. . . . A particularly problematic issue at neighbourhood level involves discovering the exact relationship between subcultural perspectives emphasising cultural diversity, pathology and transmission and a social action approach which emphasises the need for a structural analysis in turn connecting micro social constraints with their origins in wider social processes.[25]

'Vandalism'

Vandalism touches nearly all our lives. We stumble across it in the smashed up and stinking public telephone box, in the railway compartment withs the ripped seats, and walls scrawled with violent graffiti of political or footballing fanaticism. We see it in the broken windows of the housing estates, the tin of paint thrown against a wall, or the motiveless attack on some individual's private property.[26]

The Home Secretary is to hold a conference on vandalism on Tuesday. Once again police, teachers, probation officers, local authority representatives, magistrates and architects will debate what can be done to stem the plague that is costing Britain perhaps £100 million a year.[27]

It is within such terms of reference that incidents of criminal damage are popularly understood. Wilful damage to public and private property is the most visible form of juvenile crime and has received continual media attention in the post-war years. There is, however, no legal recognition of the term 'vandalism'. Rather 'vandalism' is used by the media to cluster often unrelated events under a single emotive heading:

Vandalism is not a precise behavioural description, nor a recognisable legal category, but a label attached to certain types of behaviour under certain conditions.[28]

The term itself has its origins in the behaviour of the Vandals who invaded Western Europe in the fourth and fifth centuries. They were principally regarded as destroyers of Roman art, and civilization. Indeed the adjectives which their behaviour conjured up – barbarous, ignorant, ruthless – remain part of the stereotype of contemporary vandalism. Such adjectives are still used to deny legitimacy to the motives behind some forms of property destruction and to justify punitive measures. But the label is only differentially applied. Many forms of illegal property destruction are not defined as problematic and thus are not denegrated by the label of 'vandal'. Certain groups, such as students, appear to have been given some collective licence to engage in violence and damage to public property, for example after rugby matches, during initiation rites and in inter-college rivalries. In January 1980, hundreds of students from the Jesus and Exeter Colleges in Oxford took part in a water battle in the city streets. Water bombs were later thrown at police and firemen. However, although six students were arrested, in court the prosecution decided to offer no evidence and the charges were dismissed. Or, as Cohen argues:

painting 'Fink College is the Best' on a wall is not vandalism, painting 'Stop Making Bombs' is. Destroying property during rags is 'youthful exuberance' and after all 'for a good cause' but destroying property during a political demonstration is 'thoughtless hooliganism.[29]

In other words the label of 'vandal' is a social construction and its application is politically informed. Because of the images it conjures up, it is employed to discredit the meaning of certain actions and deny them any legitimacy.

The most detailed empirical study to date which attempted to uncover the nature and extent of such behaviour was funded by the Home Office and focused particularly on housing estates in Manchester and London.[30] Its authors worked within a notion of vandalism that consisted of innumerable petty incidents of graffiti, broken windows, defaced road signs, uprooted shrubs and telephones put out of action. They concluded that only a few instances of vandalism involve large sums in repair or replacement, or lead to any real danger. It is these few cases, however, which attract a disproportionate amount of media publicity. In the London study over half the recorded incidents of damage involved breaking glass. In the Manchester housing estate, most of the estimated 940 incidents of damage occurring in a six month period involved small sums of money – usually under £20.

Their second discovery was that only a small proportion of vandalism appeared to be committed against personal or private property. Most vandalism was directed at local authority property – perhaps because it appeared impersonal and was a more vulnerable target.

Third, they found that vandalism was committed either by children under the age of 10 in the course of play, or by adolescents seeking excitement, laughs and a 'few kicks'. Occasional and petty vandalism seemed to be the rule rather than the exception. Few boys in the Manchester study denied any involvement in such destructive behaviour. For example, 85 per cent admitted to scratching desks at school, 68 per cent to breaking windows in empty houses, 65 per cent to writing graffiti on walls. In comparison, only 20 per cent admitted damaging telephone kiosks, and only 12 per cent to slashing train seats.[31]

Most vandalism appears to be associated with play. Marshall's study in Blackburn reported that the peak age of male offenders was under 10.[32] Perhaps no elaborate explanation is needed to explain why young children were so involved in vandalism. Whenever children play without supervision some damage is likely to result. Moreover Taylor and Walton argue that child vandalism is frequently purposive and creative. Their observations of children's play in Bradford revealed that, because the facilities in parks are locked during winter, children resorted to racing supermarket trolley baskets and building climbing frames from wooden pallets. What might later be described by the supermarket owner as 'malicious and non-utilitarian vandalism' was for these kids their only source of innovative play.[33]

The existence of competing definitions and meanings of vandalism was recognized by Cohen. In order to dispel the pervasive stereotype that vandalism is meaningless and senseless, he distinguished five types of conventional vandalism: acquisitive, tactical, vindictive, play and malicious.[34]

Acquisitive vandalism is in some respects akin to petty theft. Damage is done in the course of acquiring money or property, such as stripping lead, removing street signs and looting coin-boxes.

Tactical vandalism is defined as a conscious tactic used to achieve some end other than acquiring money or property. Slogans and graffiti of a political nature, or industrial sabotage to ensure regular rest periods, would be examples of this type.

Vindictive vandalism involves property destruction as a form of revenge against persons or institutions believed to be the source of personal grievance. Cohen argues that much school vandalism is of this type, the offenders being pupils of the schools, rather than outsiders. Their vandalism is usually preceded by punishments, loss of privileges or expulsions. Patrick's study of a Glasgow gang similarly reported that actions such as window smashing were not only a minor part of the gang's activity but were also neither random nor arbitrary. Rather they expressed an antagonism and hatred felt towards particular individuals.[35]

Play vandalism is motivated by curiosity and the spirit of competition and skill. The fact that property is destroyed is often a minor or incidental part of play. But as Cohen notes, 'there is also an imperceptible point at which fun becomes malice'.[36] He quotes one boy from Thrasher's study of Chicago gangs in the 1920s:

We did all kind of dirty tricks for fun. One day we put a can of glue in the engine of a man's car. We would always tear things down. That would make us laugh and feel good, to have so many jokes.[37]

Malicious vandalism is the category which most corresponds to dominant media and public images of apparently mindless and wanton destruction. Pouring acid on car roofs, strangling swans in ornamental lakes, and slashing the tyres of cars in a car park would be indicative. Cohen can only explain such actions by reference to a variety of subjective feelings – boredom, despair, failure and frustration – but stresses that such behaviour can also be rendered intelligible through understanding the context in which it occurs. When such contextualization is made, it is likely that the apparently malicious could be redefined in terms of his other four types of vandalism. Pearson also directs our attention to another form of 'vandalism' – that indirectly performed by planners and architects.[38] Following observations in a Cardiff park, he notes how juvenile vandalism became more frequent when the park was closed and re-scheduled for a development project for government offices. He rightly asks just who are the vandals in the park?

Extending the concept of vandalism in this way makes it virtually impossible to reach any workable definition. The 1981 official statistics for people cautioned for, or found guilty of criminal damage show that 15 per cent are in the 10 to 14 age group and the largest proportion (34 per cent) are over 21.[39] But if most vandalism is committed by the under-10s in the course of their play, these will be not represented in the official statistical lists. Reviewing a note prepared by the Home Office's Central Policy Review Staff for the briefing of ministers, Ward remarks:

What is vandalism? Answer: it proved virtually impossible to find a meaningful definition of vandalism. How much is there? Answer: the statistics are patchy and unreliable. How much does it cost? Answer: it is virtually impossible to measure the cost of vandalism.[40]

We should not, however, forget the power that the term 'vandal' retains, particularly in describing the actions of some working-class youth. But if the 'respectable vandalism' of planners is excused by offering reasons such as the creation of employment, then similar reasons and explanations should be applied to juvenile vandalism, rather than just calling its participants *vandals*. In the final analysis we should direct ourselves to questions of political power and social control, to understand why kids throwing stones at windows are seen as a major social problem, when planners redeveloping play areas for office development are not.

Football 'hooliganism'

At the close of the 1981–2 football season, Leeds United travelled to West Bromwich for a decisive relegation match. In the final minutes, thousands of Leeds fans demolished a nine foot high steel barrier to reach the pitch, as their team were about to lose 2–0. The pitch was invaded, rival supporters attacked each other with bricks and bottles, the police baton-charged the crowd and outside the ground the fighting continued in the streets. Forty-five people were arrested.

There was no need to wonder how these events would be reported in the press the following morning. The image of the 'football hooligan' has been an established feature of the press for at least the past fifteen years. Merely to mention the term 'football hooligan' is to evoke a whole set of accompanying characteristics: mindless, lunatic, animal, moronic minorities.

They're absolute animals, some of them. Scum. A disgrace to the human race.[41]

the disgusting mindless smashing of property and the animal terrorising of ordinary people which was last night inflicted upon London by so-called football fans'.[42]

As Hall notes, this verbal reduction of football hooligans to the level of animals has serious social consequences. It suggests that there is no rationale or reason for the actions of football supporters except some animal instinct or uncontrollable impulse of insane and 'psychopathic fans'.[43] Similarly Whannell discovered four main themes which characterized the language of football hooligan stories. These were categories of 1 mindless/senseless; 2 maniacs/lunatics; 3 foul/sub-human; 4 minority/so-called supporters.

The composite image football hooligan that the sixties gave birth to was perfectly encapsulated in one alliterative phrase by Bobby Moore when he referred to 'the mindless mentality of the moronic minority'.[44]

The source of these images, however, is not merely journalistic rhetoric, but a variety of 'official' voices from club managers, directors, supporters' club officials, officials of the football league, police, magistrates and MPs. These official sources are turned to first when an immediate reaction to any football disorder is needed to construct a media report. They become the primary definers of particular incidents and the media then transform these through codes of selection and presentation to construct their own public language.[45] In this way a stylized and predictable approach to reporting football disorders has developed. A Sports Council/SSRC report on public disorder concluded that there was no doubt that the press coverage in popular dailies sensationalized football violence and also frequently distorted the truth of particular incidents by providing inaccurate captions to photographs and by a generalized use of dismissive labelling. This tendency was epitomized by the *News of the World* caption 'Manchester United's hooligans race across the pitch brandishing the spoils of their victory' to a photograph of members of the supporters' club clearing the pitch of debris under the supervision of the police.[46]

Despite the prominence of hooliganism as one of football's major problems, the press have devoted little discussion to its causes. This is perhaps not so surprising as the phenomenon is consistently defined as irrational and thus not open to explanation. However, the press is more forthcoming in offering solutions to this 'problem', and indeed has come to play a crucial role in the demands for greater punishment and more effective measures of crowd control. In this sense the image 'football hooligan' helped to mobilize significant 'law and order' campaigns during the 1970s and, together with other moral panics about working-class youth, has justified a shift towards a more authoritarian response to troubling aspects of their behaviour.

In the wake of such publicly voiced fears about hooliganism, various sociological studies have attempted to provide a rationale or explanation for such crowd misbehaviour. The first of these was Taylor's analysis of the origins of soccer hooliganism.[47] He argued that the 'problem' can only be understood by examining changes in the game itself. First, he dismissed the public picture of hooliganism as involving a committed and organized mob of delinquent youth by referring to Matza's notion of a 'drift' into delinquency.[48] Matza had argued that there was little evidence to support the view that delinquents were organized as fully developed oppositional subcultures. Rather working-class youth *drifted* into, and out of, delinquent activities with little commitment to a permanent delinquent way of life. Above all their allegiance to the values of dominant culture remained secure. Youth justified its delinquency by pointing out that 'everyone has a racket' or that 'we all break the law sometimes'. It was only when youths were arrested for their incidental delinquencies that magistrates, police or editors constructed the picture of a continually troublesome or dangerous mob.

Within this perspective Taylor explains the transient and incidental world of soccer hooliganism as a reaction to the 'bourgeoisification' and 'internationalization' of the game by which traditional elements of working-class support and control have been consistently undermined. He points out that soccer has a particular cultural significance for the British working classes. Historically the game 'belongs' to that class in terms of social composition and organization of local teams and supporters. The rank and file supporters of the 1930s could see themselves as part of a collective and democratically structured organization united through the primary values of masculinity and collective partici-pation which were derived from their experiences of the labour process. However, during the post-war years, soccer's identifica-tion with working-class culture has been undermined by such transformations as the construction of grounds as commercial 'stadia', the elevation of certain players to media stars, the increasing hold of the petit bourgeoisie over directorships and the incorporation of soccer into the range of respectable national sports. With the development of international competitions, still further separation was engendered between local culture and the club.

The result is an uneasy coexistence between the club and the traditional working-class supporter. The latter's 'drift' into hooliganism is seen as an elementary form of protest and resistance to clubs he once helped to create and which now ignore or reject his contribution:

the centrality of soccer as a form of consciousness in sections of the working class leads those sections to locate their alienation and isolation in the soccer club itself. That is violent resistance . . . is not an arbitrary reflexion of some vague frustration. Rather the violence around soccer may be seen as a specific (if inarticulate) choice produced by the hold the game has had over generations of working class experience.[49]

Thus throughout the 1960s there were a number of pitch invasions, groups of supporters frequently called for the resignation of directors and managers and various objects were thrown at unpopular (usually non-local) players of both sides on the pitch. If such interventions were an established element of the game in the 1950s and 1960s, it was not until the late 1960s that they were defined and denegrated as 'hooliganism'. An important stage in this reaction was the commissioning of a team of psychiatrists in 1967 to research this problem.[50] The employment of psychiatrists helped to establish the idea that hooliganism was explicable only in terms of unstable and abnormal individuals who had, for some inexplicable reason, chosen soccer as the arena in which to act out their instabilities. According to Taylor, the Harrington Report and subsequent media reactions have neglected the fact that the supporters' violence is never arbitrary but has particular targets and real, historically-determined motives.

Similarly, a study by Clarke has argued that a historical perspective of the nature and importance of football to working-class culture is a necessary preliminary to understanding 'hooliganism'.[51] He relates how processes of 'spectacularization' and 'professionalization' in post-war British soccer have implied a different role and place for the traditional working-class supporter on the terraces. First, professionalism in methods of playing, planning and training for matches, has made football more systematic and routine. Second, professionalism has manifested itself in the attitudes of clubs towards attracting audiences by installing extra seating, providing new bars, restaurants and social clubs, and building enclosed boxes for the wealthy corporate spectator. These moves instigated a particular way of watching the game: seated, dispassionately critical and distant. Coupled with these developments are the attempts to make the game more of a complete spectacle and accessible to a wide audience by providing pre-match entertainment at the grounds and more pertinently by televising the 'highlights' of at least six matches every week. Through television the image of 'real' supporters was significantly altered.

in the pre-war traditions of football support ... the experience of watching football was a collective physical and emotional one, the crowd was partisanly involved in the game, involved in making their own experience of the match. For the new spectator, football is a provided entertainment – something which goes on out there; rather than something which is involved in and created by the relation between what goes on on the pitch and the crowd. The new spectator is distanced from the game, able to make critical judgements about it and able to pick and choose between this and other alternative entertainments.[52]

For Clarke, 'hooliganism' occurs when the traditional forms of watching football encounter and try to overcome these new developments. Young working-class fans are placed at the centre of this contradiction. They are seen as hooligans precisely because they contravene the new view of how football spectators should behave. But essentially their behaviour is an extension of patterns of commitment and partisanship which have always been a part of the game. The young fan now affirms his loyalty to a club by glorifying its name on subway walls and by defending it vociferously against the insults of opposing fans. However, when he acts out his emotional allegiance to a club in these ways, the club disowns him further.

While this historical perspective is important in widening the debate about hooliganism and placing it in its proper social context, neither theory has produced any firm evidence that fans do actually perceive the club as more distant than before and that their behaviour correlates with acts of resentment or hostility. In particular, Taylor's hypothesis that the game in the 1920s and 1930s was characterized by an illusion of 'participatory democracy' has yet to be verified. In addition, both studies have been criticized for ignoring the outbreaks of crowd disorder that occurred in the 1890s and it has been questioned whether analysis of these would have brought to light different causes of crowd violence.[53] Nevertheless their central insights remain valid. Hooliganism became an issue at precisely the same time that the game was undergoing significant commercial, professional and international changes.

It is to the area of understanding the social world of contemporary football fans coupled with a more thorough historical analysis of the phenomenon that most research has recently been directed.

Marsh's studies of the 'career structure' of hooligans marked a significant step in attempts to uncover the experiences of the fans themselves, and in effect to humanize their deviance.[54] Marsh, one of the few psychologists to study football violence, spent two years in close observation of crowd interaction at Oxford United. Distinguishing between aggression, as a constructive means to control physical and social space, and violence, as a subsidiary form of aggression which involves the infliction of physical pain, he argues that football aggro is neither irrational nor uncontrolled, but a finely balanced ritual display of loyalty and aggression. He concludes that left to run its own course, the aggro ritual between rival supporters ends without real trouble – honour is satisfied without physical harm being inflicted. The danger, Marsh suggests, is when external agents – club officials, the police, media reporters – intervene and interrupt the fine balance of ritual. His argument, however, rests on the theoretical premise that in the course of evolution, aggression has typically been resorted to by males to aid survival and defend terrorty. Within football crowds, he argues, this instinctive urge to aggression is again expressed, but through a set of orderly rituals which involve little or no violence. At Oxford in the 1974 season, for example, he discovered that there were only eighty-three arrests – an average of under four per game or 0.06 per cent of the total attendance. Moreover, only five of these arrests were for violent offences, the majority being to do with breaches of the peace under the Public Order Act. This was later to be substantiated by Trivizas who discovered that over 67 per cent of football crowd arrests in the Metropolitan Police Area were for the offence of 'use of threatening abusive or insulting words or behaviour'.[55]

Using such information, Marsh is able to claim that football violence is more illusory than real.[56] He does not, however, claim that aggressive behaviour (as opposed to violence) is an unimportant element in the behaviour of football fans, but that this aggression, too, is controlled and ordered by a system of implicit rules and standards. His research revealed three distinguishable groups of fans on the terraces representing something of a 'career hierarchy' – the novices, the rowdies and the town boys. The 10-year-olds (novices) are situated at the front of the crowd and observe and are entertained by the rowdies. The latter, 12- to 17-year-olds, are the stereotypical hooligans, orchestrating the chants, songs and ritualized aggression, while the older town boys are generally inactive, preferring to rest on past reputations for toughness established in their 'rowdy' days. Within the rowdy group it is the 'nutters' who, for Marsh, provide the key to the underlying order which characterizes football hooliganism.

These are individuals whose behaviour is considered to be so outrageous as to fall completely outside the range of actions based on reasons and causes. Typical of their behaviour would be 'going mad', 'going wild' or 'going crazy'. . . . It is the existence of this kind of role and the presence of notions of 'unreasoned' action, which is taken as strong corollary evidence for assuming the existence of a tacit awareness among fans of the rules governing social behaviour on the terraces.[57]

It is the 'aggro leader', rather than the 'nutters', who achieves most status by displaying an aura of fearlessness and bravery while still behaving within 'acceptable' limits. The fans are 'in no doubt as to where bravery ends and sheer lunacy begins'.[58] Football hooliganism is, therefore, contained within the parameters of an informal apprenticeship system based on age and tested by partisanship and proven ability to not back away from 'realistic' opposition. In this way increasing involvement in aggressive behaviour enables young people to achieve the sort of reputations and images denied them in mainstream society.[59] But according to Marsh, moments of real violence are rare. A thousand or more fans may chant with all sincerity 'you're gonna get your fuckin' heads kicked in', but there is a generalized restraint on actual physical contact. Similarly, when fans recall moments of violence and destruction, Marsh prefers to explain these by reference to youthful bravado. He thus paints a picture of an orderly conflict in which a lot of noise is made but little injury sustained. Fights that do occur are not random but are provoked by particular challenges such as territorial invasion or unsanctioned fouls on the pitch. Historical antecedents and local rivalries also inform the rules governing confrontation. For example in Glasgow, strong feuding traditions have long existed between Rangers (Protestant) and Celtic (Catholic). But even if such rules and order do govern conflict on the terraces, football hooliganism does provide opportunities for feats of courage and bravado – stealing the scarves of opposing fans as trophies, outwitting police, running on to the pitch, taking the opposing supporters' end. A football crowd also offers a chance to express violent emotions and collective solidarity: a moment for excitement in an otherwise drab world of routine work or unemployment. As Pearson argues:

all the evidence points to the fact that football hooliganism arises directly out of the passion and ecstacy of Britain's major working class sporting entertainment and that 'football hooligans' are amongst the staunchest and most committed supporters of the game.[60]

Nevertheless, it has been generally recognized that the noisiness and violence of soccer crowds does seem to have grown in intensity in the past decade. Clarke explains one element in the origins of such hooliganism by reference to the skinhead youth subculture of the late 1960s.[61] Their violence, both real and imaginary, is viewed as an expression of toughness and of a specific working-class self-conception of masculinity. The football ground provided one of the few avenues in which these traditional working-class values could be acted out.[62] And it is because he ignores the relevance of such specifically working-class values that the work of Marsh has been extensively criticized. While Marsh rightly stresses that the violence of football hooliganism is exaggerated in both the public and media consciousness, he drifts in the opposite direction and fails to recognize the causes and implications of a working-class youth violence that are real and serious.

Such evidence that does exist suggests that football hooliganism is the preserve of young working-class males, whose day-to-day existence is characterized by a tolerance to forms of violence condemned by other sections of society.

The present evidence suggests that they are mainly from a working class background with the special problems inherent in large industrial cities and ports where violent and delinquent subcultures are known to exist.[63]

In one dock area notorious for serious outbreaks of hooliganism we found that fighting was regarded as a way of life the inhabitants were born to, and the only proper way of settling disputes. Here to avoid a challenge was unmanly; to remain passive was looked on as wrong.[64]

Within this context Marsh's propositions have been re-examined by Murphy and Williams.[65] They conclude that Marsh has seriously under-estimated the extent of violence which pervades the values of working-class football hooligans, by failing to examine pre- and post-match activities and ignoring the significance of missile throwing inside the ground.[66] Moreover, after extensive research largely at Leicester City Football Club, they argue that injuries known to the police or St John's Ambulance only represent a minority of cases. Given the emphasis the fans place on physical toughness and the necessity to make light of injury, they conclude that many injuries never come to be officially recorded. Similarly no football hooligan will report to the police any violent confrontation which may have gone officially unnoticed.

Such an alternative reading of the official statistics on football violence and injury remains, of course, just as open to debate as Marsh's own interpretations. However the crux of Murphy and

Williams' critique is that Marsh makes no attempt to locate football violence (however extensive or not it may be) within its class specific context. As such Marsh fails to:

recognise and pursue the implications of the fact that we live in a society characterised by structural differentiation of which diverse standards of acceptable violence are both an element and a consequence.[67]

Marsh's studies may remain important in providing some order to, and rationale for, apparently mindless and irrational behaviour but do little to locate hooliganism within its wider social and historical context. There is indeed a real danger in trying to ignore or disguise elements of working-class violence. Such violence is real, but needs to be understood and responded to with reference to the history of class conflict and resistance rather than solely within a soccer/hooligan/youth scenario. As Taylor argues, if soccer hooliganism is to be recognized as a problem its resolution depends on establishing political and economic policies which will create 'real social order in working-class life, and not on the elaboration of penal measures for sections of that class by an authoritarian state'.[68]

In response to Marsh, we should also note the recent fusing of football hooliganism with the racist propaganda of the National Front. In 1980 football grounds became a priority target in the extreme right's recruitment efforts which were built around the conscious orchestration of racial tension and indiscriminate violence on the terraces. In this the activities of young skinheads have once more been central.[69]

Contemporary moral panics about hooliganism, however certainly remain uninformed of the fact that pitch invasions, terrace fights and the subsequent closure of football clubs have been a recurring element in the game since the FA tried to organize it within 'alien' rules and regulations in the late nineteenth century. Thus the degree to which the late 1960s marked a rapid escalation of the problem remains open to doubt, and popular understanding of the phenomenon has been more than tainted by sensational and overreactive media reporting.

'Mugging'

In March 1982 the Metropolitan Police released the annual crime figures for the London area. The occasion was chosen to issue a press release which concentrated on the *smallest* category of crime in London, the 3 per cent of offences constituting 'robbery and other violent theft'. These had risen by 34 per cent from 13,984 in 1980 to 18,763 in 1981. The figure included 5889 cases which were described as 'street robbery of personal property'. Although these amounted to only 0.9 per cent of all the recorded offences in London, they attracted extensive media interest because 'street robbery of personal property' is what the police also call 'mugging'. The release of these statistics will also be remembered because for the first time they were officially classified according to the race of the offender. According to the figures 55.4 per cent of all robbery and violent theft was said to have been carried out by blacks. In addition most of the victims were said to be white and nearly a quarter over 50 years old. No such descriptions of other offences were provided. Racial breakdowns of police statistics are confined to violent thefts and are not applied to the other 97 per cent of serious offences. The following day the press reacted in characteristic manner:

'BLACK CRIME: THE ALARMING FIGURES'[70]
'LONDON'S STREETS OF FEAR'[71]
'ON BRITAIN'S MOST BRUTAL STREETS'[72]

The simple equation of Black = Crime was firmly established. However, as Pierce has argued, the selective release of statistics and their interpretation by the media provided a less than accurate picture:

Realisations that will now never come to the majority of readers of newspapers or viewers of television are that 'muggings' were never the figure of 19,000 quoted last week by Scotland Yard, but instead under 6,000; that the victims were never for the most part elderly and white but in the main between the ages of 21 and 30 and on the Home Office statistics between 36 per cent and 50 per cent more likely to be West Indian or Asian; that the percentage of alleged perpetraters crudely classified as black was derived from a questionable categorisation that included many different ethnic groups.[73]

Part of this problem of 'reading' the statistics of course lies in the fact that 'mugging' is not legally recognized as a crime. But in popular idiom it has become increasingly associated with all incidents of violent theft. Moreover, from the mid 1970s an image of the mugger as *male, young, black* and usually acting alone has been continually evoked, but rarely interrogated at any great length.[74]

How has this picture of the mugger come to achieve such social prominence? What are its origins and consequences? Questions of this nature were asked by a major research project of the 'mugging' phenomenon of 1972-3 at the Centre for Contemporary Cultural Studies in Birmingham.[75] Its authors noted that the label was first used to describe a specific crime in England in August 1972 when the *Daily Mirror*, quoting a police officer, described the death of an old man outside Waterloo Station as a 'mugging gone wrong'. In October and November of 1972 a massive press coverage of 'mugging' suddenly appeared, drawing on images constructed in Nixon's election campaign in America in the late 1960s.

Chiefly involving poor, young ghetto blacks, intimately connected with drugtaking, seemingly random and often violent, 'mugging' was the perfect crystallisation of city breakdown. One of the chief electoral pledges thus became that of ridding American city streets of fear: of restoring 'law and order'. So 'mugging' entered the British press highly contextualised, highly 'connoted'. It meant from the outset, far more than a particular type of street robbery but a whole complex of images: of urban breakdown, violence, drugs and race.[76]

Above all, it was seen as a new and rapidly escalating form of youth crime. However, no statistics of 'mugging' existed in Britain before 1972. It was only by projecting the figures back to 1968 that the impression of a massive and alarming 129 per cent increase could be gained. Similarly, the newness of 'mugging' is open to question. Previously it had been popularly known as 'snatching' or 'getting rolled'. Such incidents, as Davis discovered, also have a lengthy history, traceable to the London garotting panic of 1862.[77]

Thus Hall *et al.* argue that while certain acts of street violence did occur in the early 1970s, the phenomenon was certainly not new. Neither do we know conclusively whether 'muggings' did increase in the early 1970s because of the unreliability of statistics and the re-classification of offences.

Both Hall and Davis separately concluded that 'garotting' and 'mugging' were, in themselves, initially undeserving of the media and public reaction they received. In particular any rise in the numbers of convicted offenders occurred after each of these panics had been firmly established, suggesting that we must look elsewhere to explain why such panics should arise.

Nevertheless, by the beginning of 1973 'mugging' was widely accepted as a major social problem and, as a consequence, was used to justify punitive and deterrent sanctions. As a result, in March 1973 a 16-year-old boy from Handsworth was jailed for twenty years for his part in an act of robbery with violence.

As Hall *et al.* argue, the label rather than the actual presence of 'mugging' came to represent a generalized image of lawlessness and breakdown of law and order. This in turn legitimated moves towards more coercive forms of social control and eventually the more positive policing of whole 'criminogenic' communities.

However, despite its American connotations, 'mugging' was not unequivocally defined as a racial problem until 1975. It was not until then that the equation of 'mugging' and 'black crime' became firmly established. This was triggered off by a cluster of events. First, a report on street crime in South London was prepared by Scotland Yard which (though never fully released to the public) revealed that the police now recorded the race of victims and assailants in 'mugging' cases. It argued that 80 per cent of attackers were black and 85 per cent of victims were white.[78] Second, the mid 1970s were marked by dramatic increases in black unemployment. Third, a growing hostility between West Indian youth and the police in localized areas began to develop, chiefly as a result of the police practice of SUS – arrest on suspicion. Black resistance was in turn confronted by organized National Front marches through predominantly immigrant areas. Within this socio-political context 'mugging' became specifically identified as a crime committed by West Indian youth, and as a problem specific to such immigrant areas as Lambeth and Brixton in South London. In this way Hall *et al.* explain the origins and resurgence of interest in 'mugging' with reference to the economic crisis of British capitalism and emerging control strategies of the state. Their explanation of the moral panic is firmly placed in the context of deteriorating material conditions in the inner-cities, worsening race relations and the development of a law and order state. The meaning of 'mugging' then has very little to do with the escalation of a particular crime, but is more an attempt by the state to isolate 'deviant' populations, manufacture a moral panic about them and eventually persuade the public to accept more coercive means of social control. Indeed, the construction and career of 'mugging' have played a central part in Britain's recent drift into a law and order society. It has given fuel to the fire of white racism, in that all young unemployed West Indians were seen as potential muggers. It has fostered aggressive positive and saturation policing practices in black communities. But it has also given such communities a cause for complaint and resistance:

the police have undertaken – whether willingly or no – to constrain by means which would not long stand up to inspection within the rule of law, an alienated black population: and thereby, to police the social crisis of the cities.[79]

The end result of the 'mugging' panic was seen some eight years later in the series of riots which occurred in over thirty urban areas in 1980 and 1981.

'Riot mobs' and civil disturbances

In April 1980, the morning after the disturbances in the St Paul's district of Bristol, our daily newspapers carried such headlines as:

'RIOT MOB STONE POLICE'[80]
'POLICE IN MOB FURY'[81]
'RIOT MOB TAKEOVER'[82]
'RACE MOB RUNS RIOT'[83]

The label and image of a 'riot mob' was placed firmly on the agenda of Britain's serious social problems. Immediately it stood at the head of a whole series of moral panics and derogatory labels which have characterized the media's reaction to youth behaviour on the streets. It superceded those earlier images of 'vandals', 'hooligans' and 'young thugs' and collapsed them into the more powerfully evocative notion of a 'riot mob'.

As such it carried with it, and conjured up, images of lawlessness, anarchy and irrational collective behaviour which were reminiscent of the traditional nineteenth-century bourgeois fear of the 'masses' – a fickle and violent mob lacking guidance and control. Such images were all the more powerful in the 1980s because although St Paul's was *not* a race riot, as had been suggested by one newspaper, it was sparked off by confrontations between the police and predominantly black youth.

A similar pattern of events and media reaction was evoked in the disturbances in Brixton, Liverpool 8 (Toxteth) and Moss Side in 1981. By now, however, the concept of a 'mob' on its own, with real or imagined grievances, proved to be too broad and too loosely defined to be useful in the attempts of politicians and the police to regain law and order. Thus the media and police attempted to single out criminal elements within the crowds, identify 'ringleaders', lay blame on political activists who had allegedly stirred otherwise peace loving people into action, and reduce the collective action of large communities to the actions of a few individual 'extremists'. As a result, in July 1981 the media chose the following headlines:

'HUNT FOR MASKED RIOT LEADERS'[84]
'EXTREMISTS' MASTER PLAN FOR CHAOS'[85]
'RIOTS: FOUR MEN HUNTED'[86]

Similarly Kenneth Oxford, Chief Constable of Merseyside, attempted to bypass the real grievances of British blacks by arguing that: 'This is not a racial issue as such. It is exclusively a crowd of black hooligans intent on making life unbearable and indulging in criminal activities.'[87]

Many and varied causes of the disturbances have been advanced and analysed since July 1981. These have ranged from Oxford's neo-classicist picture of hooligans and criminals who have deliberately chosen to break the law, to the unbridled pluralism of an *Observer* editorial which argued that:

The casus belli of a youth war lies in unemployment, bad housing, the breakdown of morality, of family/school discipline, a more rebellious attitude to authority in this generation, overreaction by the police, the violence of youth culture, of some rock music. The list trails into infinity, rightly so, for there is no single cause.[88]

Such pluralism was also reflected in the Scarman report – the major government-sponsored inquiry into the Brixton riots of April 1981 – when it attempted to apportion 'blame' to various sections of the community:

Nothing that I have heard or seen can excuse the unlawful behaviour of the rioters. But the police must carry some responsibility for the outbreak of disorder. . . . The failures of the police, however, were only part of the story. . . . The community and community leaders in particular must take their share of the blame for the atmosphere of distrust and mutual suspicion between the police and the community. . . .[89]

Such lists of causes may appear attractive in that no significant element appears to be omitted, but in implying many causes these analyses also require some ordering of priorities. Without this, rock music becomes as legitimate a target for criticism as unemployment. Unfortunately such multi-factor analyses, in their preoccupation with the minutiae of particular events, end up by telling us very little of general social relevance and can provide few guides for future social policy.

It would be useful to quickly recap on the events of April 1980 in Bristol, April 1981 in Brixton, and throughout Britain in July 1981 to try at least to establish priorities and explain some of these many 'causes'.

The disturbances began in April 1980 in the St Paul's area of Bristol. The 'spark' was provided by a police raid of the Black and White café, one of the few meeting places for black youth. The police cordoned off the area around the café, and for over two hours questioned people, removed crates of beer and arrested the owner. During that time an ever growing crowd of people, including some white youth, had gathered. As the owner was brought out handcuffed, the police and their vehicles were attacked by youths throwing stones, bricks and bottles. Greatly outnumbered and unprepared for the anger of the community, the police were forced to withdraw, after attempting to confront the youth with military-style tactics for two hours. For four hours while the police awaited reinforcements, St Paul's was a 'no-go' area.

In all some 130 people were arrested in the days after the disturbance. Ninety-one were charged with 'minor' offences, only one of whom was found not guilty. In July, twelve people were charged with the more serious offence of 'riotous assembly'. The police hoped for a show trial but in court their case collapsed. Half-way through the proceedings the judge directed that three of the defendants be acquitted as no case had been made out against them. The jury eventually found five not guilty, and was unable to reach a verdict on the other four. In April 1981 the DPP announced that because of lack of evidence the remaining four would not have to face retrial.

In April 1981 the Brixton police launched 'Swamp 81', a special operation to combat 'muggings' and street crime. In the first four days over 1000 people were stopped and questioned on the street, and over 100 arrests were made. The operation also included raids on homes and cafés. This time, the 'spark' occurred when a black youth who had been injured in a fight was held in a police car although he needed hospital treatment. A group of 100 black youths released him and a twenty-minute battle with police followed. Eight arrests were made before the police made a 'tactical' withdrawal. The next morning the police presence around Brixton's Railton Road was, according to the *Observer*, 'massive'.[90] When a young black was arrested by plain clothes officers, punched in the stomach and dragged to a police van, the street quickly filled with black youths who tried to release him. In the following confrontation the first petrol bombs were thrown. Besides the police and police vehicles, pubs in the area which had refused to serve blacks were set on fire. The police managed to contain the riot within an area of three square miles, but some groups of police also took matters into their own hands. A freelance photographer at Brixton police station noticed a group of about fifteen police in jeans and casual jackets carrying 'pickaxe handles, rubber tubes and a piece of chain about eighteen inches long'.[91]

The next day there were 4000 police in the area. By the end of the weekend sixty-three police vehicles had been attacked, and 286 people, mainly black, had been arrested.

These two events had striking similarities: they initially involved black youths; their targets were largely police and not the white population *per se*. They were not race riots; they occurred in areas of high unemployment and they were triggered off by heavy handed police methods – whether of harassment of individuals or saturation policing.

In July 1981, however, disturbances throughout Britain's urban centres showed that the malaise went much deeper. The youth of the working class – black and white side by side – petrol-bombed the police, their vehicles and their police stations.

The first of the July disturbances was in Southall, when coachloads of skinheads arrived for a rock concert at the Hambrough Tavern in an area largely populated by Asians. Asian shops and their owners were attacked. Inside the pub, racist hostilities within the audience were stirred up by one band making Sieg Heil salutes and singing British marching songs. Hundreds of Asian youth came on to the streets and beseiged the pub. By 10 pm the pub was on fire and the skinheads, protected by the police, withdrew. Southall differed from St Paul's and Brixton in that fighting took place mainly between black and white youths. Here, the Asian community leaders complained of a lack of police protection from racist attacks. Their common denominator, however, was a developing sense of racism within the British police force – harassing blacks in their everyday life and allowing racist attacks to go unpunished. In Southall the Asians were placed in a position where they had to police their own community in order to secure their own safety.

If these incidents were most clearly informed by a racial dimension, particularly in Southall, the disturbances in Toxteth, Liverpool 8, Moss Side, Manchester and over thirty cities during the weekend of 10–12 July added a certain class dimension. For here both black and white youths were united in attacking the police. Here again, the targets of the petrol bombs were not arbitrary. In Toxteth, for example;

It was obvious why people went for the police but there were exact reasons why each of the buildings was hit. The bank for obvious reasons, the Racquets Club because judges use it. Swainbanks furniture store because people felt he was ripping off the community.[92]

During four nights in Toxteth 150 buildings were burnt down, 258 police needed hospital treatment and 160 people were arrested. The police fired CS gas for the first time on mainland Britain, but used cartridges intended for penetrating walls and buildings rather than for dispersing street crowds.[93]

In Manchester, James Anderton, the Chief Constable, declared that it was time the police moved on to the offensive. Twenty-four police wagons, each manned by ten steel-helmeted riot police, sped through Moss Side. Black and white youths were pinned to the walls and arrested; and several youths were knocked over by the wagons.[94] These new tactics of driving vans at high speed at rioters brought their own consequences. David Moore, a disabled white youth, was run down by a police van and killed. He was the only fatal casualty of the 1981 riots.[95]

In the wake of these so-called unprecedented disturbances, it was not only the media who were mystified and bewildered by the events. Sociologists, who have long searched for the causes of youth delinquency, found few of their concepts useful in understanding the number and escalation of 'riot mobs' in 1981. The youths did not belong to any pre-existing *gangs*, with those forms of organization and codes of behaviour noted by Thrasher in Chicago. Neither were they, except in the case of the skinheads in Southall, members of any recognizable youth *subculture*.

It is to social history that we must turn to place the disturbances in their proper social and political context – a social history informed specifically by race relations and racism in Britain, and the recurring efforts of working-class youth to retain access to leisure on 'their' streets.

To accomplish this, Colin Sparks distinguished between two types of riot: race riots and class riots.[96] Class riots have been described as uprisings, usually from working-class communities, against symbols of oppression and deprivation, and occurring at times of economic crisis or decline, or when the economic and social life of whole communities is under threat. Race riots on the other hand, characteristically involve organized attempts by gangs of people to attack indiscriminately people of another ethnic origin. The latter have repeatedly taken place in Britain – and on each occasion instigated by racist attacks by white people.

In the summer of 1919 black sailors were attacked by large crowds of whites, mainly demobbed or demobilizing soldiers after the First World War. As a result of the wartime labour shortage, blacks, mainly West Indians, had settled in the dock areas of London, Liverpool, Cardiff and Glasgow, and had been sucked into the British home economy largely in the merchant marine sector. The whites' grievances centred round fears of blacks taking their work by undercutting wage levels and consorting with white women. The black sailors' lodging houses were beseiged, stormed and emptied of furniture which was then burnt in street bonfires. In London, one seige was to last several days and involved the use of guns, knives and razors.[97]

The best known example is perhaps the 1958 riots in Notting Hill and Nottingham where white youths, many of whom were Teddy boys, launched a series of street attacks on the local black community. Racial hatred had long been nurtured in Britain by Mosley's pre-war British Union of Fascists, now revived as the Union Movement, and Colin Jordan's White Defence League. It was these two organizations which loosely informed and directed the Teds' spree of 'nigger-hunting' in the 1950s.

These examples stand in sharp contrast to Brixton and St Paul's. Here there is little evidence of indiscriminate attacks on white people and property. Instead, the targets for attack were systematic – the police and symbols of oppression for whole communities, both black and white. Of all the riots in 1981, only Southall comes close to being a race riot – being sparked off by skinhead attacks on Asian shopkeepers and largely involving confrontations between Asian and white youths.

On the other hand, Britain has a rich history of class riots – directed mainly at the police force and being an elementary resistance to economic and social oppression. For example, the outbreaks of machine smashing and arson in the early nineteenth century by the Luddites were not only attempts to save employment in industries deemed to be obsolete, but were designed to resist the intrusion of officialdom in the form of magistrates, employers, parsons and spies in the daily life of working-class communities.[98]

In 1830, the so-called Swing riots involved the uprising of the rural poor and agricultural labourers in southern England. Their violence was again directed at property in the factories and fields and was largely a result of the increased poverty endured by rural labour as England shifted its economy to one based on wage-labour and withdrew customary rights to parish relief. After being eventually subdued by armed troops and special constables (there was no organized police force outside London at this time), its leaders were hanged and its members transported.[99]

Similar disturbances occurred in Wales in 1839 with the so-called 'Rebecca Riots', where young men dressed in women's clothing (the Rebeccas) attacked toll houses and destroyed crops in the name of economic and social justice.

In these events there were embryonic forms of political protest or attempts to achieve a 'collective bargaining by riot'. They were directed not only against the property of the rich, but against those representatives of the state who dismissed their protest as simply criminal and quashed their rebellion in the name of restoring law and order.

A much closer historical parallel can be found in the London youth riots of July and August 1919. These fit into a pattern of youth and working-class behaviour which (until recently) was much more common in the nineteenth century than now, and involved a collective and more or less violent resistance to the police in public places. They were mainly started as a result of attempts to control working-class leisure activities on the streets – singing, shouting and 'rowdyism'. In 1919 such groups came into conflict with the police in Greenwich, Hammersmith, Tottenham, Wood Green and Brixton. In successive weeks various police arrests were made. One night, an 18-year-old carter who had refused to 'move on' was arrested. The police were promptly attacked by a crowd of 500 youths. Five police were injured and two arrests made, both of which led to two month prison sentences with hard labour.

Similarities with the 1981 riots should not be underestimated. In 1919 the labour market had not been expanded to the extent needed to cater for the influx of servicemen returning from the First World War. In the search for jobs, it was unskilled working-class youth who were the first to be rejected by employers. War discipline and controls on entertainment had made these post-war years a particularly barren time for youth.

They came up against a police force hardened by military duties and embittered by its own failed strikes in 1918 and 1919. The right to use the streets in the way they wanted, particularly at weekends, was the cultural battleground over which youth fought the police.[100]

What these social histories tell us is that 'riot' is not some alien import of recent date (from Watts in America for example), but that its form and content, involving hostility to the police, burning and looting and the legitimate use of city streets have always been a part of the British way of life. [101] As the social historian George Rudé concluded, rather than being random, mindless and brutish, crowds are purposeful and discriminating in choosing their targets, and rational in the means they use to reach their desired ends. Crowds are not simply criminal, but seek to redress social injustice through collective action.[102]

It is in such terms, too, that the 'riots' of 1980–1 can best be analysed – as predominantly protest movements arising out of class deprivation, coupled with white racism and overreactive policing.

While Scarman's report went to great lengths to detail multi-variate causes, it gave little attention to explanations offered by the 'rioters' themselves. This omission was partly corrected by a Home Office study in 1982 of the causes of the riots that took place in the Handsworth area of Birmingham between 10–12 July 1981.[103] The Handsworth riots took place a week after Liverpool 8 and Moss Side and were generally denegrated by the media as 'copy-cat'. The researchers interviewed a sample of 532 men aged between 16 and

34 in the area. Only 4 per cent admitted to any active involvement in the riots. The major perceived cause of the riots was unemployment. A third of the sample were themselves out of work and 43 per cent suggested unemployment as the major cause. The other most frequently mentioned causes were 'copying other areas' (23 per cent) and 'boredom' (22 per cent). Of those who were actively involved in the disturbances, 25 per cent claimed that police harassment was a cause. Among the 16–24 age group 41 per cent of West Indians and 36 per cent of young whites reported that they had been subject to the police's stop and search powers in the previous twelve months.

Those involved in the disturbances tended to be young, single, unemployed and used to spending much of their leisure time on the streets. As a result it is perhaps necessary to expand the class analysis of riots to encompass those factors which apply specifically to youth. Theories which stress that riots have their basis in ongoing class conflicts have a certain pertinence, particularly when ethnic minorities are viewed as an 'underclass', but we should also beware of the overdeterminism involved in such analysis. As Paul Rock has argued:

Very few have proposed that riots are not invariably intended to convey sober meaning and political lessons. Very few have considered the possibility that some riots may be modelled on the carnival or Saturnalia, they may be fun.[104]

This theory of 'rioting mainly for fun and profit' certainly contains some truth; but its full implications are only realized if combined with a historical analysis of working-class youth leisure pursuits and successive attempts to achieve their control by 'positive' policing. And, of course, none of this 'positive' policing would have occurred without the often trivial and commonplace indiscretions of working-class youth first being defined as a 'major social problem', both historically and in the present day.

New deviancy theory and beyond

The preceding 'contemporary cases' have not only identified the major statistical or observational elements of youth involvement in crime, but have also illustrated the different ways in which American ethnographic and labelling theories informed subsequent British research. A majority of these studies has been influenced by these new perspectives on deviancy. They are rized by four interrelated features. First, they all form part

ocess in which sociological studies have gained a pre-

e within British criminology since the 1950s.[105] Second,

they have attempted to 'humanize' deviance, by granting meaning
and purpose to delinquent behaviour.[106] Third, in developing the
labelling perspective, they have directed attention away from
causal questions (why did he do it?) to definitional and consequential ones (why is that law there? how is it enforced?).[107] Fourth,
they have analysed the deviant's point of view with sympathy, and
transformed criminology 'into a kind of moral crusade on the
deviant's behalf'.[108] Together these features were believed to
amount to what has become known as a 'radical' or 'new' deviancy
theory.

This theoretical position emerged primarily in the 1960's and early 70's
and has a close relationship with the libertarian currents widespread
within Western capitalism in that period. Its influence was and still is
widespread. New deviancy theory was primarily a radical response to
positivist domination of criminology and attempted to recover the
'meaning' in human behaviour denied . . . in positivism.[109]

New deviancy theory was able to do this because it initially viewed
the social order as that of a pluralism of values. Following the
principles of labelling theory, it was argued that deviance or crime
existed only through the interaction of definer and defined. Some
groups had the power and resources to succeed in raising their
values to ascendency and enforcing their own standards on a
weakened majority. Within this context new deviancy theory was
more concerned to locate crime in its specific context and to
analyse the significance of social and media reaction, than to
explain its causes. The 'crimes' it investigated were either
'victimless' (drug abuse, abortion, homosexuality) or borne out of
media labels (vandalism, mugging, hooliganism, scrounging)
popularized by the dominant classes. Important and often
empathetic insights into the 'underworld' of deviant groups and
the 'normality' of juvenile crime were secured in this way. Crime
was viewed as ubiquitous. It was not merely the underprivileged
and marginalized groups in society that committed 'crimes'. Their
'crimes' were over-represented in official statistics because not
only were the damage, exploitation, theft and destruction carried
out by dominant classes not punished but also they were not called
crime. Within such a reappraisal of the legitimate foci of

criminology, a strong interest in working-class youth remained. Parker and Giller pick out its key elements:

Although the academics and researchers involved in all these critical studies of working class youth would probably wish to emphasise their differences, there is a clear sense in which they belong to a school of studies which has taken forward the conceptual issues borne of the re-appraisal and worked them through broadly in relation to youthful deviance. They all offer their young subjects a voice or at least implied rationality, they all find various types of conflict theory more relevant than consensual or correctional perspectives. . . .[110]

However the weakness of a loosely defined conflict theory and such concepts as social control and value pluralism were noted as early as the late 1960s. While the central thesis, that there can be no crime without an agency and mechanism of control, continued to ring true, new deviancy theory remained limited if employed without any analysis of the social and political structures in which such labels were constructed. As Hall *et al.* discovered:

The 'control-culture' approach appears too imprecise for our purposes. It identifies centres of power and their importance for the social control process; but it does not locate them historically and thus it cannot designate the significant moments of shift and change. It does not differentiate adequately between different types of state or political regime. It does not specify the kind of social formation which requires and establishes a particular kind of legal order. It does not examine the repressive functions of the state apparatuses in relation to their consensual functions. . . . It is not a historically specific concept. In short it is not premised on a theory of the state even less a theory of the state in a particular phase of capitalist development.[111]

In its concentration on street-level interactions, new deviancy theory was unable to address the more general context of class, law and *state* (as opposed to 'social') control. By characterizing society as a diversity of values, proponents of new deviancy theory blinded themselves to the existence of a very real concensus in society: that of the hegemonic domination of bourgeois values. Indeed, it was necessary to situate processes of social action and social reaction in their precise material (historical, economic and political) circumstances. Such a critique promoted and necessitated a major shift in theoretical position, and a rediscovery of Marxism. Recent analyses of crime, grounded in Marxism, have attempted to move beyond the conceptual framework of social control to examine the structural constitution of the law, the state and class relations at particular historical moments. For Hall *et al.* the British state has recently been characterized by a crisis of authority.[112] Since the late 1960s it has been in a process of transformation in which its more coercive and authoritarian aspects have been rekindled. This period in the emergence of a strong authoritarian state is of most importance because it parallels the panics over juvenile crime which characterized the 1970s and early 1980s. To date these connections between the state, class and crime have only been examined in detail in relation to mugging. However, as we have seen, these elements of Marxism are also beginning to be applied to contemporary analyses of football hooliganism.[113] Meanwhile an acknowledgement of the relevance of a Marxian concept of class (involving one's relation to the means of production) has informed the spate of studies of youth subcultures that emerged in the 1970s.

Suggested reading

There is no existing work which draws together this research on youth and crime. However, for juvenile theft see Parker (1974), for vandalism see Ward (1973) and for football hooliganism see Ingham (1978). Hall *et al.* (1978) provide by far the most comprehensive analysis of a youth crime (mugging) by situating it within its proper socio-historical context. A useful summary of the riots of the 1980s can be found in Kettle and Hodges (1982). The 'new deviancy theory' approach which has informed many of the youth crime studies is clearly laid out by Young (1981). Hall and Scraton (1981) and Young (1979) provide some important criticisms of this approach but also look forward to ways in which when, combined with Marxism, it may be employed in the future.

4 Youth in revolt

Since the Second World war, Britain has produced a number of deviant youth groups which, although not necessarily delinquent, have attracted a similar, if not more intense, degree of adult concern and reaction. In this chapter we shift our attention away from those youth legally defined as criminal, to those socially defined as deviant.

This more generalized concern about youth was intricately related to the emergence of a 'teenage' culture in the 1950s and a 'youth' culture in the 1960s. While 'teenager' was a term attached specifically to working-class youth, the notion of a 'youth' culture suggested that all young people belonged to a homogenous culture that transcended all other cultural attachments: to home, neighbourhood or class.

Of all the class struggles in modern societies, the most under-rated may prove to be those between age classes, especially those between youth and adults ... [it] is a distinctive class struggle in its own right and furthermore is one of the more serious and least tractable.[1]

Such argument was backed up by a corresponding trend in sociological theory which argued that poverty and traditional class divisions had withered away in a post-war era of unlimited affluence, equal opportunity and the welfare state. Youth was believed to have developed a rebellious autonomy, expressed not through crime but through teenage leisure pursuits. Increases in the incomes of working-class youth and changes in the education system resulting from the 1944 Butler Act were cited as significant factors in the production of a specific generational consciousness. In 1959, Abrams produced his pamphlet, 'The teenage consumer' announcing that English youth had emerged as a significant consumer grouping and a major market for records, magazines and fashions. Such spending on leisure and entertainment was moulded by 'distinctive teenage ends in a distinctive teenage world'.[2] A view of youth as living in a world apart was firmly established. Coupled with fears of adolescents' 'natural' hedonism and rebelliousness, the idea of the teenager was strongly linked with the image of the juvenile delinquent.

Above all with the coming of this new age, a new spirit was unleashed – a new wind of essentially youthful hostility to every kind of established convention and traditional authority, a wind of moral freedom and rebellion.[3]

Elements of this 'rebellion' were most dramatically seen in a variety of youth cultures – Teds, mods, rockers, hippies, skinheads and student dissenters – which emerged in the 1950s and 1960s. However, in the different life-styles and 'solutions' offered by these groups, it soon became clear that youth were not an undifferentiated and homogenous mass. There was not one youth culture, but a variety of youth subcultures. By the late 1960s, class distinctions were once more restored to the centre of the sociology of youth. The task now was to discover how age and class combined in determining the range of options open to youth. Thus in the new wave of British subcultural theory of the 1970s, class position was the starting point for analysing youthful deviance, but age remained an important factor in structuring the social position of young people.

The key concern of these studies was not, therefore, one of simply 'substituting class for age at the centre of analysis, but of examining the relations between class and age and more particularly the way in which age acts as a mediation of class'.[4]

British subcultural theory

It is significant that the most sophisticated theoretical analyses of youth in Britain have emerged not from studies of delinquency but from studies of subcultural leisure pursuits. In contrast to most American research, British subcultural theory is not primarily concerned with delinquency. The main reason for this is that post-war research in Britain has consistently been unable to discover the existence of those 'structured' gangs identified by A. Cohen (1955) and Cloward and Ohlin (1960). The first British application of American subcultural theory was provided by Downes's study of working-class youth in East London.[5] He found little evidence of Cohen's 'status frustration' or discontent with working-class status among the boys of his study. Rather they dissociated themselves from the dominant values and aspirations enshrined in school or work and deflected their interests, achievements and aspirations into leisure pursuits. Thus it is the excessive demands which working-class boys make on their leisure time which distinguishes them from middle-class boys. The connection between working-class leisure and delinquency, however, only becomes apparent when leisure aspirations also remain unfulfilled. In Downes's formulation there is a clear continuation between conventional 'teenage culture' and delinquency. This point is important because it helps to account for the processes by which aspects of subcultural behaviour have been continually subject to criminalization. Indeed Downes's study was influential in various respects. Not only did it acknowledge that youth subcultures rely on leisure and entertainment as a means of securing their own 'cultural space', but it also recognized how their experiences and opportunities are structured by the material conditions of their class.

These twin concerns were elaborated by various subcultural studies published by the Centre for Contemporary Cultural Studies during the 1970s. On the one hand the meaning of subcultural style was examined through various ethnographic and semiological analyses: on the other, the political implications of deviancy were explored through investigations of the structural and class position of various subcultures.

This complex relationship between economic structures, class, culture and subcultural meaning was first examined in detail by Clarke *et al.*[6] Working specifically within a Marxist framework they first argue for a distinction between *structures* and *cultures* when trying to understand youth life-styles. Structures refer to the material circumstances in which groups of people live. In an unequally divided society, groups occupy different positions in the various structures of inequality – inequalities in wealth, housing, education, social services and so on. These are the necessary consequences of major divisions of class and power in society. Cultures, on the other hand, refer to the way classes and social groups within classes live within these material circumstances. They are social rather than individual products and refer to the various ways in which people come to terms with their social conditions; the ways in which they either learn to live with them, or overcome them or make them, in however distorted a way, human and bearable. The content of each of these cultures is in turn related to the structures of inequality.

just as different groups and classes are unequally ranked in relation to one another in terms of their productive relations, wealth and power, so cultures are differently ranked and stand in opposition to one another in relations of domination and subordination along the scale of 'cultural power'.[7]

However, it is the dominant cultures which try to organize and remake the others to fit their own image. And it is in this context of 'cultural politics' that the life-styles of some youth become a problem. Those life-styles which appear to threaten or infringe upon the stability or 'normality' constructed by the dominant culture are the most suitable targets, whether they are young blacks standing on street corners, working-class youths singing obscene songs at football matches or middle-class youths refusing to form families, avoiding work and taking drugs. All of these are seen to theaten the conventional normality of work, leisure and family life.

But these other cultures are not only subordinate to the dominant order, they can also enter into struggle with it and seek to modify, negotiate and resist its hegemony. Indeed this is the prime function given to youth subcultures in Clarke *et al.*'s analysis: as elementary forms of resistance and opposition to the social order. But how do the particular life-styles of youth subcultures originate? These authors argue that they are first moulded by the social conditions, largely those of the class of which they are members. Attention is thus given to conditions of employment, income, housing and education which exist at that particular historical moment. So, for example, youth subcultures will be shaped in part by the prevailing possibilities and expectations of employment. The 'mod' life-style of the mid 1960s is explained by reference to the expansion of white collar employment and distributive trades which allowed access to certain symbols of affluence – the scooter, Italian suits and so on. Similarly the development of a subculture among young blacks in the late 1970s can be explained in part by recognizing the narrowness of the employment opportunities open to them. These material conditions shape the possibilities of the subculture or set the conditions for the subculture's 'focal concerns'.

In the formation of a subcultural life-style the group is also likely to draw on the cultural resources provided for it by its parent culture. Sets of traditions, habits and values provided and established by adult sections of the class are passed on to its youth through the family, neighbourhood and community. Thus, for example, the concerns of skinheads for local identity, territory and toughness involve a reworking, in subcultural form, of inherited traditions from their parent culture. Placing these elements together, Clarke *et al.* argue:

To locate youth sub-culture in this kind of analysis, we must first situate youth in the dialectic between a 'hegemonic' dominant culture and the subordinate working-class 'parent' culture of which youth is a fraction.[8]

Subcultures are ultimately viewed as active agencies involved in 'winning space' for leisure and recreation on the street, in the clubs or at football matches. If subcultures originate from problems in material conditions (such as unemployment) they develop as attempts to reach a solution to that problematic experience. However the subcultures themselves cannot overcome such problems as unemployment, low pay, and educational disadvantage, and thus their solutions remain 'imaginary' or 'symbolic'. Since their resistance operates mainly in the area of leisure, they cannot hope to transform the social formation. Instead, they offer a symbolic representation of social contradictions and a symbolic critique of the established order. They do this mainly through the creation of new styles or by appropriating old styles in order (though not necessarily consciously) to affront the 'normality' of the dominant culture.

This theoretical analysis stemmed directly from Phil Cohen's research on working-class youth subcultures in the East End of London.[9] The creation of successive styles of youthful rebellion in the 1960s – from mod to skinhead – was viewed as youth's attempted solution to problems facing the working class as a whole. The changes in the mid 1950s in housing, employment and income caught a majority of the working class in the middle of two dominant but contradictory ideologies: the new ideology of 'spectacular consumption' and affluence and the traditional ideology of work and pride in a job well done. Post-war developments in the local economy served consistently to undermine the solidarity, loyalties and traditions of working-class life. Automated techniques in manufacturing made traditional pride in craftmanship impossible. The social space of the pub, corner shop and the street was destroyed by high rise flats. The changes that accompanied 'affluence; then also threatened the very structure of working-class life. The local economy contracted, became less diverse and forced the young to travel out of the community to work, or to move away permanently. Those who remained tried – in the form of subcultures – to retrieve those socially cohesive elements that had been destroyed in the parent culture. The internal conflicts of the parent culture – between tradition and affluence – came to be worked out in terms of a generational conflict. In Phil Cohen's words, 'the latent function of subculture is to express and resolve, albeit magically, the contradictions hidden or unresolved in the parent culture'.[10]

The subcultural styles of the young reflect and act on these contradictions between working-class puritanism and the new hedonism of consumption. Cohen noted the interplay between youth's efforts to participate in affluence and their continuing position in a partly eroded working-class community. Thus the mods were seen as attempting to realize the conditions of existence of the socially mobile white collar worker (in dress, music and scooter), while simultaneously retaining certain social codes which stressed many of the traditional values of their parent culture (in language and ritual). There evolved a compromise solution between the need to create and express autonomy from parents, and the need to maintain parental identifications. The skinheads, on the other hand, were viewed by Cohen as a reaction against the contamination of the parent culture by middle-class values and a reassertion of the integral values of working-class culture through its most recessive traits – puritanism and chauvinism. Reviewing this work, Hebdige argues that:

Here at last was a reading which took into account the full interplay of ideological, economic and cultural factors which bear upon subculture. By grounding his theory in ethnographic detail Cohen was able to insert class into his analysis at a far more sophisticated level than had previously been possible. Rather than presenting class as an abstract set of external determinations, he showed it working out in practice as a material force, dressed up, as it were in experience and exhibited in style.[11]

Cohen's key insight was to view the subculture not as an anomic form resulting from alienation or 'status frustration', but as means of achieving an 'ideological resolution' to material contradictions.

Thus both Cohen and Clarke *et al.* suggested that subcultures offer solutions of a 'magical', rather than real nature to contradictions in the socio-economic system. Within youth subcultures this is perceived and responded to by the individual as a generational problem. Thus the style of each subculture allows an expression of identity and self-image which is 'magically' free from class or occupation.

While it is recognized that the analysis of such styles cannot be made in isolation from a subculture's own class position and practices, some authors have given privileged attention to a separate line of enquiry concerned primarily with how subcultures selectively appropriate symbolic objects and are engaged in processes of stylistic creation. Their attention has been so directed because it is in the generation of style that the possibility of subcultural resistance is thought to be most at work. Clarke uses Lévi-Strauss's concept of *bricolage* to explain how particular objects can be used by subcultures in such a way as to transform or subvert their original meaning.[12] For example the 'Edwardian look' of drape jackets was borrowed by the Teddy boys of the 1950s and combined with such extraneous items as the bootlace tie and brothel-creepers to produce a style in antithesis to adult sensibilities. What is involved here is a reading of subcultural style to signify or denote something beyond its surface appearance. Objects are borrowed from the world of consumer commodities and, as they are incorporated into the focal concerns of subcultures, their meaning reworked. This appropriation of style allows the subculture to express its opposition obliquely or ironically. Hebdige provides the most elaborate analysis of this process in his explanation, for example, of why mods chose to ride scooters, why skinheads wore boots and why the punks pushed safety pins through their noses.

These 'humble objects' can be magically appropriated, stolen by subordinate groups and made to carry 'secret' meanings which express in code a form of resistance to the order which guarantees their continued subordination. Style in subculture is then pregnant with significance. Its transformations go 'against nature' interrupting the process of 'normalisation'. As such they are gestures, movements towards a speech which offends the 'silent majority', which challenges the principle of unity and cohesion, which contradicts the myth of consensus.[13]

For Hebdige, then, subcultural styles act as symbolic violations of the social order. In order to explain how certain styles coalesce to create a meaningful subcultural entity, Hebdige borrows another term from Lévi-Strauss: *homology*. Contrary to popular depictions of subcultures as lawless, Hebdige illustrates how the internal structure of any particular subculture is characterized by order-liness; how different elements of style cohere into a meaningful whole.[14] He argues that there was a homological relation between the spiked hair, the amphetamines, the spitting, the trashy cut-up clothes and the raw and basic music of the punk subculture of the late 1970s. Punk styles fitted together because of their generalized 'anarchy' and refusal to cohere around a stable and permanent set of central values.

Similarly Willis has argued that there existed a homology between the intense activism, physical prowess and love of machines of motor-bike boys and their preference for rock 'n' roll music, just as there was a homology between the structurelessness, self-introspection and loose group affiliation of hippies and their choice of underground or progressive rock music.[15] The concepts of 'bricolage' and 'homology' thus explain how subcultures can alter and subvert normal expectations within a framework of meanings that is both coherent and meaningful. Through these semiotic techniques of analysis, Hebdige is able to view style as a signifier of a unified subcultural practice, rather than as a series of distinct cultural expressions. However in this concentration on the minutiae of subcultural activities, style is drawn some steps away from its followers' material existence. Whereas for Clarke *et al.* it is class that is the key to discovering subcultural resistance, for Hebdige, style is selected as the main variable in understanding how such resistance is eventually voiced. The former is an attempt to relate a set of cultural phenomena to the question of class formations and the construction of hegemony. The latter tries to establish the autonomy of the signifying practices of subcultures from any simple reduction to the interests of any single class. In both accounts, however, the relationship between subculture and leisure remains the dominant theme. It is youth's use of leisure and style which offers possibilities for subcultural resistance. Central to their approach is the assumption that the innovative in leisure style is both rebellious and a form of political protest. Thus the selective use of leisure becomes 'a source of collective power in the struggle with schools or police'.[6]

In terms of its political content them, we would characterise youth culture as being involved in a struggle fundamental to the social order – that of the control of meaning. Here one can see the significance of the media's stereotyping and thereby redefining youth cultures. It is an attempt by the dominant culture to reaffirm its own view of society, as the only correct one. It is significant that in this struggle for the control of meaning one of the most frequent adjectives used to describe disapproval of behaviour by the young is 'meaningless'.[17]

Resistance and criminalization: contemporary cases

In this section we will briefly examine the history of post-war youth subcultures in Britain, focusing in particular on aspects of protest and resistance which have been implied in their behaviour. As each subculture was believed to pose some sort of threat to the social order, it is significant that some aspects of their behaviour – for example, violence, drug usage and political radicalism – have been subject to processes of state control. These subcultures have emanated from both dominant and subordinate cultures. In particular we will examine the working-class youth subcultures of Teddy boys, mods, rockers, skinheads and punks; the middle-class youth subcultures (or countercultures) of hippies and the New Left, and that which made up a significant part of the early CND movement; and the Rudie and Rasta subcultures of black youth. It is, however, essential to remind ourselves throughout that these spectacular youth subcultures are the response of a minority of youth. While many young people are involved in following fashions, they are not all necessarily committed to the creation of nonconformist life-styles.

The 1980s would appear to be a prime moment to engage in such a review. For although these subcultures can be traced back to the mid 1950s they all, at least stylistically, have a contemporary presence and relevance.

Working-class youth subcultures

There is a very definite form to the changes in youth culture in post-war Britain, and the line of descent runs from the teddy boys through the mod to the skinhead. Each of these styles has its own distinctive flavour. Each of them is specifically the creation of working class districts in London. Each of them is associated with its own 'moral panic'.[18]

The immediate post-war years were shaped above all by the memory and aftermath of the war. Despite the austerity and rationing which lasted until the mid 1950s, Britain was believed to be entering an age of affluence epitomized by the expansion of the welfare state, equal educational opportunity and new patterns of commodity consumption. The shift in social emphasis away from work and production towards leisure and consumption was a vital base for the concensus politics of the time. By the mid 1950s Britain was supposedly riding on a wave of new affluence in which class conflict and class-based politics had little or no place.[19] However affluence also had its price. Inevitably it was those unskilled working-class youths who found they were excluded from the benefits of embourgeoisement. The post-war years also saw the 'planning blight' and the fragmentation of formerly cohesive working-class communities. It is against this background that the rise of the Teddy boys has been explained.[20] Drawn from a residue of unskilled workers after their more aspiring peers had been syphoned off into apprenticeships and white collar work, the Teds discovered that it was they who had lost out. In the wake of the new affluence it was the Teds who were first aware that there remained a general lack of public provision for leisure for the under-20s. Rather this was the heyday of the Mecca and Locarno dance halls aimed specifically at an older age group.[21] The Teds responded by moving into the only space available and claimed the local 'caff' and the street to be their 'home'. The territorial loyalty of the Teds has been read by Jefferson to be an affirmation of traditional lower working-class values.[22] Their defence of local territory in turn is seen as a symbolic attempt to keep control of their local neighbourhood in the face of urban redevelopment programmes and the influx of new immigrant populations. Identity of self and group was maintained initially by adherence to certain styles of dress and later through the music of rock 'n' roll. Their clothes were a bastardization of a style, ironically originally created by Savile Row in the early 1950s for young upper-class men. It consisted of long 'drape' jackets with velvet collars, tight 'drainpipe' trousers, bootlace ties and thick crepe-soled shoes. In all they represented an arrogant yet half-conscious parody of the upper classes and also an attempt to glorify the masculinity and slickness of the Hollywood criminal hero. It is perhaps significant that the first 'Teddy-boy murder' on Clapham Common in 1953 resulted from a fight started when one of a group of Teds had been called 'a flash cunt' by three youths. With the arrival of 'rock 'n' roll' in Britain in 1954, the Ted was able to give voice to his disenchantment. As Melly recalls it was 'a contemporary incitement to mindless fucking and arbitrary vandalism: screw and smash music'.[23] Rock 'n' roll, in the shape of Elvis Presley, Bill Haley and Little Richard, was also a blatant attack on parental sexual taboos. And the right to enjoy such leisure was violently defended. Haley's performances and the first showings of the Presley films were greeted with mass hysteria. When the adult world wanted order in the cinemas, coffee bars and streets, the Teds responded by jiving in the aisles, razoring cinema seats and attacking 'intruders'. The films 'The Wild Ones' with Marlon Brando and 'Rebel Without a Cause' with James Dean became cult movies in their celebration of teenage lawlessness. The original Teds will be most remembered, however, for their part in the 1958 'race-riots' in Nottingham and Notting Hill. Living in dilapidated inner-city areas, the Teds rationalized that their underprivileged position was due to the influx of immigrant outsiders, who also appeared to be relatively affluent. West Indians and Cypriots became 'legitimate' targets for the Teds' aggression, spurred on by the racist propaganda of the Mosleyites and the White Defence League. The nine unskilled working-class youths who were credited with starting the riots in Notting Hill were eventually each sentenced to four years imprisonment.[24] The image of the menacing and violent teenager had become neurotically imprinted on adult consciousness.

Working-class youths who reached adolescence in the early 1960s were also caught up in the desire to share the fruits of a new affluence. As Phil Cohen has argued, the mod subculture was a response to the contradictions facing the working class at this time.[25] Faced with a prevailing ideology of affluence and 'swinging London' sections of working-class youth found that they still endured class-based inequalities. The term 'mod' indeed reflected this contradiction. It was both the province of those upwardly mobile working-class youth who had made it good through art school and the commercialization of style – the Beatles, Mary Quant, David Bailey, Twiggy and so on – and also those youths who found the white collar occupations to which they had aspired just as restricting as the manual jobs they had left behind. Originating from East London and working-class estates in the suburbs, the mod was typically employed as a messenger, clerk or office boy. The mod accepted this work in so far as it allowed him a greater potential to buy style and status. Partly as a reflection of their relative affluence and partly as an attempt to emulate the 'cool' style of their West Indian neighbours, the mod style was characterized by short hair, smart Italian-cut suits and an almost narcissistic obsession with neatness. Mods were the epitome of the conspicious consumer, but they were never passive consumers. For example, the scooter, a formerly respectable means of transport, was 'appropriated and converted into a weapon and symbol of solidarity'.[26] Amphetamines, medically diagnosed for the treatment of neuroses, enabled those who used them to spend all night dancing in the clubs.

The style they created therefore constituted a parody of the consumer society in which they were situated. The mod dealt his blows by inverting and distorting the images of neatness, of short hair, so cherished by his employers and parents, to create a style which while being overtly close to the straight world was nonetheless incomprehensible to it.[27]

The mods lived for nights, weekends and bank holidays. It was on the beaches of Clacton, Margate, Brighton and Hastings on successive bank holidays in 1964 that they achieved their notoriety. The mods and rockers dichotomy was constructed by the media in the wake of some fairly trivial incidents of rowdyism and vandalism in Clacton during the Easter bank holiday.[28] Accentuating and rigidifying the opposition between the two groups, the media set the stage for the conflicts which occurred at Margate and Brighton during the Whitsun weekend, and at Hastings during the August bank holiday. Mod became synomomous with scooter, rocker with bike, but as Barker and Little's survey of offenders in Margate revealed, a majority could not afford such a means of transport and had travelled to the coast by public transport.[29] In their sample the typical rocker was an unskilled manual worker, the typical mod a semi-skilled manual worker. Both had left school at the age of 15. Most of the group were charged not with assault but with threatening behaviour. As Cohen notes:

The bulk of young people present at the resorts came down not so much to make trouble as in the hope that there would be some trouble to watch. Their very presence, their readiness to be drawn into a situation of trouble and the sheer accretion of relatively trivial incidents were found incon-venient and offensive. . . . Acts of violence and vandalism are the most tangible manifestations of what the press and public regard as hooliganism. These acts were therefore played up rather than the less melodramatic effect of being a nuisance and inconvenience to many adults.[30]

Nevertheless, mods and rockers became fused in adult minds as the folk devils of society; as posing a serious threat to the social order. In Brighton, during Easter 1965, over 100 youths were arrested and magistrates began to make use of the punitive tactic of remand in custody to provide the youths with a short taste of imprisonment.

By 1966, however, the mod subculture had all but evaporated. Its stylistic elements were incorporated into the highly commercialized period of 'Carnaby Street' and 'swinging London' which was later to evolve into hippiedom, while the hard mod found his image in the skinheads of the late 1960s.

Skinheads first appeared in East London in early 1968 and were generated from sections of the unskilled working class. The specific content of their style was largely a reaction against the softness of the early mod and the contemporary hippie, and was characterized by an exaggerated reflection of male working-class toughness. Cropped hair, braces and Doc Marten 'bovver boots' were combined in a celebration of the working class's more aggressive, puritanical and chauvinist traits. Whereas the mods had explored the upwardly mobile options of the class, the skinheads explored the lumpen. In particular they steered clear of night clubs, partly because of their expense, and partly because they identified more with the traditional working-class activities located around pubs, football and the street. For Clarke they represented:

an attempt to recreate through the 'mob' the traditional working class community as a substitution for the real decline of the latter. The underlying social dynamic for the style is the relative worsening of the situation of the lower working class, through the second half of the sixties.[31]

Football, and especially the violence articulated around it, provided one arena for the expression of the skinheads' concern with a particular collective, masculine conception of self. Concern with toughness was also involved in the two other most publicized aspects of being a skinhead – 'paki-bashing' and 'queer-bashing'. Paki-bashing was explained by Clarke as the ritualized and aggressive defence of the local community against its most visibly scapegoated outsiders. West Indian youth were seen as less of a threat, presumably because their cultural patterns were much closer to the working class. Queer-bashing was read as a reaction against the erosion of traditional stereotypes of masculinity, particularly by the hippies, but frequently extended to anyone who looked 'odd'. Similarly Pearson, in his study of paki-bashing in Accrington in 1964, attempted to explain the actions of white working-class youths as expressions of a 'resistance from below' to the forces of immigration, unemployment and working-class dislocation that had followed in the wake of the decline of the local cotton industry. Thus the youths, in attacking Pakistanis, were demonstrating their reactions to an economic slump and were waging a 'primitive form of political and economic struggle'.[32] However, the efficacy of this form of 'struggle' could hardly have been shared by the new immigrant communities, particularly when in the late 1960s skinheads were protecting Enoch Powell as he travelled the country delivering his 'rivers of blood' speeches.

During the 1970s the spectres of racism, coupled with mass unemployment and inflation, were a permanent feature of British society. Predictably the section of society that endured the highest rates of unemployment were unqualified working-class school leavers. It was against this background that punk rock, or as Marsh termed it, 'dole queue rock', developed.[33] The development of the punk subculture in 1976 was intrinsically tied to the creation of a new musical style. As in the past, the initiating centre was London, the punks congregating in a shop called Sex and a rock club called the Roxy. As the band – the Sex Pistols – achieved notoriety by swearing at an interviewer in a live TV show, the punks made their impression on the streets by dressing in plastic bin-liners, dog collars and ripped T-shirts. In contrast to the skinheads, who created a fetishism of their class position, the punks were nihilistic and saw themselves as complete outsiders – the Blank Generation. They saw 'no future' in their own or society's life and could rely on 'no heroes' from the rock culture of the past. Punk attempted to undermine and disrupt every pre-existing style of life, to reduce everything to levels of absurdity.

The punks transformed the products of society into art and society was shocked. Just as it had appropriated their bodies for its labour and rejected them, they appropriated society's rejects and made its most private property – its foulest murders, its sex sensationalism – a public feeling.[34]

Punk was seldom violent, however, despite a much publicized 'war' of Teds and punks in Chelsea in the summer of 1977.[35]

Punk's language of swear words, with its stress on collective energy and the immediate, was decidely working class, but punks also drew on influences from art school and conceptual art. Thus in opposition to Marsh's concept of dole queue rock, Frith argues that punks had connections with middle-class hippies, anarchists and the avant-garde.[36] Punk was, therefore, essentially a stratified subculture. It was made up of working-class youth who rejected the wealth and life-style of rock superstars, and middle-class art college students who attempted to satirize the bourgeoisie.

The punks' disruption of previous subcultural styles had some peculiar consequences for subcultural formation in the late 1970s and early 1980s. Hebdige has argued that punk style contained distorted reflections of all the major post-war subcultures, and it indirectly created a revival of Ted, mod and skinhead styles.[37] Reputed to have its origins in early 1960s beat music, some followers of punk rock attempted to retrace that history in a revival of a mod subculture, cemented around the band The Jam and the film 'Quadrophenia'. The harder working-class elements reacted against that element of punk that went hippie by retreating into a new skinhead subculture characterized by its association with the British Movement and the National Front.[38] Meanwhile the Teds and rockers also enjoyed something of a revival, possibly in reaction to the mods and punks. 1980 was a confusing time for the student of youth subcultures. As *The Sunday Times* argued, it was 'as though a film of the sixties is slowly playing itself back'.[39] Easter bank holiday 1980 indeed saw the replaying of familiar themes in the daily press, as these subcultures did battle with one another and the police on the beaches from Scarborough to Brighton.

'POLICE BEAT OFF INVASION BY THE MODS AND ROCKERS'.[40]
'THUGS ON AN ORGY OF TERROR IN HOLIDAY TOWNS'.[41]
'TRIBAL WARFARE' – holiday terror as Britain's young gangs invade resorts.
THE WARRING "TRIBES" – Mods, Rockers, Skinheads, Teds and soccer louts – fought with bottles, stones and chains'.[42]
'POLICE BATONS END THE MARCH OF THE MODS'.[43]
'SCOOTER THUGS IN BEACH TERROR'.[44]

Both the *Daily Mirror* and the *Daily Express* provided guides to the various subcultures that made up the 1980s version of Britain's youth 'problem'.[45] In each case their tendencies for violence and vandalism were stressed:

Who are the teenage rebels? Many are without a cause, whose sole aim is to defy authority of any kind. For others the cause is violence – to rival gangs, to people who don't dress like they do and to innocent bystanders who get in their way. A few belong to mysterious sects who guard their independence by force of arms. But most have one thing in common . . . to engender terror.[46]

In addition, a new moral panic was growing about solvent abuse – glue sniffing. The substances used are almost exclusively impact adhesives – Evostik, Thix-o-Fix, and so on – designed to induce an effect of intoxication. Although it is not known how widespread the practice is, it is believed to be taken up by some youths at around the age of 12 or 13 and dropped at 16 and 17 in preference for alcohol. The scale and dangers of the 'killer glue' portrayed by the media have, however, mystified the practice and elevated it to a point where young people who overtly indulge are seen by people around them as incomprehensible deviants. 'Parents who can cope with finding their fifteen year old sons and daughters drunk are shocked into feelings of anger and failure by finding them intoxicated through solvents.'[47]

'I WANTED TO KILL MY GLUE SNIFFING SON.'[48]

However, medical evidence regarding long-term damage from moderate glue sniffing remains inconclusive. Although a number of deaths (thirty-five in the last ten years) have been associated with glue sniffing, the actual causes of death remain inconclusive. In England and Wales, there is no law governing the sale and use of glue.[49] Moreover solvent abuse is by no means a contemporary phenomenon. It was reported in the late 1950s in America, and ether sniffing was a popular pastime in the mid nineteenth century.[50] As a *New Society* feature concluded:

Growing up is a messy process. Growing youth unemployment, plus a lack of understanding from parents, schools and police can make it messier still. Some may see glue as one way out.[51]

Certainly the continual presence of working-class youth subcultures in Britain seems assured. In their more deviant practices they seem certain to attract further adult moral censure and also be elevated by 'radical' sociologists as heroes who have the guts to question and resist adult conformity.

Middle-class countercultures

Unlike the often disguised nature of resistance present in working-class subcultures, sections of middle-class youth have indicated their own disillusionment with society by way of political organizations, liberation movements and alternative life-styles. As a result there is a tendency within the literature to view their activities as countercultural, rather than simply subcultural. Accordingly, they have been analysed more readily as political deviants, than social delinquents. Clarke *et al.*'s use of the term counterculture, to depict the political stance of the New Left and the cultural 'solution' of the hippies in the 1960s is designed to illustrate a different range of responses afforded to middle-class youths because of their preferential class position. They argue that there are:

some clear structural differences in the response of the youth of the different classes. Working class subcultures are clearly articulated collective structures – often 'near' or 'quasi' gangs. Middle class countercultures are diffuse less group-centred, more individualised. The latter precipitate typically, not tight sub-cultures but a diffuse counter culture milieu.[52]

It is important to recognize how a generalized class background does afford middle-class youth opportunities which are not usually available to their working-class peers. For example, the former tend to remain longer within the educational system and thus they are less constrained by adherence to the work ethic. While the mod may have reluctantly accepted work as a taken-for-granted fact of life, the hippie was in a position to ask 'Why work at all?'. This relative freedom has allowed middle-class subcultures to be more overtly radical and to take a more structured political form.

In the mid 1950s, for example, sections of middle-class youth in Britain were becoming increasingly concerned with such issues as the coming of the nuclear age and the H-bomb. In 1958 they were united within the Campaign for Nuclear Disarmament (CND), which organized a protest march to the atomic weapon research centre at Aldermaston.

Nominal support for C.N.D. was for many teenagers a more or less commonly accepted feature of the youth culture; like the preference for folk music, outlandish clothes and the like, it was a way of drawing a line of demarcation between adolescent and adult values. Undoubtedly too, a further attraction of the campaign for the young was its preference for political activity by way of marches and demonstrations. . . . The excitement of a four-day march, the creation of Gemeinschaft relationships . . . [and] the one occasions when the radical young stood for a brief moment at the centre of the stage of national politics.[53]

A survey in 1959 estimated that 41 per cent of CND supporters were under 21 years of age. This led *The Times* to denounce CND as being 'immature' and simply 'protesting against authority'.[54] Parkin concluded that 'the ideal type of young CND supporter could be said to come from a middle-class home with a radical leaning'.[55] The radicalism of the young middle class was, however, directed not to economic reforms but to humanitarian issues which demanded reforms which were basically *moral* in content. CND thus developed into a protest movement away from class-based politics. As such it was never deemed to be respectable, and social reaction was extreme. At the height of the campaign in 1961, on 'Battle of Britain Sunday', over 1000 people were arrested in Trafalgar Square. In particular, its young members were denegrated as long haired, beatnik and immoral. Both Nuttall and Neville have described their influence:

although teenagers made up by no means the bulk of the marchers as the square press consistently claimed they did, they nevertheless made each march into a carnival of optimism . . . with their slogan daubed crazy hats and streaming filthy hair, hammering their banjos, strumming aggressively on their guitars. . . . It was this wild public festival spirit that spread the CND symbol throughout all the jazz clubs and secondary schools in an incredibly short time. Protest was associated with festivity. . . .[56]

Duffle coats and CND badges symbolised a new generational identity. For the young, being sad about the Bomb was fun.[57]

Much of the movement's appeal for the young derived from the anti-adult and anti-authoritarian character which the campaign assumed. The bomb was held up as a symbol of the moral and political bankruptcy of the older generation. To protest against the bomb was in large part a protest against much of adult society in general.

However CND was far from politically united. By 1960 Canon Collins clashed with the Direct Action Committee (led by

Bertrand Russell) which advocated open but non-violent civil disobedience. In 1961 the Committee planned to occupy eight nuclear bases and as a result six of its leaders were tried and imprisoned for conspiracy. From this period CND went into a decline which lasted until 1980. Its policies were too vague and its pacifist, religious and radical members often politically opposed.

However CND had also helped to give birth to a movement known as the New Left. Disillusioned with the traditional politics of the Communist Party, university intellectuals advocated a socialism based not on the Leninist model of centralized political parties, but on a new libertarianism based on Trotskyite principles. During the late 1950s and early 1960s the New Left Review Group came to constitute the most important theoretical body of dissent in British youth politics.[58]

After a peak period of influence in the days of the CND demonstrations, the New Left also entered a period of decline. Five years later a very different protest style was to emerge, deriving its impetus from the American and European student revolts and from a countercultural underground. By the late 1960s the term 'New Left' was used in a general way to describe a range of distinct radical movements which were collectively to comprise the 1960s counterculture.

The term 'hippie', too, is generic, referring to a wide range of bohemian, student and radical subcultures which emerged in the mid 1960s. The immediate predecessor to the hippies was the 'beat generation'. It originated in the 1950s in California under the auspices of such poets and authors as Allan Ginsberg and Jack Kerouac. They voluntarily chose a life of material poverty and attempted to rediscover their spiritual freedom by travelling America 'on the road'. Disillusioned with a growing impersonality of social life engendered by technological and bureaucratic ordering, their solution was one of retreatism and disengagement with conventional life-styles. Jazz, poetry and marijuana use were its hallmarks. Similarly, within the hippie underground there was a hard core of artistic-literary intelligentsia, but now cemented with post-CND anti-war pacifists and political radicals. The hippies, like the beats, were deeply critical of the effect technology and bureaucracy had on the quality of human life. Accordingly, they advocated a revolution that would humanize society by reintroducing notions of romanticism, and would be based on creativity and self-expression. The rational and scientific ideology of technocracy was to be replaced by a 'new consciousness' centred on visionary experience, self-discovery and mysticism. It would be 'a political end sought by no political means':

Beyond the tactics of resistance, but shaping them at all times, there must be a stance of life which seeks not simply to muster power against the misdeeds of society, but to transform the very sense men have of reality.[59]

It is largely accepted that this particular brand of bohemianism was born in the early 1960s on the West Coast of America, and particularly in the Haight Ashbury district of San Francisco.

Hippies are many things, but most prominently the bearded and beaded inhabitants of the Haight Ashbury, a little psychedelic city-state edging Golden Gate Park. There in a daily street-fair atmosphere, upwards of 15,000 unbounded boys and girls interact in a tribal, love seeking free swinging, acid based type of society.[60]

The colony brought with it some of the trappings of the beat subculture. Of note was the use of drugs, to explore the limits of imagination and self-expression. A life-style developed based on the use of marijuana and particularly Lysergic Acid Diethylamide (LSD or 'Acid') which, because of its hallucinogenic effects, enabled the user to 'trip' through a multitude of distorted ideas, images and actions in rapid succession. The dedicated believed that such an experience enabled reality to become clearer, to be seen free from all preconceptions. The cult was notably spread by Timothy Leary who founded the so-called 'International Federation for Inner Freedom' in 1962 and by Ken Kesey and his group of 'Merry Pranksters'.[61] If Leary's interest was partly scientific and partly tied to religious awakening, Kesey's contribution was to make the acid experience spectacular, wild and playful.

At the beginning of 1967 San Francisco held its 'Human Be-In' and by the summer had attracted 100,000 young people into the district. Soon the media discovered the Haight and invented the term 'hippie'. Hippies were soon to become figures who attracted sympathy for their ideas of love and peace, but who were mistrusted for their anti-work, drug and permissive ethos. Drug abuse and permissive morality were indeed to become the main focus for moral panics in the late 1960s. In Britain, LSD was made illegal in September 1966. Regional drug squads were formed in March 1967. Later that year the Rolling Stones were arrested for possession of marijuana. From 1967 to 1969 the offices of the underground newspaper *IT* (*International Times*) were raided by police and its editors imprisoned or fined on charges of obscenity or conspiracy to corrupt public morals. The underground music clubs UFO and Middle Earth were eventually closed after police raids. And in October 1970 the infamous *OZ* obscenity trial began after raids on its offices in June. *OZ*, an underground magazine, was fined £1000 plus court costs. Prison sentences imposed on its editors, Neville, Dennis and Anderson were only dropped after a lengthy appeal.[62] Despite the hippies' liberal concerns for peace and individual freedom, their activities became consistently defined as deviant, whether because of their style of dress, length of hair, drug usage and subversive literature, or merely because of their preference for loud rock music.

Rear admirals (ret'd) from Ventnor could be sure of a couple of inches in the letter columns of the *Telegraph* inveighing against the young, quoting Horace as often as not and advocating the birch, the noose, or a third world war to deal with the menace of those who disturbed the calm of a Sunday afternoon, fornicated in public places, beat old ladies about their persons with rolled-up copies of subversive and pornographic magazines and worst of all, grew their hair.[63]

Permissiveness was assured of a universally adverse and hostile social reaction.

Drug law enforcement in particular developed dramatically throughout the 1960s. During the 1960s and early 1970s there was a marked increase in convictions for possession of marijuana in Britain – from 235 in 1960, to 4863 in 1969 and 11,111 in 1973. As the 'drug problem' expanded it took on the appearance of a youth problem in particular.[64] Marijuana remained a vital element in creating a 'moral panic' about youth, even though every major official inquiry from the La Guardia to the Wootton Report recommended greater liberality in the treatment of users. The panic culminated in 1971 when a new drugs bill – the Misuse of Drugs Act – was made law. This enabled police to have greater powers to search and hold suspects, and penalties were increased to a maximum of six months imprisonment or a £400 fine for first offenders. The results of such reaction were seen in August 1974 when the Windsor Free Festival was disrupted and halted by police action. 220 people were arrested on obstruction and drug charges, thirty-six suffered injuries, and 600 policemen were reportedly engaged in the operation to clear the festival from the park. A bystander remarked, 'I don't know why the police got so violent. People were being thrown into police vans for no reason. They were just picking people at random.'[65]

Drug control in Britain reached its apogee in 1978. On Thursday 9 March the newspapers were flooded with reports of the successful police operation code-named 'Operation Julie'. In 1976 ten provincial police forces had agreed to collaborate in tracking down LSD factories that Home Office scientists believed to exist in Britain. The whole operation cost nearly £500,000. Of more than 120 people who were arrested, seventeen key people – the chemists, manufacturers, financiers and distributors – received sentences totalling 120 years. From the popular press we were left with the impression that Operation Julie was necessary because LSD is a killer drug.

An entire city stoned on a nightmare drug – that was the crazy ambition of the masterminds behind the world's biggest LSD factory.[66]

From the serious press we learned that the operation was more concerned with controlling a vast underground network of big business. *The Times* stressed that the police were dealing here with the intelligentsia of British society. Theirs was no common drug business, but a professional organization of entrepreneurs and scientists who 'turned LSD into £sd'.[67]

The role of the law enforcement agencies was accepted unquestioningly by all the daily newspapers. Yet the thirteen-year sentences imposed on two of those involved exceeded by one year the highest sentence given in this country for heroin distribution. Yet, as Leigh established, there is no reliable evidence to suggest that LSD is harmful to the user. Unlike heroin, it is non-addictive, and while 'barbiturate and alcohol takers are strongly associated with crime, LSD takers are not'.[68] Moreover, the use of hallucinogenic drugs for purposes other than medical is by no means a contemporary phenomenon. In the early nineteenth century the Romantic poets, Coleridge and De Quincy, and the bohemians of the Latin Quarter of Paris, had used opium to awaken their artistic and spiritual consciousness. De Quincy wrote in the 1820s, 'whereas wine disorders the mental faculties, opium introduces amongst them the most exquisite order, legislation and harmony'. He referred to the drug as a form of 'intellectual intoxication'.[69] These writers, too, were concerned with the increasing rationalization and mechanization of the industrial world, and emphasized the desirability of art that denied reason and spoke of the reality of a drug- or spiritually-awakened consciousness. In the mid twentieth century, Aldous Huxley, describing his experiences with mescalin, once again argued that hallucinogens can help us to bypass the carefully selected information that we have learnt to be reality so that an insight into the true nature of things can be gained.[70] As one of the defendants in the 'Operation Julie' case had written: 'I am sustained by the total conviction of the righteousness of what we are into. I hope that all those we reached with our acid will feel united in support of truth and that vision we share of mankind living in harmony'.[71]

Meanwhile back in the late 1960s the hippie 'moment' had sown the seeds in many young minds that society needed to be changed and that alternative ways of living should be created.[72] The counterculture became not merely bohemian, but was shot through with an amorphous, New Left, political ideology in which personal and political actions were viewed as inseparable.[73] 1968 was the watershed year when bohemian disenchantment was adopted by many student bodies in universities throughout Europe and America as a basis on which a radical political movement could be built. Their contemporary origins lay in the Free Speech Movement and campus protest at Berkeley, California in September 1964, when the university authorities tried to ban all political activity on the campus. In the spring of 1965 the movement was fuelled by Lyndon Johnson's order for saturation bombing to start in North Vietnam. The three issues of American imperialism in Vietnam, black civil rights and educational control were at the centre of the spate of university sit-ins, marches and demonstrations of 1968 in which the strange agglomeration of black militants, students, dropouts, draft dodgers, mystical hippies and women's liberationists seemed to be momentarily united. In Europe, the radical student was particularly motivated by the take-over of the Sorbonne in May by a student–worker alliance and the formulation of an ideology of situationism which stressed the importance of developing revolutionary awareness and actions in everyday life. Reverberations from Paris were most felt in London at the London School of Economics and the Hornsey Art College, where students demanded more autonomy in the organization of university education. Slogans such as 'A gun in your right hand, a joint in your left' abounded. Similarly in March and

October the Vietnam Solidarity Campaign organized demonstrations outside the American Embassy in Grosvenor Square.

Student unrest was also reflected in the growth of various loosely knit anarchist movements. At the turn of 1968, when the first wave of the counterculture, based on love, drugs, and the radical arts waned, the Youth International Party – the Yippies – emerged in America. Their protest used aesthetic rather than violent means, by mocking militarism, disturbing processions and interrupting court proceedings. They first came to the public attention when a crowd of Yippies gathered together at the Pentagon to exorcize the demons from the building. Hoffman described the events:

someone gave a Marshall a leaflet on US imperialism, another squirts him with LACE, a high potency sex juice, that makes you pull your clothes off and make love . . . people are stuffing flowers in rifle barrels.[74]

Other notable events were the throwing away of money in the New York Stock Exchange and the demonstration and festival at the Democratic Convention in Chicago in 1968, for which Hoffman and Rubin were among those tried for conspiracy. Hoffman earned a five-year prison sentence for his part in organizing the joint-rolling contests, nude grope-ins and general hysteria.

Consequently, the underlying anarchism of the counterculture was brought to the surface and previously non-violent organizations began contemplating violent tactics. The Weathermen became the self-appointed 'guerilla army' of bohemianism. Courses in the free universities in USA and underground newspapers worldwide began discussing the use of small arms and the construction of bombs. This policy of agitation and provocation by 'freaking the media' and acting out the unexpected and the sensational was successful in confusing the establishment with its mixture of politics and play. For the Yippie the only way to run a revolution was to have fun while doing it. The mood was perfectly depicted by Jerry Rubin:

Clerical workers will axe their computers and put chewing gum into the machines . . . workers will seize their factories and begin running them communally without profit. . . . Yippie helicopter pilots will bomb police positions with LSD gas. Kids will lock their parents out of their suburban homes and turn them into guerilla bases storing arms. . . . At community meetings all over the land Bob Dylan will replace the National Anthem. . . . People will farm in the morning, make music in the afternoon and fuck wherever and whenever they want to.[75]

The Yippies first became widely known in Britain when a group of twenty, led by Rubin, invaded a Saturday night David Frost Show on ITV in November 1970. While Rubin was quickly deported, this was only the start of further anarchist activity in Britain for a month later the Angry Brigade came to public attention. Like the Yippies, the AB were not an organized group but more of an 'idea which anyone can join'.[76]

As early as 1968 bombs were planted at targets connected with the American, British and Spanish governments and at the close of 1970 a bomb damaged a BBC van outside the Albert Hall on the morning before the Miss World Contest. Explosions at the homes of the Attorney General, the Commissioner of the Metropolitan Police, and the Home Secretary, Robert Carr, eventually broke the previous news silence.

The A.B. is the man or woman sitting next to you. They have guns in their pockets and anger in their minds.[77]

While Prescott and Purdie were in custody on charges of conspiracy, further bombs were planted at a Biba's boutique in May 1971, the General Managers of Fords in June, and at an army recruiting station for Northern Ireland in August.

During much of the 1970s middle-class and student radicalism collapsed. A contracting market for middle-class labour ensured that universities returned to their traditional role of producing a compliant and conformist youth. However, at the close of 1979, Nato's decision to deploy Cruise and Pershing II missiles in Europe began to renew fears about nuclear warfare. The ruling Conservative Party's commitment to the Trident nuclear programme for Britain added to public anxieties and during 1980 CND once more became the 'fastest growing political organisation in the country'.[78] This 'No Nukes' movement was again able to attract considerable youth support, which came to fruition in a series of peace marches and demonstrations between 1981 and 1983. The most significant of these being the Women's Peace Camp outside the American Airforce Base at Greenham Common, which in

November 1983 received the first influx of Cruise missiles in this country.

Perhaps in tandem these years also saw the rise of a subcultural style related to a style of music popularly described as New Romantic. Within the subculture shades of a hippie revival could be seen coupled with the more outrageous stylistic aspects of punk. While the class position of the subculture thus remained ambiguous, the New Romantics provide us with a suitable epitaph to the more bohemian aspect of middle-class countercultures. Despite their infrequent association with political radicalism, their protest remained grounded in individual liberation and retreatism. Walker's description of a Spandau Ballet concert in 1981 could well have been written in 1966.

And when the stroboscope lights up, the whole thing disintegrates into a dreamy pantomine of black and white, nuns and surfers, clowns and crooners, the characters flashing on and off with bursts from the strobe freezing the action and there's nothing much else to do but to succumb to it all, to the delicious escape from whatever it is.[79]

Black youth

The thesis that subcultural styles represent a solution to living within the structural inequalities of a class society is particularly pertinent when applied to the position of black youths in post-war Britain. The majority of black youths in this country form a specifically racially stratified section of the working class. They are marked out within the working class and subject to specific pressures of deprivation and oppression because of their race. While the working class suffers from major forms of deprivation – in income, educational opportunity, life expectancy and housing – the black section of the class is likely to experience more severe disadvantage because of its colour. In education black youths have encountered various racially specific forms of disadvantage. Schools have generally failed to develop curricula which are not ethnocentric, and as a result there remains a persistent mis-conception that cultural differences are 'educational problems'. A high proportion of black children have been mis-cast as educationally subnormal. Educational disadvantage is also likely to be reproduced in the occupational structure, with blacks occupying a low status and low paid sector that has been rejected

by whites. However the vastly disproportionate level of contemporary unemployment among black youth (in comparison to
white or even Asian youth) is also the product of mechanisms of
discrimination that operate in the labour market. In a period of
general high unemployment, it is black youth who appear to bear
the severest brunt of the recession.[80] This is reinforced by their
residence in those inner-city areas which characteristically are
being stripped of employment prospects. Because of low income,
the black section of the working class is largely dependent on
cheap rented accommodation; an element of the housing market
which has gradually been eroded in recent years. This has been
particularly hard on West Indian youth who are subject to quite
strong cultural pressures to gain accommodation independent of
their families. For black youths these elements of their life
situation are encountered through the medium of race.

The present problems facing non-white youth must be seen in
the context of Britain's historical involvement in the development
of white dominance throughout the world through slave trading
and colonialism. For black people racism and prejudice are not
new. It is not a matter of black youth occasionally encountering
particular racially prejudiced individuals, but that their experiences from classroom to job centre confirm the view that racism is
a basic fact of life in British society.

The main period of black immigration to Britain during the
1950s was sponsored and encouraged by the British government
as a result of a chronic domestic labour shortage in the unskilled
sector. Since the opportunities for such work were to be found in
already overcrowded conurbations immigrants also came to
occupy some of the most inadequate housing in the country. In
this way an underclass or subproletariat was created by which the
working class was divided into an indigenous and a non-
indigenous labour force.[81] However the dominant outlook among
West Indian migrants at this time was integrationist – expecting
to be accepted as citizens of the 'mother country'. Consequently
their reception in terms of a simple black–white division and their
experiences of discrimination and racial hostility (particularly in
the 1950s from the Teds) indicated that integration was no simple
process, and, as a result, other cultural adaptations emerged.
Many denied their black identity by assimilating white values and
characteristics even to the length of straightening their hair or
lightening their skin. Others accepted their low status and

retreated into a variety of hidden West Indian cultural practices; from commitment to fundamentalist Christian sects to the creation of West Indian clubs.

But the circumstances encountered by second generation black youth have been significantly different. The cultural responses of their parent culture have become closed or unacceptable to the new generation. The continued experience of discrimination indicated that assimilation was only ever likely to be assimilation to a permanent second-class status, while commitment to fundamentalist religions was undermined by exposure to the secular liberalism of English society. As a result new cultural responses became necessary for black youth in the 1970s. These responses have centred on the construction of new and more assertive definitions of black identity, largely involving the use and reworking of cultural symbols from Jamaica. By 1973 'marginalized' young West Indians in the British ghettos were being attracted to the popular politics of Rastafari.[82]

Rastafarianism originated in the urban areas of Jamaica in the 1930s. Marcus Garvey, founder of the Universal Negro Improvement Association, had earlier awakened black people to the injustices of racism, colonialism and racial segregation. In particular he sought to return all blacks to what he considered to be their rightful birthplace in Africa. To many workers Garvey was a prophet, whose most important insight concerned the crowning of a black king in Africa. Thus when Ras Tafari was crowned Emperor of Ethiopia as Haile Selassie in 1930, he was acclaimed as the returned Messiah and Black Christ. Rastafarianism was thus influential in creating a black political consciousness linked to biblical images of salvation in Ethiopia and Africa.[83] As a political movement, however, Rastafarianism lacked clearly definable structures, being based on metaphysical and non-materialist interpretations of the social order. Nevertheless, it became influential in loosely informing black Jamaicans' experience of oppression. New cultural, and particularly musical, forms were created to promote their own culture and their own black dignity. Reggae music began to emerge in the late 1960s as an integral part of a tradition of popular resistance. The lyrics of reggae spoke of the experiences of poverty and subtle forms of resistance to oppression – parodying the dominant white culture and singing hymns of praise to those who resisted that domination. Here a central figure was the 'rudie' of mid 1960s Jamaica. Rudies were 'hustlers' who lived by dope dealing, pimping and gambling. They were figures who challenged white authority with style and panache.[84] Their petty criminality inevitably brought them into conflict with the police and Rastafarianism was likewise to be denegrated by white society because of its supposed links with violence and crime. However, as Rastafarianism became an essential reference point for the creation of black youth sub-cultures in Britain in the 1970s, it was used more to inform black youth of the history of their oppression and to promote resistance via a detachment from Babylon (white colonial capitalism). Rastafarianism stresses apocalyptic rather than violent solutions to white authority. This resistance has taken many forms. Reggae, and the rediscovery of West Indian patois, for example, have provided a cultural world which is relatively closed to outsiders. Similarly, styles of dress, of walking and of being cool have developed, which represent a positive evaluation of being black. But in turn, Rastafarianism has validated behaviours and outlooks which are more problematic to white society. The 'rudie' hints at petty crime as an acceptable cultural solution to the life situation of young blacks, embodying as it does coolness and defiance of authority. The use of marijuana (ganja) as a sacred drug has also driven black youths into situations where they will encounter the police. The organizing of 'blues' parties with 'sound systems' and the use of the streets as meeting places have in turn raised the visibility of their cultural 'deviance'. Throughout the 1970s relations between Rastas and the police noticeably deteriorated. A stereotype, that all youth wearing dreadlocks and tams in the Ethiopian colours of red, green and gold, were criminal and violent was constructed by the agencies of white authority.

In particular, Brown's police report on Handsworth concluded that the area was racked with crime, mostly of a violent nature, committed at night by a group of some 200 Rastas. They were also believed to be waging something of a minor war against the police at Handsworth's Thornhill Road station.[85] The report effectively set up a Rastafarian stereotype of the sinister night prowler engaged in a systematic attack on the police.[86] Such reaction was undoubtedly related to the moral panic equating mugging solely with black youth and was used to legitimize the selective and discriminate use of the 1824 Vagrancy Act or SUS laws. Faced with a culture that they do not understand, the agents of law and order have reacted to Rastafarianism with contempt and harassment.

But the contempt is mutual. A police raid on the Black and White café in St Paul's Bristol in 1980 to investigate alleged illegal drinking and ganja smoking, was only to provoke further racial hostility and violent confrontations.[87]

Coupled with the loudly acclaimed racism of the National Front and an almost inevitable future within the ranks of the unemployed, black youth in the 1980s have been pushed more and more into forming its own subcultural solutions. Drawing on a mixture of religion, politics and deviant style, and fed by a constant sense of rejection, black youth subcultures come closest to combining subcultural hedonism with active movements of political resistance.

In the metropolitan countries, the general economic crisis has posed additional problems for the black communities there, with the intensification of racism and exploitation. Rastafari is spreading rapidly among black youth as a culture of resistance to white society, white racist values and white education.[88]

The limits of subcultural analysis

The new wave of British subcultural theory that emerged in the 1970s was indeed influential in challenging the individual and sociological positivisms of previous criminology by combining elements of new deviancy theory and cultural studies. Its innovation was primarily to locate youthful criminality as an extension of youth leisure pursuits. It proceeded first by situating youths in relation to their economic and class position and secondly by making 'informed' readings of their leisure styles. In this way some political significance has been read into the subcultural solutions. That these 'solutions' have been identified by the dominant culture as potentially subversive and thus subjected to processes of criminalization, only added weight to the belief that subcultures are inherently political. For the student of middle-class countercultures, political protest emanates from the notion of a unified youth culture crystallized by the political demonstrations, sit-ins and festivals of the late 1960s. For the student of working-class subcultures, resistance is a crucial element in the appropriation and re-using of leisure styles as a source of symbolic struggle with parents, schools and police. In all, youth subcultures were interpreted as a political battleground between the classes. Subcultural styles became the basis of new and subversive meanings as forms of resistance to subordination. This is, however, one of the major weaknesses of these approaches to understanding subculture and crime; for there was a tendency to view all criminal activity as a form of political resistance. For example, there was a constant impulse to decode style in terms only of opposition and resistance and to ignore the more conservative aspects of subcultural style.[89]

In the rush to impute political motives, too much was asked of subcultures and consequently the limitations of, and contradictions within, their modes of protest often became pushed aside and obscured.

Most obviously, subcultural protest based on the appropriation and creation of style is limited by its inevitable interaction with the consumer and entertainment industries. The scope of revolt based on style is restricted because of the ability of the entertainment industry to incorporate and defuse oppositional symbols. Melly calls this the 'castration via trivialisation syndrome'.[90] in which 'what starts as revolt finishes as style – as mannerism'.[91] In reviewing twenty years of youth culture 'revolution' in Britain as voiced through the media of music, fashion, literature and art, he explains how this process operates. Youths' disenchantment with society is expressed at this cultural level in such questions as the élitism of highbrow culture, the boring nature of work, the meaning of freedom and the constraints of puritanical sexuality. In particular, Melly notes the role played by the Beatles and the Beat Movement, Andy Warhol and avant-garde art, and *IT* and the underground newspapers. In their time they all contained some inherently destructive criticism of society and the establishment denounced them as dangerous, subversive and a menace to youth's morality. The revolt is, however, shortlived. The consumer industries, eager to market any kind of exploitable 'subversion', move in, offering television appearances, fame and money to the rebellious. Thus, Melly argues that every new youth movement is ultimately packaged, stylized and committed more to the goals of profit than social criticism. Deviant styles must become commercially viable or else vanish into obscurity. In fact the end result is similar in both cases, for commercialism soon ignores 'old' consumer items and looks for new 'deviant' styles to promote in order to keep market demand alive. Subcultures may provide fresh meanings to existing styles or create new styles themselves, but their diffusion is ultimately dependent on marketing and commercial enterprises, over which subcultures have little or no control. Thus, for example, the 'anarchy' of punk was eventually catered for by every major record company in Britain, not as a symbol of working-class resistance, but as another youth fashion. In this context it is worth reminding ourselves of the temporary and short-lived nature of all subcultures. In concentrating on their moments of authenticity, subcultural theory has neglected to view subcultures as being continually engaged in a process which also involves commercial interests, mass appeal and trivialization. Similarly it cannot account for the processes whereby non-deviant styles are created and gain widespread popularity. The concentration on subcultures has provided an over-politicized analysis of youthful leisure pursuits. This opens up the issue of whether the formation of spectacular youth subcultures is merely the response of a minority of youth. Because of the dramatic style promoted by subcultures, vast media coverage has tended to present the spectacular at the expense of the everyday.

Most youths adopt styles from official youth provision and the teenage entertainment industry. Their culture is thus manufactured rather than innovative and rebellious. The major interests of youth, thus reflect and correspond to those of the dominant value system and are by no means deviant or in opposition. Murdock and McCron, for example, have argued that it is a realistic fatalism rather than an articulated political protest which unites working-class youth.[92] Similarly, subcultural solutions themselves are limited because they focus almost exclusively on leisure. Thus the dominant order is only occasionally confronted and then in a symbolic fashion whereby youth subcultures are only able to strike 'tangential blows'. They cannot provide a real alternative because the problems facing youth emanate largely from the workplace and the market and this is not the arena in which the collective solution is sought. As Clarke *et al.* noted, there is only compensation for, but no subcultural solution to, the problems of youth unemployment, low pay and compulsory miseducation.[93]

In a more sophisticated development of this argument, Willis's ethnographic study of boys in a Midlands comprehensive school details their opposition to authority and conformity in which the lads' specialize in a 'caged resentment which always stops just short of outright confrontation'.[94] Their counter-school culture, involving the disruption of lessons and the subversion of school work, is experienced by them as resistance but ironically contains the seeds of their own downfall. An anti-school culture of chauvinism, solidarity, masculinity and toughness inadvertently prepares them for a life of manual labour. Their symbolic resistance to authority never develops any real power, but instead reinforces the power relations involved in the labour process. The boys collude in their own domination. Rejecting educational qualifications in preference for 'mucking about' and 'skiving', these working-class 'lads' prepare themselves for a life of resisting boredom by time-wasting on the shop floor. Resistance at school ultimately leads to exploitation in the workplace.

The more overt 'political' stance of the middle-class countercultures also is weakened by their contradictory position. Their revolution was largely grounded in the ideologies of passive resistance, dissociation and subjective individualism. In many ways these solutions were class specific and only available to middle-class youth. They were thus limited in achieving the liberation of subordinate cultures. Disenchanted with established politics, the countercultures protest was based on a revived romanticism that if love prevailed all problems would be solved. This apolitical ignoring of the state allowed expressive values and idealism to be seen as an alternative to rationality. However this concern for the *quality* of life was made possible only for those who did not endure scarcity, poverty and labour alienation in their daily lives. Their ignoring of power in political struggle remained an anathema to working-class experience and politics. Similarly, the hippies' concern to travel, both geographically and symbolically via drugs, and to discover new 'realities', came to be easily equated solely with hedonism, retreatism and solipsism. In effect, such expressive alternatives allowed them to reassert their own middle-class position as different and liberating. In this way the counterculture smacked of class élitism and arrogance and was dependent on a relatively secure economic position. When rising unemployment and inflation in the early 1970s began to undermine this security, the counterculture entered its decline. Above all, the emphasis on individual solutions and the belief that freedom could be found 'in your head' denied collective political action. The importance given to individualism also created space for hip entrepreneurs to market and unwittingly defuse the counterculture's 'radical' styles. The swift rise of the underground press, rock music, and a drug culture were all a tribute to the ethics of private enterprise and *laissez-faire*. The counterculture's needs were supplied by profit-making organizations which claimed to support the 'new' community but in fact performed a role no different than that of any other consumer industry in the wider society.

In many ways the counterculture was exuberantly capitalist. In the early 1960s LSD was still obtainable legally and for some was seen as 'revolutionary' in its own right. This revolution was only made available, however, through the transformation of acid manufacture from a domestic industry into big business. The *Village Voice* in August 1974 reported how the manufacture of acid in America in the early 1960s was always designed as a profit-making enterprise 'marketing a product whose time had come', largely because of William Hitchcock and his associate Timothy Leary, who found they had wealth, connections and a ready market for their product.[95]

it becomes immediately evident how both the established firms within the entertainment world and a newer breed of trendy young capitalists, sometimes sporting velvet trousers, long hair and tinted spectacles, have sought to exploit every conceivable object for profit, from drugs and pop festivals to Che and revolution.[96]

In this way cultural radicalism is easily defused, packaged and merchandised to youth.[97] We should question whether all such interventions at the level of culture are likely, on their own, to provide any challenge to the dominant order. As a result, Clarke *et al*. have argued that the counterculture should be considered as a crisis *within* dominant culture, rather than as a conspiracy *against* dominant culture.[98] The counterculture may have reflected a definite stage in the maturation of the crisis of capitalism, in that seemingly large numbers of the population were beginning to find their place intolerable, but the forms in which this conflict was analysed and articulated were not conducive to mass unrest and the development of labour movement politics.

Subcultural solutions are therefore limited by their lack of concern for the politics of work and the labour process. Youths' consciousness of their position is 'negotiated' rather than being truly oppositional and political. Opposition is only expressed in the limited area of leisure which is an inappropriate base for the widespread mobilization of subordinates. Similarly, dominant culture can recuperate from the potentially subversive by reducing it to commodity status.

Nevertheless, subcultural theory has maintained that subcultures are never totally subjugated to commercialism. Even if the commodities of subculture are incorporated, the dominant order can never gain complete control over the more deviant remnants of subcultural action. Thus Teds ripping up cinema seats, skinheads disrupting football marches or hippies refusing to work are elements which still retain an essence of political protest. For Willis, subcultural politics derive from transforming the everyday and commonplace and making them 'answerable to their own collective identity and praxis'.[99]

Subcultures, it is argued, raise the possibility of the revolutionary in the small, detailed and everday. This may, however, be but another, albeit more sophisticated, version of a left romanticism or idealism, which has tended to identify working-class crime and deviancy as forms of quasi-rebellion, thus neglecting that the *reality* of crime on the streets can also be the reality of human suffering and personal disaster.[100]

While subcultures have been reluctant to attach themselves to established political parties, their history is nevertheless rich in their association with numerous political issues. In the late 1950s and early 1980s, sections of middle-class youth were influential in the development of CND. In the mid 1960s many hippies supported the Vietnam Solidarity Campaign. In 1978, black youth and punks were united in the Anti-Nazi League and Rock Against Racism carnivals. Thus Tickell has argued that the tying of subcultures to particular socialist and libertarian causes has been influential in bringing many young people into a situation in which they may be politicized.[101] However, while the Anti-Nazi League gave the anti-racist message an anti-authoritarian and populist image, its chosen medium of music made its transmission dependent on the all too volatile affinities of subcultural politics. The attempt to forge an alliance, between skinheads, mods, punks and black youth, had no real organizational base. Its symbols – a badge, a T-shirt, a hair-style, slang – remained free of any fixed ideological context and allowed endless permutations in which 'youth could follow anti-racist Two-Tone bands but also join racist groups without experiencing any sense of contradiction'.[102]

Subcultures, then, are not automatically synonomous with a progressive outlook on life. Subcultural style can find its practical expression in support of the Right as well as the broad Left. In particular, the solutions preferred by the Teds and skinheads have involved the threatening and attack of immigrant communities. Subcultural theory has sought to explain such behaviour as a rational reaction to the 'invasion' of working-class territory. In this way it has tended to move such problems as mugging, paki-bashing and queer-bashing away from the personal responsibility of the individuals involved and has over-romanticized elements of their violence. Murdoch and Troyna have catalogued the rise of youth wings within such fascist organizations as the National Front, the British Movement, Column 88 and Viking Youth in the late 1970s. For example, in 1978, 21 per cent of NF supporters were aged between 15 and 20. These organizations have added a political dimension to existing working-class youth subcultures, particularly the skinheads, and provided them with a platform for their racist attitudes.[103]

The implicit and everyday politics of subcultures are not therefore the same and are open to both socialist and reactionary appeals. The available evidence clearly shows that most working-class adolescents are deeply conservative and that their radicalism is most likely to be reactionary. For example, a National Opinion Poll in 1978 found that 89 per cent of 15- to 21-year-olds thought that vandals and hooligans should be dealt with more severely.[104] Thus, the subcultural accounts have generally failed to interrogate sufficiently the more conservative aspects of each subculture. For example, violence is presented mainly in instrumental terms as a means of pursuing such goals as the defence of threatened identities and community homogeneity. The intention is to demonstrate that violence is not senseless or animalistic, but is essentially ordered, rational and meaningful. As a result, subcultural theories have tended to underplay the extent of violence in some subcultures, and failed to recognize its effects on victims and on vulnerable, particularly immigrant, communities. There is indeed a problem in inferring that such degrees of rationality exist within subcultural violence, particularly when the participants would not recognize themselves in the offered explanations.[105] The terms 'magical', 'symbolic' and 'imaginary' to describe solutions in effect allow subcultural theory to infer a potentially infinite range of meanings to subcultural action. While these analyses are certainly imaginative, they also appear free-floating, unstructured and ambiguous. We do not know when or how one symbolic interpretation is more adequate than another. This problem is further exacerbated by the concepts of bricolage and homology. Rather than providing us with a fresh understanding of the origins and development of subcultures, they appear merely as devices to explain away subcultural inconsistencies and thus disguise their contradictions. Subcultural theory often appears content to find meanings (magic, recovery of community, resistance or whatever) quite independent of intent and awareness. The danger is of getting lost in the 'forest of symbols'.[106] This problem is epitomized by the often debated meaning lying behind the wearing of the swastika emblem both by punks and fascist skinheads. Are its wearers ironically distancing themselves from the very message that the symbol is intended to convey, or is it a rather more simple matter of conformity, ignorance and overt racism?[107]

Finally, and arguably, the most significant weakness of the 'new deviancy' studies lies in their stress on class and style and a consequent neglect of gender divisions. There are still very few studies either of the participation of girls in subcultures or of female delinquency.[108] In the discussions of youth and crime and youth subcultures, existing research has spoken overwhelmingly of *male* youth cultural forms. When the causes of girl delinquency have been discussed in orthodox criminology, it is usually with recourse to psychological and individualistic theories. Thus girls who break the law do so because they are 'unloved', have had 'poor mothering' or are 'maladjusted' to their roles as prospective wives and mothers. The significance of culture, class and community, which are now established parameters in recognizing boys' delinquency, is ignored in discussing female delinquency. Delinquent girls have not, generally, been portrayed in the same way as their male counterparts as imaginative and important critics of the social order. Part of this problem lies in the fact that subcultures do tend to be male-dominated forms concerned with, among other things, an exploitation and glorification of masculinity. But if it is more difficult for girls to achieve subcultural affiliation, then this should also be explained within the theory.

In documenting the temporary flights of the Teds, Mods or Rockers, they fail to show that it is monstrously more difficult for women to escape (even temporarily) and that these symbolic flights have often been at the expense of women (especially mothers) and girls. The lads may get by with – and get off on – each other alone on the streets, but they did not eat, sleep, or make love there. Their peer-group consciousness and pleasure frequently seem to hinge on a collective disregard for women and the sexual exploitation of girls.[109]

Indeed, most subcultural studies have failed to adopt a critical attitude to the overt sexism of their subjects, and have unwittingly reinforced stereotypical images of women as passive, dependent and subordinate. McRobbie and Garber argue that girls are not necessarily absent from subcultures, but, because of their different structural position within the home, they are pushed by male dominance to the periphery of social activity.[110] In addition, girls' potential income and spending power is lower than that of boys. Parents guard girls' leisure time much more closely and, through a variety of moral constraints, their behaviour outside the home is carefully controlled. Much of this is linked to dominant ideologies about women's 'natural' place being in the home, revolving around a culture of domesticity rather than paid employment. As a result, Frith has argued that:

girl culture becomes a culture of the bedroom, the place where girls meet, listen to music and teach each other make up skills, practise their dancing, compare sexual notes, criticise each other's clothes, and gossip.[111]

Girls' leisure thus operates more within the invisible space of the home than on the streets. While boys might sexually and socially 'sow their wild oats' in the neighbourhood, the consequences for girls of getting known as a receiver of the 'wild oats' is drastic and irreversible.[112] This does not mean that girls have played no part in the history of subcultures but, as Brake argues, they occupied a more passive and subordinated position:

During the period of the Teds, girls would be present during the social activities but absent from the street corner culture. With the Mods, girls were subordinate but the mod 'cool' style allowed them to go out in groups or alone. With bikers they never penetrated the central masculine core, riding or owning a bike; they were always a pillion rider. In the hippy subculture they were still contained within the sphere of traditional femininity, even though it allowed a moratorium which suspended marriage (but not steady relationships).[113]

Sexual divisions within society are simply replicated by subcultures. Whatever 'solutions' to class inequalities and deprivation they may have offered to boys, these were certainly not shared by girls. Subcultures offered them no alternative to their ever-impending 'career' of marriage, home and children.

New deviancy and subcultural theory indeed overlooked vital aspects of youth socialization in its continual celebration of male delinquency. The ignoring of sexual divisions was mirrored by the absence of any discussion of work and relations within the family, the ways in which girls and women can respond to male violence and the sexual practices of youth. Given the undoubted significance of sexual feelings for both boys and girls (and the media's repeated interest in such relations), this omission is doubly surprising.[114]

Future research will need to give more attention to these issues if new deviancy theory is to achieve its stated intention of situating youthful (mis)behaviour in its full and complete social context.

Suggested reading

An exposition of 'new subcultural theory' and its application to various case studies is the subject of Hall and Jefferson (1976). This book is a major landmark in the development of youth studies in Britain in the 1970s. Hebdige (1979) develops the analysis by concentrating on the significance of style in informing subcultural practice. Mungham and Pearson (1976) offer another representative series of case studies, while Brake (1980) provides a 'textbook' review of both the American and British subcultural studies. To date the most telling critiques of this work have been McRobbie (1980), Dorn and South (1982), and S. Cohen (1980).

5 The practice of youth control 1: regulation and restraint

The preceding chapters have attempted to identify and interrogate the major problems, crimes and deviant behaviours associated with youth. However, these arguments, of whether juvenile crime is misrepresented, miscategorized or misunderstood, have little relevance in the operation of contemporary juvenile justice. The post-war years witnessed a massive growth in the amount of state intervention devoted to tackling the 'problem'. As delinquency came to be regarded as a dramatic problem, it inevitably attracted extreme solutions. The calls for 'birching of vandals', 'corporal punishment for muggers' and 'stocks for hooligans' have to date found their practical implementation in the provision of 'short, sharp shock' detention centres and curfew orders for young offenders. On the other hand, there is, and has been since the nineteenth century, a concurrent concern to 'treat' the delinquent through various non-custodial means and to prevent 'those most at risk' from becoming delinquent. This element of social policy, while attempting a positive promotion of welfare, has indirectly enabled a greater surveillance and regulation of youthful behaviour. In particular, the use of more segregated and institutionalized means of socialization in state schools and the juvenile justice system has prolonged a view of adolescence as a distinct and special period of life in which youth is vulnerable and needs careful guidance and direction. The practice of youth control, then, extends beyond the more 'exceptional' interventions of the juvenile justice system and into the continuum of 'everyday' interventions offered by compulsory schooling, the workplace, 'new' training schemes for the unemployed and the general policing of youth's leisure. This chapter draws together some of the most recent and 'critical' research that has been done in these areas.

Schooling

Youthful behaviour is not only controlled by the ultimate threat of incarceration in detention centres, youth custody centres and secure units, but also by systems of surveillance, regulation and discipline which operate in the wider community. The most prominent institutional form of control of the latter type lies within the educational system. One often forgotten, though central, feature of schooling is that it is *compulsory*. While discussions of the development of compulsory education since 1870 are frequently couched in liberal and democratic arguments to do with the beneficial effects of the dissemination of literacy and knowledge, we should not forget that educational institutions also contain a real substratum of coercion. Today, although schooling generally operates with the consent of the pupils, if that consent is withdrawn, school can be experienced as a much more coercive and total institution.

The compulsory schooling of youth has become so institutionalized that it appears both natural and inevitable. However, analysis of the political debates prior to the 1870 Education Act reveals that the particular nature and function of the education to be offered the working classes was far from universally agreed. Similar to the attempts to reform youth through industrial schools and reformatories in the mid nineteenth century, the instigation of state education was born out of a conflicting number of motivations including humanitarianism, bourgeois charity, religious commitment, fear of disorder and revolution, and utilitarianism. State schooling is thus an area of intervention which simultaneously tries to educate neglected youth, control delinquent youth, enforce particular moral standards as universal, and ensure that the labour force is both adequately trained and willing. The extension of elementary schooling in the late nineteenth century was designed not only to provide opportunities for some working-class children to achieve social success, but also to combat those aspects of working-class socialization which were believed to create juvenile crime and street gang violence, through an infusion of bourgeois values of hard work, discipline and thrift. As Humphries argues:

The state schooling system was conceived as potentially the most powerful instrument with which to inculcate in successive generations of working-class children values and attitudes that were thought necessary for the reproduction and reinvigoration of an industrial-capitalist society. It was not designed to impart literacy, skills and knowledge as ends in themselves. Instead learning was conceived as a means to an end – it made the pupil more amenable to a socialisation process, through which his or her character and future lifestyle might be shaped.[1]

The state education system was born as much from questions of how to achieve social order (and quell fears of crime and disorder) as attempts to 'civilize' the working classes through literacy and learning. The particular content of the education destined for the working class thus included the provision of particular bourgeois ideologies, and moral and religious codes to counter 'revolutionary' tendencies. It was designed to create both a disciplined and punctual labour force and ultimately a 'hierarchy of civilisation based upon education and refinement which the working class would respect and of which they would find themselves at the very bottom'.[2] A commitment to schooling thus required the working classes to reject their own cultural heritage, styles of speech and behaviour in favour of those from a higher and alien social class. The instigation of a national education was not simply a way of providing some education to a class which would have otherwise been intellectually bankrupt. Prior to 1870 the working classes had organized educational institutions by and for themselves without recourse to philanthropic or state provision.[3] Far from promising an extension of knowledge, state-provided education thus threatened to be an 'imposition from above', enabling a greater surveillance and control of working-class culture and radicalism. Between 1840 and 1870, the state produced a complex machinery, via school inspectorates, training and certification of teachers, and withholding school grants, to regulate and eventually destroy the working class's own education:

From the mid-nineteenth century onwards the power of the state was used to create the structures which provided the bourgeois definition of education and to discredit and destroy alternatives; this was the process through which the hearts and the minds of the working class were 'captured by' bourgeois ideology, through which the class was incorporated.[4]

However, incorporation within an imposed and compulsory institution did not necessarily mean acceptance. Oral histories of working-class experience in the late nineteenth century clearly show how school routine was experienced as an imposition with little relevance to the working-class child. Compulsory schooling was thus met with various forms of resistance – disobedience, 'dissocation' and school strikes – instigated by pupils *and* their parents.

Opposition to the authoritarian and bureaucratic form of rational state schooling was rooted in three principal grievances. Its compulsory nature threatened the domestic economy and survival of many families: its regimented and repressive form abused the fundamental personal liberties that most working-class parents accorded to their children: and its removal of character development and work from the community to a depersonalised and bureaucratic setting was widely felt to be an infringement of the customary rights of the family.[5]

It is with reference to this historical context that Corrigan attempts to rationalize contemporary practices of working-class truancy, 'mucking about in class' and 'dolling off'.[6] Such classroom misbehaviour has become of increasing concern with the apparent growth in violence against teachers and damage to school property. In February 1982 a junior school in Liverpool was temporarily closed following a 'riot' by some of its pupils.[7] While this may be an extreme reaction, Corrigan's interviews with a group of 14- to 15-year-old boys in a Sunderland School revealed that deeply engrained feelings of hostility and resentment towards the institution exist in the minds of many working-class pupils. Concentrating his analysis on ninety-three boys, Corrigan found that fifty-two only went to school because they had to: thirteen went to 'muck teacher about': eighteen went to learn: and only five went because they enjoyed it.[8] The major values of the school are thus barely supported, or complied with, by the majority of the boys. While frequent truancy was found to be rare, this was born not out of moral compliance but from a recognition of the consequences of getting caught. However truancy was but one of a number of tactics the boys employed to overcome compulsory attendance and thus remains a very imprecise measure of their rejection of school. Following registration the boys skip some lessons or disrupt those at which they are present:

truancy must be seen as an extreme action: 'dolling off' as less extreme: 'mucking about' as a major activity and 'not paying attention' as endemic.[9]

In this way they avoided the more punitive sanctions of the law and their actions became a matter solely for the control of individual teachers. Asked how often teachers resorted to physical violence to achieve this control, thirty-nine of the boys replied 'every day'.[10] Such sanctions were applied largely to cases of minor misbehaviour, such as talking or being cheeky. Violence is thus used to create the necessary conditions under which discipline, rather than any academic subject, can be taught.

A similar picture of working-class schooling experience is painted by Willis's ethnographic study of 'the lads' at a Midlands secondary school. The educational paradigm, structure and organization of the school attempts to model each pupil through a mixture of consent and coercion. School is experienced as an agency of compulsion and punishment designed to achieve the deference and compliance of its pupils.

The careful bell rung timetable; the elaborate rituals of patience and respect outside the staff room door and in the classroom where even cheeky comments are prefaced with 'sir', compulsory attendance and visible staff hierarchies – all these things assert the superiority of staff and their world.[11]

Willis discovered relatively little direct coercion or repression, but rather 'an enormous constriction of the range of moral possibilities'. The continual attempts to induce discipline, obedience and conformity reveals to some students that the school is more of a total institution than a means for self-advancement through the acquisition of knowledge. The infusion of a multitude of petty school rules which are often arbitrarily enforced is the main source of the 'lads'' grievances. But their insubordination and undermining of authority would not be seen as a problem if control and regulation was not the axis on which the relations between students and staff turned. It is no surprise then that 'the lads' frequently described the school as 'a prison camp', teachers as enemies and looked eagerly to the day when they could leave and achieve some independence. Meanwhile they continue to express their opposition to school by thwarting its formal organizational and educational aims:

As 'the lads' enter the classroom or assembly, there are conspiratorial nods to each other saying 'Come and sit here with us for a laff', sidelong glances to check where the teacher is and smirking smiles. . . . After assembly has started the kid still marooned from his mates crawls along the back of the chairs or behind a curtain down the side of the hall, kicking other kids, or trying to dismantle a chair with somebody on it as he passes.... Settled in class there is a continuous scraping of chairs, a bad tempered 'tut-tutting' at the simplest request . . . an aimless air of insubordination with spurious justification and impossible to nail down.[12]

Their opposition is directed also at the school conformists – the 'ear 'oles' – who have invested some support in the formal aims of education. 'The lads' ' counter-school culture is then set against the school, teachers and other students.

The existence of different student subcultures in schools has long been recorded. Hargreaves's analysis of the status systems of fourth year boys at a secondary modern school in the 1960s revealed two distinct value climates – the academic and what he called the delinquescent. Hard work and discipline characterized the former, nonconformist dress, smoking and fighting the latter. A number of factors combined to associate these two subcultures with the system of school streams. The lower the stream the greater the propensity towards delinquent behaviour. Through streaming and peer group pressure these two subcultures became cemented and highly differentiated. The school then played an important part in providing the conditions necessary for the emergence of a delinquent group which found a solution to its lack of status by rejecting the pupil role.[13] Similarly Power *et al.*'s study of secondary schools in Tower Hamlets indicated that there were large differences in delinquency rates between similar secondary modern schools which could not be explained by differences in the delinquency rates of the areas from which the schools drew their pupils. They suggested that the type of social education and the kind of social relationships within the school and between school, parents and community were significant determinants of pupil delinquency.[14] Reynolds's research of delinquency rates in nine secondary modern schools in South Wales certainly appeared to substantiate this view.[15] He argued that in schools with low delinquency rates, teachers and working-class pupils with low aspirations had negotiated a truce to their classroom conflicts:

A truce situation means simply that the teachers will go easy on the pupils and that the pupils will go easy with the teacher. On the teachers' side, they will no longer proceed against the pupils to any great extent to ensure compliance with expressive, non-pedagogic or character moulding goals since they know that to do so will only produce rebellion, a rebellion that by lowering pupils' overall level of commitment to the school will make it even more difficult for the school to maintain control.[16]

Those schools where no such truce existed were predictably characterized by teacher coercion and pupil dissociation, thus producing a greater propensity towards vandalism within the school, truanting from it and delinquency outside it. The particular way in which control is achieved in schools thus has important implications for the future behaviour of youth. Reducing the stress on rules and the desire to achieve pupil deference may prevent the non-academic pupil from being subjected to the ultimate form of control in schools – special units and withdrawal sanctuaries. In 1977 there were an estimated 239 education units providing nearly 4000 places. By 1982 these had increased to 400 units providing more than 7000 places. These are either on site, incorporated in the school building, or 'off site' in separate buildings.[17] The units are designed to relieve teachers of 'troublesome' pupils. They provide a temporary retreat in which pupils are closely supervised in small groups under the guidance of teachers and social workers. If 'behavioural problems' are resolved, by the pupils showing some compliance with the values and constraints of learning, they will be returned to the school.

In whatever ways resistance to school is negotiated or controlled, however, the desire for independence on the part of the working-class pupil is never achieved. For, as Willis notes, resistance to schooling means that 'the lads' are destined for the unskilled labour market where their subordination is reinforced. The meaningless and irrelevant nature of school for much working-class youth is replicated in their future (un)employment.

Work and unemployment

The transition from school to work holds certain continuities for nonconformist working-class students. In terms of job choice, it is their own culture, rather than that offered by qualifications and official careers advice, which provides their most influential reference point. The informal shop-floor culture of the factory has some marked similarities with the counter-school culture. 'Skiving off', male sexual and physical bravado, and opposition to authority all have their place on the shopfloor.[18] Social divisions in school are replicated at work. The working-class youth enters work not from a matter of a particular job choice, but as a realistic fatalism towards a future of generalized labour.

Most work – or the 'grafting' they accept they will face – is equilibrated by the overwhelming need for instant money, the assumption that all work is unpleasant and that what really matters is the potential particular work situations hold for self and particularly masculine expression, diversion and 'laffs' as learnt in the counter-school culture. These things are quite separate from the intrinsic nature of any task.[19]

The constraints of school and industry act together to *reproduce* major class and cultural divisions in society. If schools were indeed successful in producing working-class youth who had absorbed the rubric of self-development and interest in work, greater demand would be placed on the few meaningful jobs available and employers would be struggling to persuade working-class youth to accept meaningless work in the factories. As this is not yet the case, Willis suggests that 'some of the real functions of institutions work counter to their stated aims'.[20] Thus working-class dissociation from school actually achieves for education its main objective – the placing of working-class kids 'voluntarily' in semi-skilled and unskilled manual work.[21] Indeed, apart from traditional apprenticeships and some clerical work, the youth labour market has been characterized by the existence of a large number of unskilled 'dead-end' occupations. The unqualified and unskilled have a special relationship to production. Job changing is frequent. The young are also always at risk of being jettisoned by employers at the point at which they become entitled to an adult wage, to be replaced by younger and cheaper labour. The 'job mobility' of unskilled youth, according to Frith, thus reflects both their own readiness to leave when 'fed up', and their employers' readiness to sack them for 'disciplinary problems'.[22]

Indeed, Willis's 'lads' all ended up in jobs – fitting tyres, laying carpets, painting, decorating, acting as plumber's and bricklayer's mates or as trainee machinists in a local factory. That was in 1975. Five years later, they could be considered to be particularly fortunate. Unskilled youth have always constituted one of the most vulnerable sections of the workforce. In times of falling employment it is those groups considered to be marginal to the labour market – unskilled youth, women and immigrants – who will find themselves to be part of the 'reserve army of labour'. Triggered by economic recession and technological changes which reduced the demand for young unskilled labour, the numbers of unemployed school leavers rose dramatically in the mid 1970s. In September 1973 there were 14,000 school leavers (under 18s) without a job. By July 1980 this had risen to 368,000.[23] This almost thirty fold increase took place despite higher numbers of young people avoiding the labour market by going into higher and further education.[24] The unemployment rate of 18- to 25-year-olds is even greater. In July 1982 some 926,499 young people between 18 and 25 were registered as unemployed – almost one in six of this section of the population. A quarter of a million had been out of work for a year or more; over 75,000 for over two years, and almost 20,000 for three years.[25] Overall, some 30 per cent of the unemployed were under 25. The situation was even more acute for black youth. In November 1982, the Commission for Racial Equality reported that 60 per cent of young Afro-Caribbeans who were available for work in the 16–20 age group were without a job.[26] At that time some 40 per cent of whites and Asians were also out of work. Unemployment has always tended to hit the young hardest. Every rise in adult unemployment since the 1960s has been accompanied by a greater rise in the youth rate. In May 1983 the rate for all ages was some 13 per cent, but for under 18s it was over 50 per cent. Regional unemployment is even more substantial. In Liverpool, where overall unemployment was 20 per cent in 1983, unemployment of under 18-year-olds was nearly 90 per cent.[27]

Since 1975, when youth unemployment first became a major political issue, the state has poured resources into various job creation, work experience and improved training schemes. The bulk of this effort has been directed towards the 16-year-old school leavers. This is hardly surprising. Nearly 50 per cent of Britain's 16-year-olds leave school to find work. In July 1983 over 50 per cent of these school leavers were either unemployed or on a government sponsored training scheme.

In 1978 the Youth Opportunities Programme (YOP) was launched by the Labour government under the guidance of the Manpower Services Commission (MSC). Initially some 86,000 school leavers were involved, and 69 per cent of YOP trainees later found full-time employment.[28] In 1981 the scheme was expanded, providing places for 180,000 young people. In the same year, the

Conservative government disclosed plans to put a new youth training scheme (YTS) into operation by September 1983, whereby *all* unemployed school leavers would be required to undertake a one year period of post-school work 'training'. This involved finding suitable placements for some 460,000 young people.

The YOP consisted of four different elements: work experience on employer's premises (WEEP), community projects (community service schemes); training workshops (manufacture of consumer products from wood, metal or fabrics); and various kinds of work preparation courses. Its aim was to prepare young people for work by making them more acceptable to employers. This was to be achieved by providing not only work experience but also 'life and social skills' related to work discipline, appearance and punctuality. The basic premise of the programme was that youth unemployment had risen because of a sudden failure of youth to be suitable candidates for employment. But as Phil Cohen argues, the aim of the programme could not realistically be to expand job opportunities as these depend on an uplift in the market economy. Rather its:

real effect is limited to ideology – to represent youth unemployment as a problem of faulty supply rather than demand; a failure of the educational system rather than capitalism; a personal problem of joblessness due to lack of motivation, experience or skill, rather than the position youth occupies in the market economy.[29]

In fact, as the YOP expanded its 'success rate' noticeably declined. By 1981 the numbers of trainees subsequently finding full-time employment fell to about 36 per cent. By far the largest element in the YOP was the WEEP scheme which accounted for three-quarters of YOP places. It was also the element that received most criticism. Rather than providing secure future job opportunities, the scheme artificially created a demand for youth labour which in market terms was no longer profitable. Trainees worked for up to six months with one employer, often in unskilled, repetitive and dirty jobs for which they were paid an allowance by the government (in 1983 this was £25 per week). The scheme was therefore cheap to run but lent itself to the possibility of employers replacing paid employees with a succession of YOP trainees.[30] Despite assurances that employers who sought to abuse the scheme in order to obtain cheap labour would be excluded, by 1981 the MSC conceded that one in three of the positions created had cost a permanent worker a job.[31] The provision of six months free non-unionized labour also resulted in many employers simply taking on YOP workers rather than employing school leavers full time. Above all, the scheme was used not so much for the training but for the vetting of youth by employers. The MSC's booklet 'Instructional guide to social and life skills' emphasized the need 'to adjust trainees to normal working conditions', to check for 'signs of alienation in matters of timekeeping, discipline etc' and 'any unsatisfactory relationships'.[32] Essentially the young unemployed were viewed as deviants who needed 'treatment' in the form of work discipline, regulation and surveillance. As Morgan concludes:

the Youth Opportunities Programme offers a chance to experience the discipline of work without being allowed any of the advantages that go with it. . . . (Young people) are, through the 'training programme', encouraged to believe that it is their personal inadequacies which create unemployment. They are, in effect, less powerful and more atomised on the programme than off it.[33]

In essence, YOPs acted as a form of social control by attempting to reassert the value of the work ethic to those who find work unavailable. Such a benefit, however, came to be increasingly lost on the young and unemployed. For a majority, WEEP only provided a temporary respite from the dole queue. Many learnt that because of low allowances they were as well, if not better, off receiving supplementary benefit than a YOP allowance.[34] Others questioned the dubious amount of training they received as cheap labour in menial jobs. There is no evidence that the YOP made any difference whatsoever to the amount of regular employment available to school leavers. But the programme did have two clear political attractions. It helped to keep some 300,000 people off the official unemployment register and also off the streets, every year. The social order implications of high youth unemployment were noted as early as 1978. A minister at the DES in the last Labour government warned that, without jobs:

a growing number of youngsters are bound to develop the feeling that society has betrayed them. Such feelings can very easily lead to crime and even more sinister, can provide a fertile ground for the breeding of various kinds of political extremism. I do not think it is exaggerating to suggest that these factors pose a threat to the fabric of society potentially as serious as that of armed conflict between nations.[35]

When a MORI poll, conducted among the young employed in 1981 to establish their views of the 1980–1 riots, found that two-thirds blamed unemployment for the riots and 28 per cent thought they were justified, such fears appeared to be vindicated.[36]

A number of studies have examined the relationship between crime and unemployment. Although these have yet to establish that there is a direct link between joblessness and criminality, Box and Hale confirmed that:

Unemployment among young males results in more frequent prison sentences than among older males. It appears, after controlling for other related factors that for every 1,000 increase in youth unemployment 23 additional young males get sent to prison.[37]

Those working in probation also increasingly came to view the problems of unemployment and criminality as closely related. In Cambridgeshire it was noticed that whenever unemployment in the region increased, then so did the number of unemployed offenders. Cambridgeshire's probation service noted that 68 per cent of juvenile offenders in 1982 were unemployed at the time of the offence.[38]

It was thus partly in response to questions of social order that the government unveiled a new training scheme for youth which aimed to overcome the failures of the YOP. The Youth Training Scheme (YTS), which replaced YOP in September 1983, is a twelve-month training programme directed at 16- and 17-year-old school leavers. It aims at the eventual provision of a permanent bridge between school and work by offering all young people under the age of 18 the opportunity to either continue in full-time education or to enter a period of planned work experience combined with related training and education. At the end of the year, 'trainees' will have their progress and achievements recorded in a personal profile to serve as a reference and recommendation for future employers. YTS is intended to be a comprehensive scheme covering both employed and unemployed young people. It thus seeks to influence the way industry trains its own workforce, as well as providing a scheme to cope with the unemployed. However, the scheme is unlikely to solve some of the problems of YOP. Like YOP it is open to abuse by employers and its acceptance by employers and trainees depends on the level of grant that both parties eventually receive from the government. In addition, there is no guarantee that all young people will receive a

similar 'training'. 'All manner of types and levels of provision' will
exist 'determined not by informed planning but rather by the
accident of where they live and the short term preferences of
employers'.[39] In the final analysis young people will be expected to
display all the qualities that were formerly the products of
experience when they are thrown into the labour market after their
one year of training.

YTS thus remains a logical continuation of the government's
and the MSC's attempts to provide a permanent structural
resolution to the crisis of youth unemployment by tightening the
control over school leavers. As Dan Finn concludes, 'state
agencies are increasingly going to determine what it means to be
young'.[40] YTS also continues to interpret the problem of employment for young people as a problem about young people. By
insisting that the young working class now have special develop-
mental needs, their exclusion from the labour market, their
redefinition as trainees and their exposure to new forms of
educational experience are spuriously justified. YTS's primary
fallacy lies in its premise that a programme of vocational
preparation will enable the young to be better equipped to
compete for jobs, without actually expanding real job opportunities. Rather, even if youth are persuaded to accept their status as a
new client group in need of a further year's education and training,
at the end of the new scheme, the trainees will face the same future
as most YOP graduates – the dole. As Anne Stafford concludes, the
integration of youth into the labour market will depend on their
willingness to accept any alternative to the dole. It is an integration
then which 'is precarious and rests on a promise which must
surely turn sour'.[41]

The political rationale for these employment schemes thus lies
elsewhere than in the actual creation of jobs. The young and
unemployed working classes have been understood as both a
potential threat to the social order and, partly as a consequence, in
need of special provision from and direction by that same social
order if they are to assume their role as the next generation of adult
workers. In this context, policies around working-class youth
display a Janus-face where what is altruistically proclaimed to be
meeting their needs also contains the potential for their direction
and control.

Policing leisure

The street has always provided the main arena for the leisure activities of working-class youth. It is on the streets, too, where troubling aspects of their behaviour are at their most visible, and contact with the police is most likely. As Corrigan's conversations with 'the boys' from Sunderland revealed, alternative arenas for leisure were likely to be rejected because they 'are not open to the boys as real choices'.[42] The official provision of the youth service – the youth club – may have been used as an initial meeting-place, but compliance with its rules and regulations is likely to be resisted. The formality of applying for membership, paying subs and being subject to some supervision, placed some youth out on to the fringe of the youth service. The cinema, disco and dance hall were frequently too expensive. The home was constrained by the presence of parents. The boys were left with nothing but the street – the place that offered them a limited degree of freedom. The boys described their main leisure activity on the streets as 'doing nothing' or 'just hanging about', yet it still offered the most potential for something exciting *to* happen:

given nothing to do, something happens, even if it is a yawn, or someone setting down on somebody else's foot, or someone turning over an old insult or an old injury and it's this in the context of 'nothing' that leads to fights – something diminutive and unimportant outside the context of 'doing nothing' yet raging and vital within that context.[43]

'Doing nothing' may, however, be interpreted by external observers as 'loitering with intent'. The boys' experience of leisure was thus likely to involve contact with the police at some time. This was how they got into trouble:

The boys see trouble as something connected purely with the police, or other social control agents; one cannot get into trouble without the presence of one of these groups. At no stage do they perceive it as doing wrong or breaking rules. . . . What wrongs are they doing if they just walk around the streets and the police harrass them? The reasons for the harrassment lie with the police, and NOT inside any rule that the boys are breaking since for the boys the streets are a 'natural' meeting place.[44]

'Keeping the streets safe' is, however, high on the list of the police's priorities. In policing practice an imaginary connection is made between a dangerous place (the streets of the working-class city) and a dangerous time (youth).[45] Central to this ongoing dispute for control of the streets is the discretionary use of police powers to stop on suspicion. Until 1981, Section 4 of the Vagrancy Act 1824 allowed police to arrest a person on suspicion of loitering with intent to commit an arrestable offence. During the 1970s the issue of the infamous 'SUS' offence came to a head after repeated claims that the police used the law selectively to 'harass' black youth.[46] SUS was used extensively in London, Merseyside and Greater Manchester, but very little elsewhere. In 1978, black arrests accounted for 44 per cent of London's SUS arrests. In Lambeth, 77 per cent of those arrested for SUS were black.[47] Despite police denials that the law was used discriminately against blacks, the government repealed the law in 1981. However, its replacement by stop and search proceedings (SAS) has not reduced the likelihood of youth being stopped on the streets. In 1978, police in Liverpool had already preferred to use SAS in place of SUS. As one local black youth recalled:

I've been stopped and searched loads whilst playing football at night. 'Don't be on the street at 11 o'clock, Stand in your own paths' they say. You're not allowed to leave your gate. It's like a curfew. When I got picked up for SPL (Suspected Person Loitering) five of us were walking home, just talking. The police thought they recognised one of my mates and searched us. We started laughing and it was then that they threw us into the van.[48]

The repeal of SUS appears, therefore, to be a change in name only. Certainly a sense of 'vulnerability' continues to be felt by young people themselves. At a 'Youth in the City' conference organized by the Leicester City Council in 1983, young people voiced their complaints that the police show little respect to youth, that they pick on groups of youth, and that young policemen in particular are too aggressive. They advocated a less intensive police response to youthful behaviour.[49]

Other aspects of police practice have also become increasingly questioned. During the 1970s, football crowd control became increasingly coercive. Fans were segregated and broken down into smaller units by 'cattle penning'; more police were on duty at matches in the form of 'snatch squads' and 'mobile squads'; restrictions were placed on road and rail travel to away games; and helicopters and video cameras have enabled greater surveillance.[50]

Saturation policing methods, such as Operation Swamp in Brixton in 1981, involving the drafting in of extra police to police *selected* communities, once again raised questions of racism and control. In 1982, the decision to equip police forces with CS gas, plastic bullets and water cannons was taken by chief constables without a thorough public debate, and epitomized the shift to a more 'reactive' style of policing to which black youth and black communities feel particularly vulnerable. Such increases in police surveillance of 'targeted populations' inevitably lead to more arrests, thus providing the raw material to which proponents of the 'crime wave' lobby can turn.

Jock Young's study of the enforcement of drug laws in Notting Hill was the first British research to show how police practices create, rather than control, deviant behaviour.[51] He argued that the police, from the nature of their work, and to some extent as a matter of policy, were relatively isolated from the general public. This made them particularly prone to stereotyping such groups as marijuana smokers as deviant and immoral outsiders. Police action on drug-law enforcement – the people they look for, the way they perceive and treat them – was determined by these stereotypes. The intensification of such action by the formation of drug squads not only increasingly marginalized the drug-takers, but intensified and amplified their identity as deviant. They were thus transformed from an integrated community where drug-taking was peripheral into isolated groups of fearful deviants within which the meaning and practice of drug-taking became central. Similarly, Gill's study of the relation between police and youths in Liverpool concluded that, by concentrating surveillance in particular areas of the city, the nature of youthful crime was determined by police expectations and actions.[52]

Crime waves among sections of the population simply reflect the deployment of police resources in tracking down certain offenders. In this process working-class youth are particularly vulnerable. As a targeted group they conform perfectly to Chambliss's observations:

persons are arrested, tried and sentenced who can offer the fewest rewards for nonenforcement of the laws and who can be processed without creating any undue strain for the organisations which comprise the legal system. The lower class person is more likely to be scrutinised and therefore to be observed in any violation of the law; more likely to be arrested if discovered under suspicious circumstances; . . . and if found guilty more likely to receive harsh punishment than his middle or upper class counterpart.[53]

Suggested reading

The most comprehensive study, both in ethnographic detail and theoretical insight, of the impact of schooling and the labour market on youth socialization is that of Willis (1980). Corrigan (1979) provides another useful ethnographic study of working-class schooling. On youth unemployment see Finn (1983), Morgan (1981), and the Youthaid bulletins (from December 1981). Useful discussions on police/youth relations are more sporadic. Young's (1971) study of drug-law enforcement includes a discussion of how the police can act as amplifiers of deviance and police/black youth relations are analysed by Kettle and Hodges (1982) and Roberts (1982).

6 The practice of youth control 2: correction and confinement

The starting point for much of the contemporary debate on juvenile justice policy is the identification of the incompatibility between policies of punishment and a judicial approach to delinquency on the one hand, and welfare and treatment on the other. The former focuses on the offence committed and determining appropriate punishment, while the latter is ostensibly more concerned with child welfare and meeting the social needs of the delinquent and the 'predelinquent'. Both approaches have been extensively criticized; the punitive approach for thwarting welfare reforms, and the welfare approach for legitimating inappropriate forms of state intervention into working-class family life. The debates of the mid nineteenth century between care and control, prevention and punishment are still the centre of controversy today.

This chapter examines how the arrested delinquent is received by the English juvenile court and what forms of treatment and punishment have been used to cure, care for or control those who are subsequently convicted. In particular, it questions the impact that the ideology of 'treatment' has had in securing a more liberal approach to young offenders. It examines how far such liberalism has been subsumed by the goal of control and the ways in which techniques of 'treatment' may ultimately offer potentially stronger forms of control. First, it is necessary to situate these debates in their proper historical and socio-legal context.

Juvenile justice

The age of criminal responsibility in England and Wales currently stands at 10 years old. Children and young persons under the age of 17 who have been charged with a criminal offence are dealt with within a justice system that is, in the main, separated from adult criminal justice. By way of various Acts of Parliament during the twentieth century, juvenile justice has developed into a highly complex and often contradictory state apparatus. Persons within the system are classified as 'juvenile' if under the age of 17; as 'child' if under the age of 14, and as 'young person' if between the ages of 14 and 17.

The system is designed not only to punish offenders but also to protect juveniles who may be in some physical or 'moral' danger at home. It is therefore the province not only of police, magistrates and the prison service, but also of social workers, residential childcare officers and probation officers.

Since the war, the legislation of juvenile justice has developed out of a growth of political pressure from the increasingly powerful middle-class population employed in social work and social welfare. It has consistently argued for the adoption of a 'treatment' perspective towards juveniles who were previously dealt with only by the legal process. In 1948 local authorities were assigned the duty to provide care for children where the parents were unable or unwilling to provide 'proper accommodation, maintenance and upbringing'. Local authority children's departments could also assume parental rights over a child if the parents were considered unfit. In 1963 the work of the Children's departments was extended into 'preventive work' with families. This was designed to reduce the need to receive children into care, or to bring them before a juvenile court. The 1969 Children and Young Persons Act was heralded as the next step in this process of decriminalization. It advocated that care proceedings should take precedence over criminal hearings in court. The Act itself was born out of several years of compromise and argument which began with the Ingleby Committee in 1956. Its report in 1960 recommended that the age of criminal responsibility be raised from 8 to 12 and eventually to 14, and that below 14 criminal prosecution should be replaced by some form of civil proceedings. Although the committee was set up by a Conservative government, there was a marked reluctance to move on these proposals because of their implied decriminalization. But the issue it raised, that criminal prosecution was not only irrelevant to controlling delinquency but was also likely to generate even more delinquency, remains the pivot around which many contemporary debates still revolve.

When the Labour Party came to power in 1965 a new White Paper 'The Child, the Family and the Young Offender' was published from the findings of a private committee chaired by

Lord Longford. This recommended the abolition of juvenile courts and advocated the development of family services to deal informally with children in trouble. This time the proposals received tough opposition from lawyers, magistrates and probation officers and the White Paper was eventually dropped.[1] Three years later a new White Paper, 'Children in Trouble', was published which a year later became the 1969 Children and Young Persons Act. While the two themes of decriminalization and service provision reappeared, the decriminalization proposals were less radical. The juvenile courts were to remain, but the service provision proposals were extended to include a range of services designed to provide alternatives to custodial sentences. This represented a major victory for the social work profession. At almost every stage of the proposed new system, social work discretion was to play a central role in the definition of the delinquent. In particular, care proceedings were to replace criminal hearings for children and were recommended for young persons. The Act was claimed to be the most definite 'decriminalizing' instance of post-war penal policy. However as Thorpe *et al.* remarked:

The tragedy that has occurred since can be best described as a situation in which the worst of all possible worlds came into existence – people have been persistently led to believe that the juvenile criminal justice system has become softer and softer, while the reality has been that it has become harder and harder.[2]

During the 1970s, vital elements of the Act were never implemented and government concern has been characteristically directed to providing more and more secure places for convicted juvenile offenders.

The Conservative government of 1970 declared that it would not implement sections four and five of the Act which were intended to raise the age of criminal responsibility. Magistrates responded by sentencing more juveniles to institutions and the use of community-based services declined. This refusal to implement the Act was based on the popular belief that the 1970s witnessed a massive and rapid growth in juvenile crime, characterized by a core of 'vicious and hardened young criminals'. Statistically, however, indictable offences for juveniles remained constant throughout the decade, with a slight rise in burglaries and a reduction in violent and sexual offences.[3]

Analysis of the Portsmouth juvenile court records in 1980, for example, revealed that fewer serious crimes such as burglary or assault were being committed and while theft had increased, the items stolen were often of trivial value. One quarter of the offences of theft involved sums of less than £10. Nevertheless a significant proportion of first offenders were sent directly to detention centres without alternative means of disposal having first been tried. 33 per cent of those who were given detention centre orders were first offenders.[4] In direct opposition to the 1969 Act's intentions, the number of juveniles given custodial centres rose dramatically during the 1970s and 1980s and much more rapidly than the rise in juvenile crime. As a 1981 DHSS report concluded, the number of juveniles sent to borstal and detention centres increased fivefold between 1965 and 1980. However, less than a fifth of this rise could be attributed to increased offending. Rather the increase in incarceration was believed to reflect the growing tendency to give custodial sentences for almost all types of offence.[5]

While magistrates were committed to incarcerating the young offender, social workers extended their preventive work with the families of the 'predelinquent'. Ironically, this development meant many more children were under surveillance, the market for the courts was widened and more offenders were placed in care for relatively trivial offences.[6] In practice, preventive work meant that children were being sent to institutions at a younger age. As in the past, new institutions which were supposed to reform youth instead created new categories of delinquency.

These contradictions were reflected in the Criminal Justice Act which became law in October 1982. The Act abolished the indeterminate borstal sentence of up to two years and replaced it with a determinate sentence of youth custody, restricted, in the juvenile court, to between four months and one year. The length of detention centre sentences was also reduced from six months to between three weeks and four months. The Act thus gave more power to the courts to determine length of sentence, and also gave them new powers to impose very short sentences which, as Cavadino argues, 'must tempt them to use custody on a much wider scale than ever before'.[7] Moreover, the Act officially abandoned those parts of the 1969 Act which advocated a phasing out of custody for the under 17s, and established in law a firm commitment to custodial provision for juvenile offenders. On the other hand, the Act also advocated the wider use of non-custodial measures. It gave the courts the power to include 'curfew' requirements in supervision orders. These specify that young offenders should stay indoors for up to ten hours between 6 pm and 6 am. The scheme, supported by the Magistrates' Association and the Lord Chief Justice, was designed to reinforce parental responsibility. However, how it should be implemented remains unclear, particularly in its suggestion that social workers and probation officers should take a more apparent policing role in their supervision of juveniles.

To some degree the current legal framework of juvenile justice continues to reflect the contradictions inherent in a system which attempts to pursue two ideologies at once. However, whatever gains the welfare lobby achieved in the 1960s (in principle, if not in practice), these were overturned by the 1980s. In many aspects, juvenile justice can be seen as merely a reflection of dominant political ideologies. In the late 1960s a welfare lobby was influential in attempts to decriminalize some aspects of juvenile offending, while in the 1970s and early 1980s a law and order lobby was able to accelerate the number and places available within programmes of 'short, sharp shock' and extend the range of penalties available to the courts.

As Pitts concluded, the 1982 Act effectively demolished 'the remaining barriers which keep juveniles out of the mainstream of the penal system and for good or ill abandons the notions that young people are sent to penal establishments for treatment or rehabilitation'.[8] Indeed the 1980s are likely to see more working-class young people having a 'taste' of custody, as welfarism recedes and state authoritarianism becomes more strident.

The juvenile court

The need for special jurisdiction over young offenders was first mooted in the early nineteenth century. However it was not until the 1908 Children's Act that the principle was established that young offenders should be heard separately from adults by way of juvenile courts. These were courts of summary jurisdiction; primarily special sittings of the magistrates' courts held at a separate time from the normal criminal court business and usually in a separate building. They were empowered to act upon both the young offender and also the destitute child who may have been found begging, vagrant or whose parents were considered to be unworthy. In 1933 the courts were directed to construct a specially selected panel of magistrates from which three were chosen to hear each individual case. Today, at least one of these three must be a woman. The courts' powers and procedures are further governed by the Children and Young Persons Act of 1969. This stipulated that care proceedings should replace criminal proceedings for all *children* aged between 10 and 14 and should be optional for *young people* aged between 14 and 17. The court is thus designed to provide both welfare and judicial functions. The reconciliation of these two principles has never proved easy and in theory is perhaps the single most contradictory and ambiguous element in the courts' role and function today. In practice, however, as we shall see, the 1969 Act has been barely implemented and the last decade has witnessed a growth, rather than reduction in punitive policies. Between 1971 and 1974 the Conservative government suspended key clauses in the 1969 Act. They dropped measures to raise the criminal responsibility age from 10 to 14, to abolish penal sentences for those under 17 and to require wider consultation before the police could prosecute juveniles. The 'caring' concerns of welfarism were again bypassed in the 1982 Criminal Justice Act. This concentrated on providing the juvenile court with a broader range of sentences designed primarily to *control* the young delinquent.

Most criminal cases heard before the juvenile court have been initially referred by the police. The first phase of prosecution revolves around the extensive police discretionary powers to sift, divert or prosecute juveniles. Any consultation between the police and social services or education agencies is largely controlled and defined by the police and although 'officially encouraged' is not required by law. The police thus play a key role in defining the court's workload. The raw material for any juvenile court is in part a construction of the ideological and organizational preferences of the local police force. Research by Priestley *et al*. in Bristol and Wiltshire[9] and Parker *et al*. in Merseyside[10] concluded that there is a pervading ideological outlook within the police to catch juveniles and send them directly to court, known as the 'push-in' tendency. Various juvenile liaison schemes between police and social services operate haphazardly and are unable to counteract this tendency, and many juveniles are cautioned or prosecuted for increasingly trivial offences. The 1969 Act gave the first legal recognition of the police caution which can be administered where a juvenile admits an offence and the police feel it appropriate not to proceed but to warn. The number of cautions delivered to offenders in the 10–17 age group increased from 36,000 in 1970 to 104,000 in 1980. As a result many more juveniles have had their cases recorded in a police juvenile index, whereas previously there may have been no further action (NFA). Certainly Ditchfield has suggested that the creation of a quasi-social services arm of the police through the juvenile bureau has only served to inflate the figures.[11] Similarly, as a result of the 'push-in tendency', about two-thirds of arrests pass through the police filter and enter the juvenile court.

Juvenile courts differ from normal sittings of the magistrates' court in certain crucial respects. Additional powers are provided to social services departments to determine the meaning of court-made 'care orders' according to their own interpretations of a child's needs. In court, evidence of this nature is offered in a social inquiry report (SER) prepared by a social worker acting for the client-defendant. At least one of the individual's parents or guardians must also be present in court.

Restrictions are placed on the number of people allowed to be present. The public are excluded and representatives of the media, while allowed to be present, are forbidden to publish particulars which would identify the defendant. However, this apart, it has been suggested that 'the juvenile court in action still retains the look and the feel of some of the dramatic ritual which dignifies adult justice'.[12]

Before 1975, in a majority of cases there was no legal representative for the client-defendant (not until the 1975 Children Act did any provision exist for juveniles to be legally represented at public expense), and the configuration of personnel in court was largely one of magistrate, police and child. Today, courtroom procedure has been more efficiently streamlined within the more 'adult' configuration of clerk of the court (representing the magistrate), prosecutor (representing the police or other referral agency), and defence solicitor (representing the child). These three key figures are likely to be the most active in processes of pre-court, out of court and in-court bargaining and negotiating. It still remains unlikely, however, that many of the children or their parents will have been fully briefed by anybody about what to except in the courtroom situation, prior to their entry.

It is around the role of the social worker(s) in court that further controversy is aroused. Parker's research on Merseyside found that while the social work role was perceived as crucial by both worker and family alike in care proceedings, in criminal cases families saw the police, their solicitor(s), magistrates and clerks as the key figures.[13] The social work role was only invoked in these cases if the individual and family found themselves the subject of a social inquiry report. Such reports are officially required in all cases unless there is a positive reason for not providing them, and the 1982 Act made it a general requirement that a social inquiry report must be obtained before a custodial sentence is imposed. However there is no requirement that the reports be made available to the children or their parents prior to the hearing. Unlike adult proceedings, children may enter the court without fully knowing the case which they have to answer. Most reports are divided into two sections. The first contains details of the offender's personality and family background, and the second, recommendations for action. Leaving aside arguments concerning the nature of the assessment included in the reports, Parker *et al.* discovered that the weight they carry with magistrates varies greatly from region to region and from courtroom to courtroom.[14] Similarly it has been found that if the report contains no firm recommendation, then it is less likely to be taken seriously in determining sentence and will offer little check or counter-argument to those magistrates who are predisposed to sending juveniles down as a matter of routine.[15]

The way in which such information about the juvenile, his/her family and background is received ultimately rests with the discretion of the magistrates. Although welfare considerations are present, particularly in care cases, the 'duty to safeguard the public interest may take precedence'.[16]

We should certainly not be surprised that court workers and particularly magistrates with their predominantly affluent, upper middle class backgrounds should hold ideological views including moral judgements about 'deviant' working class youth.[17]

After reviewing police evidence and hearing deputations from the defence and from social workers, the magistrates proceed to give 'sentence'. Although the words 'conviction' and 'sentence' cannot be used in juvenile court proceedings, the range of *orders* available in criminal and in some care cases are largely punitive and may involve removing children from their home environment to other places of accommodation provided by the local authority or

Home Office. In this context the term 'sentencing' remains arguably the most appropriate.

In terms of custody or long-term duration in a place of residence, the range of options open to the juvenile court, in ascending order of severity is:

Absolute discharge
Conditional discharge
Fine
Deferred sentence
Attendance centre
Supervision order
Detention centre
Care order
Youth custody (borstal) order

Absolute or conditional discharges are available as in the adults' magistrates court. In 1981, 18 per cent of boys and 30 per cent of girls between the ages of 14 and 17 received conditional discharges, compared to 32 per cent and 38 per cent respectively for those under 14.

For all age groups a fine was the sentence most frequently imposed, although its proportionate use has decreased in the past decade. The parent of a child will be ordered to pay any fine, costs or compensation, while the parent or guardian of a young person will normally only be so ordered if they are thought to have been negligent in the care or control of the juvenile.

As in the adult court, the court may defer making any order at all so that the offender's subsequent conduct may be taken into account. This can only be done once, and deferment may not exceed six months. It is, however, invoked very infrequently.

If a centre has been allocated for the use of the court, the court may give an attendance centre order provided the defendant has not previously served a custodial sentence. The usual period is twelve hours, normally completed in two-hour spells on Saturdays. The centres, which are run by the police, operate as a form of probationary supervision and are 'to provide a constructive use of leisure time'.[18] They are primarily available for boys under 17, but from January 1979 were also made available for girls. In 1981 about 18 per cent of boys were dealt with in this way, and 3 per cent of girls.

Supervision orders and care orders are usually used in care

proceedings, but are also available in criminal cases if the court decides that 'welfare' measures are the more appropriate. Decisions of this nature are usually dependent on the nature and quality of the social inquiry report, and other evidence which may suggest that the juvenile's development is being avoidably prevented or neglected, s/he is being ill treated, is exposed to 'moral danger', or is beyond the control of parents or guardians.

The supervision order can be applied for a maximum of three years and has two general requirements: 1 to keep in touch with and receive visits from a supervisor; 2 to report any change of address. On the courts' discretion further requirements can be included: 1 the individual to remain in residence with a named person; 2 mental treatment on medical advice; 3 intermediate treatment if a scheme is locally available, and 4 a 'curfew' or 'night restriction' on the consent of the offender's parents, and of the offender if s/he is over 14. Failure to comply with supervision orders, unlike a failure with adult probation requirements, is not punishable through the court. The supervisor can, however, act in such cases to apply to the court for the substitution of a care order.

Care orders give a local authority powers to override parental powers and duties and remove the juvenile to a community home, foster home or hostel. The order runs until the juvenile is 18 (or 19 if s/he was already 16 when the order was made). During this time the authority, juvenile or parent may apply to the juvenile court for discharge which may be granted completely or a supervision order substituted. The 1982 Act, however, significantly strengthened the courts' arm by introducing a residential care order. This enables the court to require a local authority to automatically remove a young person from home for a period up to six months if an offence is committed while already subject to a care order.

Detention centre orders are available for boys over the age of 13. They are intended to be more punitive than reformative. Orders are made for a fixed period of between three weeks and four months. The proportionate use of the detention centre for boys increased from 4 per cent in 1971 to 10 per cent in 1981. There are no detention centres for girls.

Finally, the court may decide to make a youth custody order. Prior to the 1982 Act, the hearing of these cases was transferred to the Crown court. The juvenile court had no power to commit an offender direct to borstal; it could only make a recommendation for borstal training to be reconsidered by the higher court. The 1982 Act effectively bypassed this safeguard. The change in the name of sentence from 'borstal training recommendation' to 'youth custody order' is also significant. It reflects the view that containment is more appropriate than attempts to rehabilitate via 'training'. The new sentence of youth custody is available for young offenders between the ages of 15 and 21. Before the 1982 Act the court could not determine the length of sentence. Now the juvenile court can provide a shorter, but determinate sentence of between four months and one year for 15- and 16-year-olds. Older offenders are, of course, dealt with in normal sittings of the magistrates' court. Juvenile and older offenders can receive youth custody sentences of over a year but only after their cases have been referred to the Crown court. In 1981, 8500 boys and some 300 girls were sentenced to borstal training. If bail is not allowed, the juvenile must be admitted directly to a remand centre or an adult prison to await allocation. On release the inmate/trainee is subject to up to twelve months supervision and may be recalled to the youth custody centre for a thirty day period or fined if the requirements of supervision are not met.

In 1981 the juvenile court sentenced some 16,800 children and some 69,400 young persons with these variety of measures. During the decade 1971–81 the use of fines and care orders gradually decreased, while that of attendance centres increased. Similarly the use of custodial sentences increased both in numbers and as a proportion of the total over the decade.

In this context the role of the juvenile court has consistently become more punitive, abandoning the ideology of care in favour of institutional custody and coercion. Indeed both Morris *et al.* and Parker *et al.*'s research concluded that for those on the receiving end, the court's prime task was regarded as one of punishment and control.[19] The 'offence' and 'punishment' view of the juvenile court held by parents and children may be a far more accurate reflection of what occurs in court than the formal accounts of policies and practices would suggest. Research suggests that magistrates concentrate more on details of the offence than on personal circumstances in deciding sentence. Removing a child from home also represents not so much a commitment to 'treatment' but a way of delivering a punitive warning to the 'predelinquent' and delinquent child.[20] Various court cases noted by Rohrer in the early 1980s brought this punitive function into sharp focus. For example:

Thames Valley Police charged two boys after they had been caught playing 'knock me down ginger' – ringing door bells and running away. They were fined £25 each.

A boy who robbed a fellow football fan of 10p was sent to detention centre for three months in Wallasey.

A soccer fan aged nineteen was jailed for three months at Hereford for stealing the match ball at a Hereford v. Doncaster game.

In 1980 thirty-two boys under seventeen were convicted under local bye-laws for playing in the street. Fifty-four juveniles were convicted of allowing a chimney to be on fire. 412 were convicted of 'simple drunkenness'.[21]

Magistrates' sentences also reflect oscillations in official and public opinion about what constitutes a serious crime at any particular historical moment. Magistrates may hand out exemplary sentences when particular categories of offenders, such as the mods and rockers of 1964 and the youthful rioters of 1981, are singled out for special treatment. Sentencing is then a highly discretionary process. Magistrates have continually resisted attempts to set fixed sentences and thus disparities between courts are always likely to occur. The image of justice as impartial and universal is consistently undermined by its actual practice.[22]

In custody

In this section we will examine the range of institutions in which 'disturbed' and 'delinquent' young people have found themselves as a result of decisions taken by the juvenile courts and other administrative bodies. Such institutions range from observation and assessment centres, to community homes, detention centres and borstals. During the past decade the courts have resorted to punitive control far more readily than opting for non-custodial measures, despite the fact that a range of 'softer' options was made available and recommended for use in the 1969 Children and Young Persons Act. The number of juveniles (under-17s) committed to borstal rose from 818 in 1969 to some 1800 in 1981. The numbers sent to detention centres increased from 2228 in 1969 to some 6000 in 1981. Over 5000 fewer supervision orders were made in 1981 (15,900) than probation orders for juveniles in 1969 (21,652).[23] Perhaps most alarming is the number of young people under the age of 17 being placed in local adult prisons or remand centres while awaiting trial, sentence or allocation to a borstal.

Observation and assessment centres

O and A (observation and assessment) centres were established by the 1969 Children and Young Persons Act to provide a 'sophisticated analysis' of a child's needs by 'skilled staff of all the necessary disciplines' to determine the most appropriate course of future action. Officially the centres are used for children aged 10 to 17 who have been convicted in a juvenile court and are thought to need further detailed analysis of their own individual case. The centres are also used to house children who have committed no crime but, as a result of mistreatment at home, are given a place of safety order of up to twenty-eight days. Administrators of the centres claim that the maximum amount of time needed to observe and assess individuals in this way is six to eight weeks, culminating in a case conference and a placement recommendation (return to home, removal to community home, borstal, detention centre, etc). The distribution of O and A centres is far from uniform, however, being dependent on local authority policy decisions and available resources.

This official picture has, however, been seriously undermined by researchers and some residential childcare officers. First, many children who are the subject of magistrates' care orders are immediately sent to community homes, without the benefit of the 'analysis' available at an assessment centre. Second, rather than acting as a place for analysis of particular needs, there is much evidence that many of those held in assessment centres are distinguished not by the complexity of their needs, but by the fact that no other institution is prepared to take them. The centres act more as places to hold those children who cannot be absorbed by other facilities within the system.[24] Such claims are strengthened by evidence that over half the children remain in the centres for longer than the prescribed two months, 13 per cent being still in residence after six months. This places doubt on the stated objective of providing a 'sophisticated analysis', and it illustrates that in many cases there is no other institution willing to take the 'more difficult' children. The centres thus act more for the purposes of remand than assessment, particularly for those under 14 who cannot be sent to detention centres or borstals. Further criticism has been levelled at each centre's ability or intention to provide assessment, given the fact that most of its employees are unqualified residential childcare officers. Nationally, only 5 per cent of all residential workers are professionally qualified. Even if some assessment is undertaken its value may be seen as particularly limited. The problem remains of how an objective assessment can be made of a child's normal style of working, playing and sleeping when that person is incarcerated in an abnormal – and often rule-oriented and repressive – environment. As a result, distribution to final placements is in many cases highly random, dependent on decisions based more on who will take the child than on where the child might be most suitably placed. On surveying all available evidence Taylor *et al.* describe this remarkable divergence between the theory and actual practice of O and A centres by concluding that they: 'contain inappropriate children supervised by under qualified staff faced with inadequate placement opportunities'.[25]

Community homes

In 1932 juvenile reformatories, which had survived for seventy-five years, were reconstituted and given the name 'approved schools'. They were designed for the education and corrective training of young people who had appeared before a juvenile court. Reflecting the welfare lobby behind the Children and Young Persons Act they were again renamed, as community homes, in 1969. Within the Act, local authorities were empowered to develop a wide range of institutions of different types for all children in need. Magistrates were no longer to be involved in detailed decisions about the kind of treatment appropriate for the child. As in the case of O and A centres, social workers were to determine the most suitable placement. It is not possible to provide a generalized picture of these regimes, for not only is there a wide variety of institutions which fall under the general heading of community home, but there is also considerable difference between those which are classified together. What is clear is that in the past decade the numbers sent to community homes have risen from 29,800 in 1972 to 33,700 in 1977. Whether they have fulfilled the aim of providing special education and corrective training is also open to doubt. In 1977 only 6400 of these children attended homes with educational facilities on the premises (CHEs). The remainder attended normal schools while 'living in' the community home. In this context it is important to remember again that a majority of children in community homes have committed no offence at all, but are there because it is believed that they would suffer from neglect if they remained in their own home. However, with the conflation of those 'in care' and those sentenced by a court, the regimes of each home are the same for the 'deprived' and the offender alike. And the 'penal' character of many homes is compounded by an obsession with petty restrictions, filing of case history records and details of 'behavioural problems'. In this way community homes tend to see themselves (and are seen by their inmates) to be more concerned with delinquency and its control, and less with providing a range of opportunities which would normally be available to children outside the institution.

The most obvious motive is that of 'containment'; there is always an anxious preoccupation with custodial security and orderliness which suggests that the schools (like so many of our residential institutions) are used by society primarily as a way of 'disposing of' its more burdensome fellow citizens – an opportunity to brush the dust under the carpet.[26]

There are no national statistics documenting re-entry rates after community home care. However, research by Tutt indicated a wide variation in the reconviction rate of senior boys in community homes in one region ranging from 15 per cent to above 60 per cent.[27] A Home Office Research Study at the Kingswood CHE at Bristol in 1975 found that one house unit – based on therapeutic community principles – had a 70 per cent reconviction rate within two years, and a second unit – based on conventional approved school principles – had a 69 per cent rate.[28] Thorpe's Rochdale research discovered a 66 per cent rate of re-offending[29] and Cawson's report, based on an analysis of postal questionnaires sent to local authorities in England and Wales in 1975, found that 177 young offenders from an intake of 497 (25 per cent) committed further offences within nine months of receiving the care order.[30] The failure of residential care to prevent re-offending is thus well established. Given these research findings, the new residential care order included in the 1982 criminal justice act appears to be even more anomalous. Furthermore Zander's study of 224 young offenders committed to care in Inner London in 1975 had found that re-offending was *less* likely to occur when the offender was returned home. Of those sent home, 30 per cent committed further offences but of those sent to some form of institution, 66 per cent re-offended.[31]

Although the homes are designed mainly for rehabilitative purposes, the degree of treatment each inmate can expect to receive is limited. Often treatment is couched in experimental schemes such as token economy management systems (TEMS). Under one such system fifteen boys in an 'intensive care' unit of a Birmingham community home earned tokens by conforming to personalized behavioural targets. Tokens are then exchangeable for various benefits such as extra home leave, sweets, toys, cigarettes and so on. Failure to reach the 'target' is punished by awarding punishment tokens which must be redeemed before re-entry into the main programme can be achieved. As a treatment programme TEMS rely on a simple behaviourist learning theory of reward and punishment. It operates more as a crude programme of day-to-day control in which normal rights are redefined as privileges.[32]

More alarming are the sporadic reports of the use of drugs – particularly the 'liquid cosh' largactil – to control behaviour deemed to be unruly. One such case reported in February 1981 concerned a girl of 14 who was given the drug because her behaviour at school was thought to be sexually provocative and distracting boys from their school work.[33]

In 1982 it cost up to £360 per child per week to keep a child in a community home with education.

Detention centres

Perhaps the most controversial element within the juvenile justice system is the use of detention centres, first established by the 1948 Criminal Justice Act. They are categorized as junior, for 14- to 17-year-old boys, of which there were seven in 1982; and senior, for boys over 17, of which there were thirteen. The only detention centre for girls, Moor Court, was closed in 1969. The 1969 Act was intended to remove this more penal option for those under 17 and rely instead on the system of community homes; the assumption being that an offence by a child was evidence that his/her needs were not being met and therefore welfare intervention was justified. In this respect the Act was never implemented. During the 1970s magistrates made increasing use of detention centres. In 1969 2228 juveniles were sent to detention centres compared to

5757 in 1977. This was a much faster increase than the rise in juvenile crime during that period.[34] The average daily population in the junior centres in 1981 was 691, and 1476 in the senior detention centres.[35] Offenders are sent to such institutions for a period of between three weeks and four months, to endure what has become known as a 'short, sharp shock'. They are run by the prison department rather than local authorities, and this is reflected in their regime. They are based primarily on farming, market gardening, physical education, drill sessions, parades, and inspections.

The ability of detention centre policy to 'jolt inmates back to normality' is, however, far from encouraging. Of those discharged in 1974, 73 per cent of juniors and 50 per cent of seniors were reconvicted within two years. Nevertheless, in 1979 William Whitelaw, the Home Secretary, promised a new and rigorous regime in detention centres as a central part of the Conservative Party's law and order campaign. In April 1980 two experimental Home Office detention centres were set up at Send in Surrey for 14- to 17-year-olds, and at New Hall near Wakefield for 17- to 21-year-olds. Together, the two centres deal with approximately 1000 offenders a year. The number of staff, parades and inspections has increased, while the time given to training courses has decreased. On arrival the boys get a haircut (except skinheads who must grow their hair to a regulation length), earrings are removed and uniforms issued. The schedule for each day is the same:[36]

6.15 am	Reveille, cleaning of dormitory, kit inspection
6.45 am	Wash
7.30 am	Breakfast
8.00 am	Parade and division of working parties
8.00–12.00	Work (gardening, feeding pigs, digging fields)
12.00–12.30	Lunch
12.30–6.00 pm	Drill, physical education, work and tea
6.00 pm	Woodwork, metalwork classes
8.00 pm	Polishing shoes and buttons
9.30 pm	Lights out

There is little doubt that detention centres exist mainly as a vehicle to satisfy popular demands for retribution. Any commitment to treatment has all but disappeared. Yet is such a response clearly justified? Research by the Social Research Unit at Dartington Hall shows quite clearly that persistent offenders who make up the population of detention centres are not merely 'hard core young thugs'. Many of them have experienced extremes of family disturbance and abuse, for example 38 per cent of their sample had been abused or neglected by parents, 38 per cent were mentally unstable, 43 per cent had parents who were frequently absent from home.[37] In this context the escalation of detention centre philosophy appears both overreactive and misguided. As for the two new experimental centres, it is worth remembering that the original centres of the 1950s were also initially designed as 'experiments'. The average weekly cost of keeping a boy in a detention centre in 1980 was £125.[38] In March 1981 the Home Office announced it would be opening two more strict regime detention centres at Foston Hall near Derby, and Haslar near Gosport, providing an additional 155 places.[39]

Youth custody centres (borstals)

When the first specialized detention centre for young offenders was set up by the Crime Prevention Act of 1908 at Borstal in Kent it was heralded as a major liberal breakthrough. The separation from adult criminals of the under 21s in their own closed institutions was seen as a major step towards the retraining and rehabilitation of the young convicted offender. In 1961, the Criminal Justice Act reduced the minimum age for borstal training to 15 years. It also made it easier to transfer young people from approved schools to borstal and integrated borstals into the prison system. As such, borstals acted largely as prisons for the young. This was even more the case for young offenders who were committed immediately from court to a borstal. The offender was sent to either an open or a closed institution and this decision was taken while the convicted was held at a remand centre or an allocation centre, the latter usually being in a wing of an adult prison. On entry to borstal the 'trainee' could be detained for a minimum of six months and a maximum of two years. The length of sentence was indeterminate and date of release was at the discretion of each particular borstal.

As well as providing borstals with a new name, the 1982 Act provided determinate but shorter sentences of youth custody, thus enabling a greater number of places to be available each year. While the regime of each institution varies to some degree, there are certain common features. As in detention centres, trainees awake at 6.00 am and, following a head-counting parade, will be at work by 8.00 am sewing mail bags, gardening, servicing the institutions and so on. There is work on Saturday mornings and church on Sunday mornings.

In many ways the borstal system acts as a mirror image of the prison system for adults. During the 1960s their regimes became more punitive and expanded to act as an additional outlet for the under-resourced child care system. Consequently 'younger and less difficult young people have increasingly been subject to tougher punishment'.[40] Like prison, borstal inmates are subject to a punishment and reward system. Minor infringements of rules can lead to a review board operated by a prison officer and can result in loss of 'association', loss of money earned for work undertaken and reduced privileges. Major infringement of rules can lead to the inmate being placed on the Governor's report or appearing before a board of visitors, and may result in an extension of the borstal sentence, and being sent 'down the block' (solitary confinement in a bare cell for up to twenty-eight days).

Borstal regimes have received many damning criticisms from both trainees and staff, culminating in Roy Minton's 1979 film 'Scum'. But there has been little public debate. The Home Office and the Prison Officers' Association dismissed the film and related criticisms as sensationalism. Yet the recent record of borstal successes is far from encouraging. During the 1930s, reconviction rates stayed at around 30 per cent, but in the 1970s 70 per cent of trainees were later re-admitted, and in 1981 84 per cent were reconvicted within two years.[41] This suggests that there is something about the borstal experience which generates the criminality it is supposed to eradicate.

Taylor *et al.* describe how the structure of the institution leads to confusion of the functions of care and control. Offers of help and support are provided inconsistently, and arbitrarily withdrawn. Thus some boys prefer solitary confinement to living on a wing, some passively accept being physically and verbally abused by prison officers and other trainees for fear of retribution if justice is sought, while others turn their anxiety on to themselves, cutting their wrists or burning themselves in the hope of being removed to hospital. A picture emerges of largely punitive regimes in which re-training is minimal, and the possibility of being permanently institutionalized is forever present.[42] On release each trainee is supervized by a probation officer for two years and can be returned to borstal if another offence is committed. Because of the lack of training offered, first, fear of the outside world, and then the prospect of unemployment looms large. These authors pessimistically conclude that: 'Common humanity, statistical evidence and above all, common sense demand the abolition of the Borstal institution'.[43]

In 1980–1 the average weekly cost of keeping a person in a borstal was £180.[44]

Prisons and secure units

The 1969 Act specifies that if someone under 17 is remanded in custody, not on bail, then that person must be placed in the care of the local authority. However, if the child is deemed to be unruly, then 'guardianship' is handed over to the prison department. Thus, although it is not possible to sentence a person under 17 to imprisonment, on 31 May 1982, 118 juveniles were being held in adult prisons either awaiting borstal allocation or sentence,[45] and a further 260 were locked up in remand centres. This practice has long been a cause for concern. In 1979 girls under 17 could no longer be remanded to prisons by the procedure of 'certificates of unruliness'. However, for boys, the use of imprisonment continues unabated, often in the most under-resourced and overcrowded institutions of the prison service.

It is well known that the worst conditions in our prison system are to be found in the squalid, overcrowded local prisons. Yet it is here that many juveniles are held. In a number of instances they are the only juveniles in an establishment and have no company of their own age. . . . One juvenile, sentenced to borstal training was in Gloucester prison, a place where conditions have been described by the Chief Inspector of Prisons as 'degrading and deplorable'. Many youngsters are also held in Manchester's Strangeways prison. Conditions there have been described as 'oppressive and despondent' by Manchester MPs. . . .[46]

Holding juveniles in prison is, however, only one element in the juvenile justice system where young offenders can find themselves subject to secure accommodation. Various other 'secure units' have been built into the system during the 1970s to place certain individuals within a prison-like institution while avoiding the 'moral outrage' of holding children in adult prisons. Secure units are to be found in CHEs, youth treatment centres and in assessment centres. Their provision is developing rapidly, despite the fact that in 1982 it cost somewhere between £300 and £600 per head per week to contain juveniles in this fashion.[47]

In 1979 there were 244 long-term and 126 short-term security places in community homes in England and Wales. At that time a further 170 places were being constructed and 57 others were being planned. In addition, two youth treatment centres – special secure residential homes – were established to deal with 'severely disturbed' boys and girls. In 1971, St Charles YTC was opened at Brentwood in Essex and in 1978 Glenthorne YTC opened in Birmingham. These offered the system a further seventy-eight secure places. By June 1981 there were at least 537 officially approved secure places available,[48] compared with 150 such places in 1971. The major argument for expanding prison-like conditions within community homes is that their referrals are more difficult than in the past. However Millham *et al.*'s research concluded that there was no significant change in the backgrounds and characters of the boys that justified this extension of secure provision.[49] Indeed, because greater numbers of the more difficult juveniles were being sent to borstal, those in the childcare system were arguably *less* difficult than previously. Confusion also appears to exist over whether the child is sent to a secure unit for punishment, treatment, or both; or merely because no other suitable place is available. Whatever the reason for their construction, secure units closely resemble conditions in prison cells, with inmates locked up for considerable periods of the day. While secure units stress the imperative of continuous and effective control, they are also supposed to encourage creative outlets to avoid frustration and disruptive behaviour. On both accounts, researchers seem to agree that secure units fail to modify behaviour. In Millham *et al.*'s sample, 76 per cent of those released from the units re-offended. Similarly, experience of a secure unit appears to increase the chance of re-offending for younger children and for those who had not committed offences prior to going in.

Lawson and Martell's DHSS report argued that both boys and girls were being referred to secure units despite having considerably less problematic backgrounds than those referred prior to the 1969 Children and Young Persons Act. Moreover, except in a small number of cases, troublesome behaviour was produced by the institution itself rather than being an attribute of the individual. They concluded that:

In many instances the children referred seemed to have little need for placement in closed institutions. There was no evidence of a large increase in the number of violent or seriously disruptive children in care, and, equally, no evidence that closed units were particularly effective in reducing violent, disruptive or delinquent behaviour.[50]

Moreover the safeguards against unnecessary incarceration are limited. The Children's Legal Centre's 1982 report expressed concern that childcare staff and social service directors decide to detain children without any recourse to the courts, and that the very existence of places to be filled creates the risk that children will be found to fill them. The report's criticism of present practice was far reaching:

The Children's Legal Centre is concerned at the increasing use of secure accomodation; at the confused state of the law; at the way in which major research findings have been ignored by politicians and practitioners in the child care system; at the lack of publicly available information and statistics. We find the restriction of children's liberty without judicial review contrary to the principles of natural justice, reflected in articles in the European Convention on Human Rights.[51]

This often uncontrolled use of secure units once more highlights the increasing slide into widespread custody that currently characterizes contemporary juvenile justice.

Community corrections

The 1969 Children and Young Person's Act anticipated an end to a custodial system for juveniles, and its replacement by care and treatment in the community. Although this part of the Act has never been fully implemented, some 'diversionary' or 'preventive' forms of 'treatment' have been made available to the courts. The major forms are attendance centres, various forms of supervision order (with or without such attached conditions as a 'night restriction' order) and intermediate treatment.

A non-custodial penalty of deprivation of leisure has in fact been available to juvenile courts since the Criminal Justice Act, 1948. Attendance centre orders can be made for any person aged between 10 and 21 who has been found guilty of an offence, for which an adult could be sent to prison. The orders range from twelve to fourteen hours in periods of not less than one hour and not more than three hours on any one occasion. Attendance is usually on Saturday afternoons, aimed specifically at combating football hooliganism. A period of physical exercise is usually followed by a lecture or other instruction in first aid, vehicle maintenance and so on. Firm discipline is maintained throughout the period of attendance. Those who fail to attend or who break the rules of the centre may be brought back to court for the original offence as though an attendance centre order had not previously been made.[52] The centres are run and organized by the police, rather than the social services.

In 1972 there were sixty centres in England and Wales handling about 7 per cent of the cases heard in the juvenile court. This proportion increased dramatically with the opening of ten more centres in 1978, eleven more in 1979 and thirteen in 1980. The number of young persons given an attendance centre order accordingly rose from about 3500 in the early 1970s to 14,000 in 1981. By the end of 1982 there were 106 junior attendance centres for the under-17s (ninety for boys, six for girls and ten mixed), and fourteen senior attendance centres for older boys aged between 17 and 21.[53] Contrary to the popular image of attendance centres' main function being to deal with 'hooliganism' offences, a Home Office study of junior centres in 1976 found that almost 60 per cent of the boys' offences involved theft, burglary and handling stolen goods. Only 5 per cent entailed disorderly behaviour.[54]

Probation orders for juveniles were renamed supervision orders by the 1969 Children and Young Persons Act. The order places a child or young person thought to be in need of care under the supervision of a probation officer or local authority. While it was intended to place all juvenile 'probation' work in the hands of the local authority social services departments, the 1969 Act retained a clause allowing the court to decide what type of supervision was the most appropriate. The tendency has been for the probation service to continue in its traditional supervisory role.[55] The court may, in addition, attach certain conditions to the supervision. This can include the use of traditional 'treatment' methods such as social casework with juvenile and parents, the removal of the juvenile from home for specific periods at the discretion of the social worker, restricting the movement of juveniles between 6 pm and 6 am, and intermediate treatment.

Intermediate treatment (IT) was established by the 1969 Act to provide a half-way stage between a supervision order and a care order, and as an alternative to custody. The court is allowed to instruct the juvenile's supervisor to remove the juvenile from home for a period not exceeding ninety days. If a supervision order has been made for the maximum of three years, IT will usually be ordered for thirty days in each year. The length of order is at the discretion of the court and at the request of the social worker. The nature and purpose of intermediate treatment, however, remains far from clear. Its original formulation in the 1969 White Paper 'Children in Trouble' was to provide supervision and partial residential treatment in order to 'bring the young person into contact with a new environment and to secure his participation in some constructive activity'. Such activities include attendance at youth clubs, sports clubs, adventure playgrounds, holiday camps, outward bound schemes, weekend centres and traditional attendance centres. Some combination of these schemes is now variously available in many local authorities.

However, instead of reading 'Children in Trouble' as a move towards non-institutional care, social workers took its concepts to imply a treatment strategy appropriate to a younger or less delinquent population. IT thus operates to identify 'children at risk' and prevent them realizing their full delinquent potential.[56] Its development coincided with the rise of a social work 'prevention theory' which argued that the sources of delinquency are identifiable and treatable if the 'vulnerable' child can be reached early enough. Attention is thus shifted to 'prevention' rather than 'cure'. Certainly the rationale behind a majority of IT schemes is to reduce the numbers of juvenile offenders in residential care. The schemes are attractive not only because they are set in the mould of delinquency prevention, but also because they are cheaper to operate. The cost of IT programmes ranges from £100 per child per year to £4000 for the more intensive programmes, compared with an average cost of £10,000 a year for a CHE place, £9000 for a borstal place and £8000 for a detention centre place.[57] However these new services have not led to a reduction in the numbers receiving residential care orders, partly through lack of political will or resources to finance such 'experiments', and partly because no clear criteria has been established whereby those in need of IT can be distinguished from others who have been 'reached too late'. Such decisions are at present based on the discretionary powers of social workers.

Despite their liberal appearance, such community-based

treatment programmes have been criticized because ultimately their main functions appear to be ones of widening the net for potential delinquents and justifying an expansion of social work surveillance and assessment of working-class family socialization. The end result may well be that more and more children are discovered to be 'at risk' and enter the juvenile justice system before they have even committed any offences.

Rather than becoming an instrument with which to reform the juvenile criminal justice system preventive intermediate treatment has effectively allowed correctional agents to penetrate even further into the lives of 'deviant' adolescents.[58]

While these 'new' non-custodial measures remain available to the courts, they have not, as was intended by the 1969 Act, replaced the more punitive measures. Rather, the new has been grafted on to its predecessor. The range of intervention and surveillance has thus been extended, widening the potential market for the courts, and offering no threat to the established system. Thus Thorpe has argued that IT should only be used as a specific alternative to custody and necessitates a reduction in the number of custodial places available. The development of intermediate treatment is presumed to owe much to the growth in influence of welfare state programmes and ideology in the 1960s. It is based on the assumption that young offenders are not fully responsible for their actions. The primary objective remains to produce conformity to the social order by 'treating' with 'more humane means' the individual or social pathology of the offender.[59]

One of the most detailed examinations of this treatment ethic was made by Lerman in California. He analysed two projects set up by the Californian Youth Authority in the 1960s – the Community Treatment Project and the Probation Subsidy Project.[60] While both projects were designed to reduce the use of institutionalization, Lerman found that there was no evidence to suggest that juveniles released into the community, on either of the projects studied, actually spent more time in non-institutional treatment than those sent into institutions and released on parole. Rather, he suggested that the creation of new 'diversionary' measures expanded the number of offenders subject to forms of surveillance and detention. This resulted not just from courtroom decisions but from an increased willingness on the part of social workers to use their discretionary power to intervene on the offenders' behalf. Moreover the development of 'treatment' practices in California resulted in a considerable decline in the legal protection afforded to the young offender. By strengthening the discretionary powers of social workers, decisions over a juvenile's future were taken without regard to the due process of the law or the juvenile's own constitutional rights.

The 'treatment' focus of the 1969 Act has also come under increasing criticism. Both Morris *et al.* and Taylor *et al.* have remarked that the treatment philosophy and the individual pathology model of the causes of delinquency have acted as justifications for the exercising of greater coercive intervention in the lives of 'delinquent' children and their families.[61] They argue that investigation of social background is an imposition and that social work discretion not only preserves explanations of individual pathology, but also undermines the juvenile's right to natural justice. On the experience of the 1970s, in which more children were incarcerated than ever before, they argue that children's rights would be better upheld by returning to principles of eighteenth-century liberal criminal justice. Thus while it may be seen as politically repressive to advocate a return to the 'rule of law' (as in a law and order society) it is equally possible to raise the issue of the rule of law as a progressive demand.

Under English law the child enjoys very few of the rights taken for granted by adults under the principles of natural justice. The law's reference to the child's 'best interests' reflects the benevolent paternalism of its approach. Essentially as far as the courts are concerned, the 'best interests' principle empowers social workers, psychologists, psychiatrists and others to define on the basis of their opinions what is good for the child . . . (the law) does not require that the experts should substantiate their opinions or prove to the court that any course of action they propose will be more effective in promoting the best interests of the child than those taken by the parent or by the child acting on his own behalf . . . a child may find that his/her arguments against being committed to care are perceived as evidence of their need for treatment as a sign, for example, that they have 'authority problems'.[62]

In some respects such an argument marks a return to eighteenth-century principles of viewing the juvenile as a young adult. The approach is complemented by proposals for law reform which would decriminalize such juvenile crimes as drink and drugs offences, and homosexual or heterosexual behaviour under the age of consent, and remove the force of law from such misdemeanours as running away from home and truancy.

Such arguments are, however, by no means unproblematic, for the concept of 'juvenile responsibility for law breaking' is also ideologically effective in general reactionary arguments for increasing order and control. If the concept were to be adopted without the necessary instances of decriminalization, then places of secure accommodation for youth would, arguably, be even more expanded. It remains indicative, however, that a majority of children placed in community homes since 1969 have committed no offence whatsoever, but are present in them as a result of the belief that they would suffer from neglect if they remained in their own home.[63] At present both the treatment and punishment options ultimately reach the same conclusion, as can be seen by the increasing numbers of juveniles incarcerated in institutions.

Intermediate treatment thus reflects the continuing contradictions of a justice system for juveniles which oscillates between welfare and punishment. What appears as one of the few 'humanitarian' elements of the system can in practice be a more insidious form of control. As Thorpe *et al.* remarked:

> Rather than arguing about the relative merits of 'justice' and 'welfare' we ought perhaps to take a step backwards and survey the framework which effectively supports them both. The beads may be of different colours and situated at opposite ends. But they are on the same thread.[64]

Indeed the debate over the proportionate role of law and welfare is limited because both are contained with a system devoted to discovering the most legitimate and effective way in which to *control* juvenile behaviour. Concentrating inquiry solely on the operation of justice systems for juveniles tends to neglect the 'real nature and loci of domination – that which is expressed in the norms, techniques and strategies operating throughout the social body'.[65] Thus a comprehensive analysis of how kids get into trouble, and what to do with them when they do, should also understand how forms of regulation and control have been extended in the post-war years to include a multiplicity of institutional sites – family, school, training programmes, social work, probation, juvenile courts and the various forms of secure accommodation.

Approaching the question of 'youth as a social problem' from such a socio-political viewpoint does indeed raise the crucial question of whether 'justice' for juveniles can ever be achieved, while principles of social justice and egalitarianism remain peripheral to social relations elsewhere in the social structure.

Suggested reading

A number of 'critical' socio-legal and social policy studies have recently been made of the contemporary juvenile justice system. Parker *et al.* (1981) compare the operation of two juvenile courts and offer a qualitative analysis of juveniles' perceptions of the judicial process. Taylor *et al.* (1979) provide a critical overview of the way young people are treated in institutions. Morris *et al.* (1980) and Thorpe *et al.* (1980) complement this with a critique of treatment methods in general and intermediate treatment in particular. Pitts (1982) traces developments in post-war juvenile justice and provides an important social and political background to current debates.

Conclusion:
youth in the 1980s

The young have consistently been identified in the post-war years as a major social problem. Many of these fears have clustered around the image of a 'vicious young criminal' or 'hooligan' intent on 'meaningless' violence, who has made the streets unsafe for 'law abiding citizens'. Such notions are repeatedly employed by the media, and as we have seen the state has responded by adopting an increasingly punitive attitude to young offenders.

British youth research since the 1950s has, however, come to question the legitimacy of this dominant model of delinquency definition and government reaction. The critique of 'youth as a social problem' has come from many quarters. From each there are lessons to be learned with implications for the future direction of both social policy and delinquency research.

We began our review of these youth studies with the media. Here we found a general tendency for the sensational and unusual to be exaggerated to the detriment of the ordinary and everyday behaviour of young people. Public knowledge about youth misbehaviour is contained within the parameters of a debate concerned more with discovering what is 'wrong' with young people, rather than interrogating the multitude of ways in which youthful behaviour is already constrained and circumscribed. In the terms of 'news values' and 'newsworthiness', the 'unusual' and 'exaggerated' seem automatically to focus on crime. Crime is repeatedly a source of news; the bread and butter of popular journalism.

Following on from this we could rightly expect the 'unusual' to become normalized. But not so. Rather the 'unusual' is consistently taken as a cause for concern; the higher the reportage, the greater the intensity of such concern. The media then, unwittingly or no, have an inbuilt tendency to raise the level of public anxiety about youth into quite unwarranted degrees of fear and panic about criminality. The 'trouble with kids today' is characteristically viewed as a problem *of* youth, rather than as a series of problems created *for* youth. This partiality is further reflected in the almost commonplace argument that whenever young people are arrested and convicted of crime, then this is a general sign that their behaviour is becoming progressively more unruly, dangerous and uncontrollable. Consequently, as youth violence is perceived to be reaching 'epidemic proportions'; then stronger measures of crime control become all the more 'justified'.

By contrast socio-historical research has revealed how such panics about youth are by no means unprecedented. British history is replete with recurring incidents of youth disorder and accompanying fears about their future. Indeed, this was officially recognized in a number of commissions of inquiry in the early nineteenth century, and surfaces again most prominently in the fears surrounding adolescence at the turn of this century. Such explorations of the past reveal how the very categories employed to describe young people – child, delinquent, adolescent, teenager, young offender – are social constructions which clearly demarcate (and in the same process problematize) a particular period in one's life. The early theoretical formulations of this 'problem' tended to be largely deterministic. That is, they denied rationality to youthful behaviour and explained criminality as an inevitable feature of the moral bankruptcy of working-class socialization. The post-war wedding of sociology to criminology has, however, considerably widened the frames of reference to understanding the twin concepts of youth and crime. Rather than viewing crime as pathological, a cluster of studies reported that crime was ubiquitous. Moreover, certain patterns of crime were considered as quite natural and normal when viewed in the context of a society based on inequality and class difference.

Sociological research of delinquency in Britain has maintained that the 'crimes' of the young are overwhelmingly trivial and undeserving of so much censorious attention. In the 1960s, a 'labelling' perspective emerged in which it could be argued that the problem of youth was only a problem created by law enforcement agencies in an overreactive drive to establish their own sense of social order. Essentially, the kids were seen as being alright. Within new deviancy theory, the 'crimes' of young people were seen to derive not from an innate criminality or moral impoverishment, but from their attempts to overcome their own sense of powerlessness. This line of reasoning was eventually able to propose that deviance is politically, rather than criminally, inspired. Here the kids were viewed as being proto-political actors. Such theoretical premises were most notably employed in various examinations of post-war youth subcultures. In contrast to official pronouncements, British subcultural theory was more inclined to view subcultural criminality as an element of resistance to parent and dominant cultures. The 'hooligan' was viewed more as a 'hero'; the nonconformist as a political rebel. The strength of such theory indeed lay in its reconstruction of the 'deviants'' own understanding and definition of their actions and situations so that 'meaning' and 'authenticity' could be granted to their behaviour. This stood – and continues to stand – in marked contrast to the dominant social characterization of such behaviour as 'mindless' and 'meaningless'.

New deviancy theory was, however, not without its own problems. Whilst rationalizing criminality and deviancy, new deviancy theorists provided a non-judgemental analysis of youth's behaviour which seemed particularly inappropriate in assessing the more extreme forms of violence and its effect on victims. This problem was more acute when youth violence was celebrated as a primitive form of political warfare. New deviancy theory appeared to be offering unconditional justifications for youthful behaviour even when that behaviour might have serious consequences for 'vulnerable' individuals and communities. For example, British subcultural theory tended to omit from its analysis any considera-tion of the social consequences of sexism and racism which characterized many forms of subcultural action. The analysis of youth violence as either illusory or purposeful may solve the problem of merely condemning youth as pathological, but it does not exhaust the problems. Rather it clears the ground, but only for new problems to be raised. Instead of maintaining that youth is not a problem, contemporary research has begun to argue that the problem with youth should be differently phrased. Thus schooling, experiences of the labour market and restrictions on leisure activities can, quite legitimately, now be seen as part of the 'problem'. The question of violence can be approached in much the same way too. As the most disturbing incidents of violence are perpetrated mainly by males, then the impact of sexually specific forms of socialization needs also to be considered when trying to understand why youthful behaviour takes its present forms. The aim of trying to develop a full social theory of delinquency has not been aided by the fact that, with few exceptions, every research project has concentrated solely on boys' behaviour and has barely acknowledged the existence of girls or the significance of male/female interrelationships. For instance, a reluctance to view girl delinquency as equally politically inspired underlines the point that to date the sociology of delinquency informs us only of male delinquency – and white, working-class, male delinquency at that.

New deviancy theory has, however, remained alive to interrogating the interrelationships of age and class, and their significance in ordering the lives of young people. For a majority of young people, their interaction with adults exists within the parameters of a legally condoned control. Police, parents, teachers and social workers are all legally required to exercise control over youth. The forms in which this control becomes manifested have received extensive criticism from various socio-legal and social policy studies. They conclude that many of the problems surrounding youth are created by inappropriate forms of reaction. Increased police resources are only likely to bring more trivial and hidden indiscretions to light. Increased professional services are not likely to 'reform' the delinquent. The juvenile justice system has clearly proved to be ineffective in correcting, deterring or preventing delinquency. However, despite these conclusions, when young people refuse to adhere to these forms, this is generally taken as evidence that they require *more*, rather than less, control.

There has now emerged a major disjuncture between this growing body of theoretical, ethnographic and policy research, and contemporary government responses to the 'problem'. The state, it seems, refuses to allow youth responsibility for itself or autonomy in determining its own future. Young people are characteristically viewed as being less than fully developed individuals, and dependent both on the family and on the state. When this status of dependency is questioned or rejected by young people then youth becomes dangerous, not only to itself, but to the very moral fabric and stability of society. Within the terms of such contemporary political law 'n' order ideology, the state 'defends' itself by incarcerating more and more young people. As the 'problem' continues to grow, the reactions of the state become more severe, thus increasing the magnitude of the 'problem'.

The inescapable conclusion of the studies reviewed in this book is that this dominant model of delinquency definition and 'prevention' is not only self-defeating; but that the stability of society would be no more threatened if we did not give youth so much privileged attention.

However, the state remains more inclined to ignore social scientific research than it does 'problem youth'. Present social relations continue to place a high stake on the imposition of authority, discipline and passivity on the young. A reduction of intervention remains a forgotten strategy while the media, police, government and welfare agencies continue to afford youth such critical attention. Similarly intervention, which might sponsor youth autonomy as a desirable response to their situation, is rejected in favour of the continuing stress on supervision and discipline. Part of this problem lies in the concept of 'youth' itself.

Through two centuries of alarmist fears, muddled policies and urgent 'remedies', 'youth' has now become a well-established category in ordering our images of others. The category serves a dominant ideological function of maintaining a period in our lives as either dependent or dangerous and thus in continual need of careful control and guidance. While the concept of youth continues to serve this global function, it is, however, differentially enforced. 'Youth' is an inoperable category unless interrogated by specific sets of class, racial and sexual relations. In fact when the government, media or indeed social science researchers speak of problem youth, they are more usually directing attention to one section of youth – male and working class. It is this section that is believed to be most 'at risk' and deserving of critical attention. For government, the concern is not just one of maintaining social order, but of ensuring a stable social reproduction of future generations of labour power. The control of working-class youth crime and deviance has, in the final analysis, two major rationales of both 'keeping the streets safe' and also 'keeping the factories filled'. These twin concerns have once more placed working-class youth in the centre of controversy in the 1980s.

Faced with an economic situation in which there no longer seems to be any place at work for youth, the debate concerning the 'youth problem' has once more taken a significant shift. No longer are youth a source of envy for their apparent affluence, but feared as a potential source of resistance to a society that has turned its back on them. The official response is to attempt to make young people *more* dependent by introducing work-training schemes which will keep them off the streets for a year after leaving school.

A similar strategy was attempted in 1972 by raising the school leaving age to 16 and only succeeded in making this the peak age for convicted offenders. Coupled with this is an expansion of custodial and punitive measures to deter youth from not conforming to their new found 'status'. To date, sections of youth have responded by organizing strikes against this 'enforced' training and by taking their demonstration on to the streets, albeit in the form of disorganized 'riots'. Similarly, many young people respond to their exclusion from work and the right to determine their own lives by engaging in such deviant behaviours as absenteeism, petty theft, drug usage and challenges to authority. While such behaviour is common among adults, it is all the more visible and detectable among youth because the only available 'space' for their deviance is in the communal areas of the street, football ground or shopping centre. It is to be expected that working-class youth will continue to make up a significant proportion of the annual crime statistics which are repeatedly referred to to justify an escalation in forms of coercive intervention. In turn we can be assured that the crime rate will not come down just because the state has decided to offer youth more lessons in the 'benefit' of a short, sharp shock. This is a vicious circle which at present only shows signs of being tightened.

The dislocation of traditional working-class communities in the course of economic decline, urban redevelopment and inner city decay will ensure a continuation in the relative material impoverishment of working-class life. In the past the young have generated a succession of spectacular subcultural styles to voice their resistance to these processes. The 1980s have above all been characterized by a splintering of these styles and the launching of a romantic and escapist reaction to the realities of economic recession. Both are symptoms of youth's contemporary political disaffection. Disaffection with politics is represented in a general disregarding of the social order. If the 'riots' of black and white youth can be seen as a quasi-socialist form of resistance, then skinhead violence against immigrant communities stands at the reactionary pole of youth 'politics'. Both are the product of a growing contraction of British industrial capitalism in which marginalized youth are among the first to find that they have no useful role to play.

A growing state authoritarianism which fails to recognize the long-term, precarious, economic position of youth and only seems able to respond by escalating the means of youth control and custody, would seem to offer them little hope for their future either.

References

Chapter 1   Media images of youth

1   *Daily Mirror*, 11 February 1982.
2   *Sun*, 2 August 1982.
3   *Guardian*, 13 April 1982.
4   *Daily Express*, 26 June 1982.
5   *Daily Mail*, 7 April 1980.
6   P. Morgan, *Delinquent Fantasies* (Temple-Smith 1978), p. 13.
7   *The Sunday Times*, 29 August 1982.
8   New Society, 'The law 'n' order vote', *New Society* (12 June 1980), p. 220.
9   M. A. Porteous and N. J. Colston, 'How adolescents are reported in the British press', *Journal of Adolescence*, no. 3 (1980), pp. 197–207.
10   ibid., p. 202.
11   ibid., p. 206.
12   *Daily Mirror*, 24 February 1982.
13   *The Sunday Times*, 28 February 1982.
14   *Daily Star*, 24 February 1982.
15   S. Chibnall, *Law and Order News* (Tavistock 1977), p. 77.
16   ibid., p. 78.
17   *Daily Express*, 8 April 1980.
18   S. Hall, 'The determinations of news photographs', in S. Cohen and J. Young (eds.), *The Manufacture of News: Deviance, Social Problems and the Mass Media* (Constable 1973), p. 188.
19   S. Hall, 'The treatment of football hooliganism in the press', in R. Ingham *et al.*, *Football Hooliganism* (Inter-Action Inprint 1978), p. 22.
20   D. Hebdige, *Subculture: the meaning of style* (Methuen 1979), p. 92.
21   *Daily Mirror*, 2 December 1976.
22   S. Hall, 'Culture the media and the ideological effect', in J. Curran, *et al.* (eds.), *Mass Communication and Society* (Edward Arnold 1977), p. 344.
23   S. Hall *et al.*, *Newsmaking and Crime*, Stencilled Occasional Papers (Centre for Contemporary Cultural Studies 1975), p. 9.

24   S. Cohen, *Folk Devils and Moral Panics: the creation of mods and rockers* (Paladin 1973).
25   ibid., p. 108.
26   S. Hall *et al., Newsmaking and Crime*, p. 12.
27   J. Young, 'Mass media, drugs and deviance', in P. Rock and M. McIntosh (eds.), *Deviance and Social Control* (Tavistock 1974), p. 241.
28   *Sunday People*, 21 September 1969, quoted by Young, 'Mass media, drugs and deviance', p. 242.
29   *Daily Mirror*, 29 March 1982.
30   Cohen, *Folk Devils and Moral Panics*.
31   *Daily Telegraph*, quoted by Cohen, *Folk Devils and Moral Panics*, p. 30.
32   *Daily Express*, quoted by Cohen, *Folk Devils and Moral Panics*, p. 30.
33   *Daily Mirror*, quoted by Cohen, *Folk Devils and Moral Panics*, p. 30.
34   L. Wilkins, *Social Deviance* (Tavistock 1964).
35   Young, 'Mass media, drugs and deviance', p. 243.
36   Cohen, *Folk Devils and Moral Panics*, p. 204.
37   S. Hall *et al., Policing the Crisis: Mugging, the State and Law and Order* (Macmillan 1978), pp. 238–306 and pp. 16–17.
38   S. Hall, 'The treatment of football hooliganism in the press', p. 34.
39   G. Pearson, *Hooligan. A History of Respectable Fears* (Macmillan 1983), pp. 3–11.
40   ibid., p. 231.

Chapter 2   Studies in the history and theory of youth

1   E. P. Thompson, *The Making of the English Working Class* (Penguin 1963), pp. 367–8.
2   P. Aries, *Centuries of Childhood* (Jonathan Cape 1962).
3   ibid., p. 47.
4   P. Thane, 'Childhood in history' in M. King (ed.), *Childhood, Welfare and Justice* (Batsford 1981), pp. 10–11.
5   A. Morris and M. McIsaac, *Juvenile Justice?* (Heinemann 1978), p. 1.
6   J. R. Gillis, *Youth and History* (Academic Press 1974), p. 56.
7   I. Pinchbeck and M. Hewitt, *Children in English Society*, 2 (Routledge and Kegan Paul 1973), p. 348.
8   Thompson, *The Making of the English Working Class*, p. 367.
9   ibid., p. 370.
10   Pinchbeck and Hewitt, *Children in English Society*, p. 352.
11   ibid.

12 P. Boss, *Social Policy and the Young Delinquent* (Routledge and Kegan Paul 1967), p. 21.

13 M. May, 'Innocence and experience: the evolution of the concept of juvenile delinquency in the mid-nineteenth century', *Victorian Studies*, 17 no. 1 (1973), p. 10.

14 H. Mayhew, *London Labour and London Poor* (Griffin, Bohn and Co. 1861), pp. 468–79.

15 Gillis, *Youth and History*, pp. 63–4.

16 Pinchbeck and Hewitt, *Children in English Society*, p. 435.

17 May, 'Innocence and experience', p. 12.

18 Report of the Inspectors of Prisons 1843, quoted by May, 'Innocence and Experience', p. 12.

19 A. Platt, *The Child Savers* (University of Chicago 1969), p. 18.

20 M. Carpenter, *Reformatory Schools for the Children of the Perishing and Dangerous Classes and for Juvenile Offenders* (Gilpin 1851).

21 M. Carpenter, *Juvenile Delinquents, their Condition and Treatment* (Cash 1853).

22 Carpenter, *Reformatory Schools*, p. 321.

23 Carpenter, *Juvenile Delinquents*, p. 298.

24 J. Clarke, 'The three R's: repression, rescue and rehabilitation, ideologies of control for working class youth' (unpublished paper, University of Birmingham 1975), p. 7.

25 Mathew Davenport Hill, quoted by May, 'Innocence and experience', p. 7.

26 Quoted by May, 'Innocence and experience', p. 28.

27 Boss, *Social Policy and the Young Delinquent*, pp. 26–7.

28 J. Carlebach, *Caring for Children in Trouble* (Routledge and Kegan Paul 1970), p. 68.

29 May, 'Innocence and experience', p. 29.

30 Clarke, 'The three R's', p. 13.

31 see V. A. C. Gatrell, 'The decline of theft and violence in Victorian England', in V. A. C. Gatrell, B. Lenman and G. Parker (eds.), *Crime and the Law, The Social History of Crime in Western Europe since 1500* (Europa 1980), and J. Stevenson, *Popular Disturbances in England* (Longman 1979).

32 J. R. Gillis, 'The evolution of juvenile delinquency in England 1890–1914' *Past and Present*, no. 67 (May 1975), p. 99.

33 Gillis, *Youth and History*, p. 114.

34 G. S. Hall, *Adolescence: its psychology and its relation to physiology, anthropology, sociology, sex, crime, religion and education*, 1 (New York: Appleton 1904), p. 325.

35 ibid., p. 338.

36 Gillis, 'The evolution of juvenile delinquency', p. 97.

37 M. Blanch, 'Imperialism, nationalism and organised youth', in

J. Clarke, C. Critcher and R. Johnson, *Working Class Culture: Studies in history and theory* (Hutchinson 1979), p. 116.

38   Gillis, 'The evolution of juvenile delinquency', p. 122.

39   Blanch, 'Imperialism', pp. 104–5.

40   Gillis, *Youth and History*, p. 182.

41   A. Morris, *et al.*, *Justice for Children* (Macmillan 1980), p. 21.

42   C. Burt, *The Young Delinquent* (University of London 1925: 4th and revised edition 1945), p. 564.

43   ibid., p. 422.

44   ibid., p. 495.

45   ibid., p. 95.

46   see J. Conger, *Adolescence and Youth* (New York: Harper and Row 1973), pp. 19–27.

47   S. Humphries, 'Steal to survive: the social crime of working class children 1890–1940', *Oral History Journal*, **9**, no. 1, 1981.

48   ibid., p. 24.

49   ibid., p. 31.

50   W. G. Carson and P. Wiles (eds.), *Crime and Delinquency in Britain* (Martin Robertson 1971), p. 48.

51   C. Shaw and H. McKay, *Juvenile Delinquency and Urban Areas* (Chicago: University of Chicago Press 1929).

52   F. M. Thrasher, *The Gang* (University of Chicago Press 1927), p. 20.

53   C. Shaw, *The Jack Roller* (University of Chicago Press 1930), C. Shaw, *The Natural History of a Deviant Career* (University of Chicago Press 1931) and C. Shaw, *Brothers in Crime* (University of Chicago Press 1938).

54   L. Taylor, *Deviance and Society* (Michael Joseph 1971), p. 130.

55   H. Finestone, *Victims of Change: Juvenile Delinquents in American Society* (Connecticut: Greenwood Press 1976), p. 80.

56   A. Cohen, *Delinquent boys: the Culture of the Gang* (Chicago Free Press 1955).

57   R. Cloward and L. Ohlin, *Delinquency and Opportunity: a theory of Delinquent Gangs* (New York: Free Press 1960).

58   ibid., p. 82.

59   R. Merton, 'Social structure and anomie', *American Sociological Review*, **3**, 1938, pp. 672–82.

60   E. Lemert, *Human Deviance, Social Problems and Social Control* (Englewood Cliffs: Prentice-Hall 1967).

61   D. Matza and G. Sykes, 'Juvenile delinquency and subterranean values', *American Sociological Review*, **26**, 1961, pp. 712–19.

62   ibid., p. 717.

63   D. Matza and G. Sykes, 'Techniques of neutralisation: a theory of delinquency', *American Sociological Review*, **22**, 1957.

64   W. Miller, 'Lower class culture as a generating milieu of gang delinquency', *Journal of Social Issues*, **14**, 1958.

65   Finestone, *Victims of Change*, p. 190.
66   H. Becker, *Outsiders: Studies in the sociology of Deviance* (New York: Free Press 1963).
67   E. Sutherland and D. Cressey, *Principles of Criminology*, 8th edition (Philadelphia: Lippincott 1974), first published, 1947.
68   E. Lemert, *Instead of Court* (Washington DC: National Institute of Mental Health 1971).
69   Becker, *Outsiders*, p. 8.

Chapter 3   Youth and crime

1   'New approaches to juvenile crime', *Some Facts about Juvenile Crime*, Briefing Paper, no. 3, 1980, p. 3.
2   Home Office, *Criminal Statistics for England and Wales* (HMSO 1981), p. 85.
3   ibid., p. 84.
4   J. Pitts, 'Policy, delinquency and the practice of youth control 1964–1981', *Youth and Policy*, 1, no. 1, 1982, p. 8.
5   See Chapter 6.
6   R. Rohrer, 'Lost in the myths of crime', *New Statesman*, 22 January 1982, p. 6.
7   ibid., p. 6.
8   L. Radzinowicz, 'The criminal in society', *Journal of the Royal Society of Arts*, no. 112, 1964.
9   see L. Taylor and B. Coles, 'Crime and the fear of Crime', *New Society*, 3 March 1983, p. 338.
10   W. A. Belson, *Juvenile Theft: the Causal Factors* (Harper and Row 1975), pp. 73–122.
11   P. Wiles, 'Criminal statistics and sociological explanations of crime', in W. Carson and P. Wiles, (eds.), *Crime and Delinquency in Britain* (Martin Robertson 1971), p. 174–192.
12   G. Murdock, 'Mass communication and social violence', in P. Marsh and A. Campbell (eds.), *Aggression and Violence* (Blackwell 1982), p. 74.
13   J. B. Mays, *Growing up in the city* (Liverpool University Press 1954).
14   P. Willmott, *Adolescent Boys of East London* (Routledge and Kegan Paul 1966).
15   D. Downes, *The Delinquent Solution* (Routledge and Kegan Paul 1966).
16   H. Parker, *View from the Boys* (David and Charles 1974).
17   Mays, *Growing up in the city*, p. 147.
18   Willmott, *Adolescent Boys*, p. 145.
19   For an analysis of this possible connection see J. Ditton, *Part Time Crime* (Macmillan 1977) and S. Henry, *The Hidden Economy* (Martin Robertson 1978).
20   Willmott, *Adolescent Boys*, p. 142.

21   Downes, *The Delinquent Solution*, p. 259.
22   ibid., p. 134.
23   Parker, *View from the Boys*, p. 160.
24   ibid., p. 194.
25   H. Parker, 'Boys will be men: brief adolescence in a down-town neighbourhood' in G. Mungham and G. Pearson (eds.), *Working Class Youth Culture* (Routledge and Kegan Paul 1976), pp. 44–5.
26   *Sunday Telegraph*, 29 October 1978.
27   *The Sunday Times*, 29 October 1978.
28   S. Cohen, 'Property destruction: motives and meanings', in C. Ward (ed.), *Vandalism* (Architectural Press 1973), p. 23.
29   S. Cohen, 'The politics of vandalism', *New Society*, 12 December 1968, p. 17.
30   R. V. G. Clarke, (ed.), *Tackling Vandalism*, Home Office Research Study, no. 47 (HMSO 1978).
31   ibid., p. 23.
32   T. Marshall, 'Vandalism: the seeds of destruction', *New Society*, 17 June 1976.
33   I. Taylor and P. Walton, 'Hey mister this is what we really do', *Social Work Today*, 2, no. 10, 1971.
34   Cohen, 'Property destruction', pp. 41–51.
35   J. Patrick, *A Glasgow Gang Observed* (Methuen 1973).
36   Cohen, 'Property destruction', p. 48.
37   ibid., p. 48.
38   G. Pearson, 'Vandals in the park', *New Society*, 9 October 1975.
39   Home Office, *Criminal Statistics*, p. 85.
40   C. Ward, 'Vandalism: don't panic', *New Society*, 19 October 1978, p. 140.
41   *Sunday Mirror*, 12 October 1980.
42   *Sunday Mirror*, 23 March 1969.
43   S. Hall, 'The treatment of football hooliganism in the press', in R. Ingham, *et al.*, *Football Hooliganism* (Inter-Action Inprint 1978), p. 28.
44.   G. Whannel, 'Football crowd behaviour and the press', *Media Culture and Society*, 2, no. 4, 1979, p. 332.
45   See Chapter 1.
46   Sports Council/SSRC, *Public disorder and sporting events* (Sports Council 1978), pp. 32–3.
47   I. Taylor, 'Soccer consciousness and soccer hooliganism', in S. Cohen (ed.), *Images of Deviance* (Penguin 1971).
48   D. Matza, *Delinquency and Drift* (New York: Wiley 1964) and see Chapter 2.
49   Taylor, 'Soccer consciousness', pp. 155–6.
50   J. Harrington, *Soccer Hooliganism* (John Wright and Sons 1968).

51   J. Clarke, 'Football and working class fans: tradition and change', in R. Ingham *et al.*, pp. 37–60.

52   ibid., p. 49.

53   E. Dunning, *Soccer: The social origins of the sport and its development as a spectacle and profession* (Sports Council/SSRC 1979), pp. 23–5.

54   P. Marsh, 'Understanding aggro', *New Society*, 3 April 1975; P. Marsh, 'Life and careers on the soccer terraces', in R. Ingham *et al.*, pp. 61–82; P. Marsh, E. Rosser and R. Harré, *The Rules of Disorder* (Routledge and Kegan Paul 1978), and P. Marsh, 'Careers for boys: nutters, hooligans, and hardcases', *New Society*, 13 May 1976.

55   E. Trivizas, 'Offences and offenders in football crowd disorders', *British Journal of Criminology*, **20**, no. 3, 1980, p. 278.

56   Marsh, Rosser and Harré, *The Rules of Disorder*, p. 116.

57   ibid., p. 70.

58   ibid.

59   ibid., p. 64.

60   G. Pearson, 'Does hooliganism make sense?', *Community Care*, 20 August 1975, p. 16.

61   J. Clarke, 'Football hooliganism and the skinheads', Stencilled Occasional Papers (Centre for Contemporary Cultural Studies 1973).

62   See also R. Robins and P. Cohen, *Knuckle Sandwich* (Penguin 1978), pp. 139–41.

63   Harrington, *Soccer Hooliganism*, p. 25.

64   Harrington, ibid., p. 26.

65   P. Murphy and J. Williams, 'Football hooliganism: an illusion of violence' (unpublished paper, University of Leicester 1981).

66   See also P. Harrison, 'Soccer's tribal wars', *New Society*, 5 September 1974.

67   Murphy and Williams, 'Football hooliganism', p. 35.

68   I. Taylor, 'on the sports violence question: soccer hooliganism revisted', in J. Hargreaves (ed.), *Sport, Culture and Ideology* (Routledge and Kegan Paul 1982), p. 188.

69   See Contemporary Affairs Briefing Paper, 'Football and the Fascists' 1, no. 3 (Centre for Contemporary Studies, January 1981).

70   *Daily Mail*, 11 March 1982.

71   *Daily Mirror*, 11 March 1982.

72   *Daily Express*, 11 March 1982.

73   G. Pierce, 'Unleashing an uncritical press', *Guardian*, 15 March 1982, p. 10.

74   See M. Pratt, *Mugging as a social problem* (Routledge and Kegan Paul 1980), p. 163.

75   S. Hall *et al.*, *Policing the Crisis: Mugging, the State and Law and Order* (Macmillan 1978).

76   T. Jefferson *et al.*, 'Mugging and law 'n' order', Stencilled Occasional Paper (Centre for Contemporary Cultural Studies 1975), p. 4.

77   J. Davis, 'The London garotting panic of 1862', in V. A. C. Gatrell, B. Lenman and G. Parker (eds.), *Crime and the Law* (Europa 1980).

78   Hall *et al.*, *Policing the Crisis*, pp. 330–1.

79   S. Hall, 'The Law's out of Order', *Guardian*, 5 January 1980.

80   *Daily Mail*, 3 April 1980.

81   *Daily Mirror*, 3 April 1980.

82   *Daily Express*, 3 April 1980.

83   *Daily Star*, 3 April 1980.

84   *Daily Mirror*, 11 July 1981.

85   *Daily Mail*, 12 July 1981.

86   *The Standard*, 12 July 1981.

87   Kenneth Oxford, quoted in the *Guardian*, 6 July 1981.

88   *Observer*, 12 July 1981.

89   *The Scarman Report* (Penguin 1982), pp. 118–19.

90   *Observer*, 19 April 1981.

91   *The Sunday Times*, 19 April 1981.

92   *New Society*, 16 July 1981.

93   *New Statesman*, 17 July 1981.

94   *Daily Mirror*, 10 July 1981.

95   For a more detailed chronology of the 'riots', see *Race and Class*, **23**, nos. 2/3, pp. 223–32; S. Spencer, 'Chronology 1981', in D. Cowell, T. Jones and J. Young, *Policing the Riots* (Junction 1982); or M. Kettle and L. Hodges, *Uprising* (Pan 1982).

96   C. Sparks, 'A class riot not a race riot', *Socialist Review*, 16 May 1981, p. 7.

97   J. White, 'The summer riots of 1919', *New Society*, 13 August 1981, p. 260.

98   E. P. Thompson, *The Making of the English Working class* (Penguin 1968), p. 531.

99   E. M. Hobsbawn and R. Rudé, *Captain Swing* (Penquin 1973).

100   White, 'The summer riots', p. 261.

101   A similar point is made by G. Pearson, *Hooligan. A History of Respectable Fears* (Macmillan 1983), in his survey of incidents of 'hooliganism' over the past three centuries in Britain.

102   G. Rudé, *The Crowd in History* (New York: Wiley 1967).

103   S. Field and P. Southgate, *Public Disorder*, Home Office Research Study no. 72, (HMSO 1982).

104   P. Rock, 'Rioting', *London Review of Books*, 17–30, September 1981, p. 3.

105   P. Wiles (ed.), *The Sociology of Crime and Delinquency in Britain*, **2** (Martin Robertson 1976), p. 14.

106   J. Muncie and M. Fitzgerald, 'Humanising the deviant', in M. Fitzgerald, G. McLennan and J. Pawson (eds.), *Crime and Society* (Routledge and Kegan Paul 1981), p. 421.
107   S. Cohen, 'The failures of criminology', *The Listener*, 8 November 1973, p. 623.
108   Wiles, *The Sociology of Crime*, p. 25.
109   J. Young, 'Thinking seriously about crime' in Fitzgerald, McLennan and Pawson, *Crime and Society*, pp. 286–7.
110   H. Parker and H. Giller, 'British delinquency research since the sixties', *British Journal of Criminology*, **21**, no. 3 (July 1981), p. 235.
111   S. Hall *et al.*, *Policing the Crisis*, p. 195.
112   ibid., chapters 8 and 9, pp. 218–323.
113   Taylor, 'On the sports violence question', pp. 180–8.

Chapter 4   Youth in revolt

1   G. Lenski, *Power and Privilege* (New York: McGraw Hill 1966), p. 426.
2   M. Abrams, *The Teenage Consumer* (London Press Exchange 1959), p. 10.
3   C. Booker, *The Neophiliacs* (Fontana 1970), p. 33.
4   G. Murdock and R. McCron, 'Youth and class: the career of a confusion', in G. Mungham and G. Pearson, (eds.), *Working Class Youth Culture* (Routledge and Kegan Paul 1976), p. 24.
5   D. Downes, *The Delinquent Solution* (Routledge and Kegan Paul 1966).
6   J. Clarke *et al.*, 'Subcultures, cultures and class', *Working Papers in Cultural Studies*, nos. 7/8 (Summer 1975), pp. 9–74.
7   ibid., p. 11.
8   ibid., p. 38.
9   P. Cohen, 'Subcultural conflict and working class community', *Working Papers in Cultural Studies*, no. 2 (Spring 1972).
10   ibid., p. 10.
11   D. Hebdige, *Subculture: the meaning of style* (Methuen 1979), p. 78.
12   J. Clarke, 'Style', *Working Papers in Cultural Studies*, nos. 7/8 (Summer 1975), pp. 177–9.
13   Hebdige, *Subculture*, p. 18.
14   ibid., pp. 113–17.
15   P. Willis, *Profane Culture* (Routledge and Kegan Paul 1978).
16   P. Corrigan and S. Frith, 'The Politics of Youth Culture', *Working Papers in Cultural Studies*, nos. 7/8 (Summer 1975), p. 237.
17   J. Clarke and T. Jefferson, *The Politics of Popular Culture:*

cultures and subcultures, Stencilled Occasional Papers (Centre for Contemporary Cultural Studies 1973), p. 9.

18   Mungham and Pearson (eds.), p. 4.

19   J. Clarke and T. Jefferson, 'Working class youth cultures', in Mungham and Pearson (eds.), p. 140.

20   See P. Rock and S. Cohen, 'The Teddy boys', in J. Bogdanor and R. Skidelsky (eds.), *The Age of Affluence* (Macmillan 1970).

21   J. Nuttall, *Bomb Culture* (Paladin 1969), p. 21.

22   T. Jefferson, 'Cultural responses of the Teds', *Working Papers in Cultural Studies*, nos. 7/8 (Summer 1975), pp. 81–6.

23   G. Melly, *Revolt into Style* (Penguin 1972), p. 36.

24   Jefferson, 'Cultural responses of the Teds', p. 83.

25   Cohen, 'Subcultural conflict', p. 24.

26   D. Hebdige, 'The meaning of Mod', *Working Papers in Cultural Studies*, nos. 7/8 (Summer 1975), p. 93.

27   ibid., p. 93.

28   S. Cohen, *Folk Devils and Moral Panics* (Paladin 1973), p. 29.

29   P. Barker and A. Little, 'The Margate offenders – a survey', *New Society*, 30 July 1964.

30   Cohen, *Folk Devils and Moral Panics*, p. 36.

31   J. Clarke, 'The skinheads and the magical recovery of community', *Working Papers in Cultural Studies*, nos. 7/8 (Summer 1975), p. 99.

32   G. Pearson, 'Paki-bashing in a north east Lancashire cotton town: a case study and its history', in Mungham and Pearson (eds.), p. 69.

33   P. Marsh, 'Dole Queue Rock', *New Society*, 20 January 1977.

34   T. Kiernan and K. Kiernan, 'Punk: self styled politics', *Youth in Society* (March 1981), p. 17.

35   M. Brake, *The Sociology of Youth Culture and Youth Subcultures* (Routledge and Kegan Paul 1980), p. 81.

36   S. Frith, 'The punk bohemians', *New Society*, 9 March 1978.

37   Hebdige, *Subculture*, p. 26.

38   See I. Walker, 'Skinheads: the cult of trouble', *New Society*, 26 June 1980, and D. Hebdige, 'Skinheads and the search for white working class identity', *New Socialist*, no. 1 (September/October 1981).

39   *The Sunday Times*, 23 March 1980.

40   The *Sun*, 8 April 1980.

41   *Daily Express*, 8 April 1980.

42   *Daily Mirror*, 8 April 1980.

43   *Daily Mail*, 7 April 1980.

44   *Daily Mirror*, 7 April 1980.

45   *Daily Mirror*, 10 April 1980, and *Daily Express*, 8 April 1980.

46   *Daily Express*, 8 April 1980.

47   J. Marr, 'Solvent Abuse', *Youth in Society* (July 1982), pp. 18–19.

48   *Daily Mirror*, 20 February 1982.

49   This situation may soon be changed following increased 'panic' about glue sniffing in England and Wales. In July 1983 a Solvent Abuse Act came into effect in Scotland and marked the first statutory recognition of glue sniffing as a problem which requires specific treatment. The Act made solvent abuse a ground for referring a juvenile to the reporter to the children's panel (the Scottish equivalent of the English juvenile court); see A. Crine, 'Stuck with the law', *Community Care*, 16 June 1983, pp. 13–15.

50   C. Thomas, 'High Society', *Youth in Society* (July 1982), p. 10.

51   *New Society*, 12 March 1981, p. 463.

52   Clarke *et al.*, 'Subcultures', cultures and class', p. 60.

53   F. Parkin, *Middle-Class Radicalism* (Manchester University Press 1968), pp. 158–9.

54   *The Times*, quoted by K. Leech, *Youthquake* (Sheldon 1973), p. 19.

55   Parkin, *Middle-Class Radicalism*, p. 166.

56   Nuttall, *Bomb Culture*, p. 47.

57   R. Neville, *Playpower* (Paladin 1971), p. 19.

58   Brake, *The Sociology of Youth Culture*, p. 106.

59   T. Roszak, *The Making of a Counter-Culture* (New York: Doubleday 1971), p. 267.

60   W. Hinckle, 'The coming of the hippies' in *Ramparts* (eds.), *Conversations with the New Reality* (San Francisco: Canfield 1971), p. 3.

61   See T. Leary, *The Politics of Ecstacy* (Paladin 1970); and T. Wolfe, *The Electric Kool-Aid Acid Test* (Bantam 1969).

62   See T. Palmer, *The Trials of OZ* (Blond and Briggs 1971).

63   D. Benedictus, 'Defeated youth', *The Sunday Times*, 8 June 1975.

64   N. Dorn, 'The conservatism of the cannabis debate', in NDC (eds.), *Permissiveness and Control* (Macmillan 1980), p. 53.

65   *The Times*, 30 August 1974.

66   *Daily Mirror*, 9 March 1978.

67   *The Times*, 9 March 1978.

68   D. Leigh, 'LSD: the real risks', *New Society*, 16 March 1978, p. 606.

69   T. De Quincy, *Confessions of an Opium Eater* (Penguin 1975), p. 73.

70   A. Huxley, *The Doors of Perception* (Penguin 1972).

71   *Daily Express*, 9 March 1978.
72   S. Hall, 'The hippies: an American moment', in J. Nagel (ed.), *Student Power* (Merlin 1969).
73   See H. Marcuse, *One-Dimensional Man* (Abacus 1972); and H. Marcuse, *An Essay on Liberation* (Penguin 1972).
74   A. Hoffman, *Revolution for the Hell of it* (Pocket 1970), p. 46.
75   J. Rubin, *Do It!* (Simon and Schuster 1970), p. 255.
76   *Inside Story*, no. 4, 1972.
77   Angry Brigade Communique in *IT*, no. 106, 1971.
78   see R. Taylor, 'The born-again CND', *New Society*, 10 September 1981.
79   I. Walker, 'The delicious escape', *New Society*, 8 January 1981, p. 42.
80   See Chapter 5.
81   A. Sivanandan, 'Race, class and the state', *Race and Class*, **18** (Spring 1976), p. 357.
82   A. Sivanandan, 'From resistance to rebellion: Asian and Afro-Carribean struggles in Britain', *Race and Class*, **23** (Autumn 1981), p. 140.
83   H. Campbell, 'Rastafari: culture of resistance', *Race and Class*, **22** (1980), p. 6.
84   P. Hebdige, 'Reggae, Rastas and Rudies', *Working Papers in Cultural Studies*, nos 7/8 (Summer 1975), p. 145.
85   J. Brown, *Shades of Grey* (Cranfield: Institute of Technology 1977).
86   E. Cashmore, 'After the Rastas', *New Community*, **19**, no. 2, 1981, p. 177.
87   See Chapter 3.
88   Campbell, *Rastafari*, p. 20.
89   S. Cohen, 'Symbols of Trouble', introduction to second edition of *Folk Devils and Moral Panics* (Martin Robertson 1980), p. xii.
90   Melly, *Revolt into style*, p. 107.
91   ibid., p. 43.
92   Murdock and McCron, 'Youth and class', p. 25.
93   Clarke *et al.*, 'Subcultures, cultures and class', p. 47.
94   P. Willis, *Learning to Labour* (Gower 1980), pp. 12–13.
95   M. J. Warth, 'The story of the acid profiteers', *Village Voice*, **19**, no. 32, 1974.
96   M. Jacques, 'Trends in youth culture: some aspects', *Marxism Today*, **17**, no. 9 (September 1973), p. 277.
97   L. Leamer, *The Paper Revolutionaries* (New York: Simon and Schuster 1972), p. 159.
98   Clarke *et al.*, 'Subcultures, cultures and class', p. 65.

99   Willis, *Profane Culture*, p. 121.
100   J. Young, 'Working class criminology', in I. Taylor, P. Walton and J. Young (eds.), *Critical Criminology* (Routledge and Kegan Paul 1975), p. 89.
101   P. Tickell, 'Mass Culture and Rock', *Socialist Challenge*, 12 October 1978, p. 15.
102   P. Cohen, 'Sore thumb: knuckle sandwich revisted; *Youth in Society* (August 1980), p. 10.
103   G. Murdock and B. Troyna, 'Recruiting racists', *Youth in Society* (November 1981), p. 9.
104   Cited by G. Murdock, 'Mass communication and social violence', in P. Marsh and A. Campbell (eds.), *Aggression and Violence* (Blackwell 1982), p. 78.
105   See, for example, the critique of Pearson's 'Paki-bashing' study by J. Tierney, 'Political deviance: a critical commentary on a case study', *Sociological Review*, 28, no. 4, 1980, pp. 829–48.
106   S. Cohen, 'Symbols of trouble', p. xiv.
107   ibid., p. xvii.
108   See A. Campbell, *Girl Delinquents* (Blackwell 1981).
109   A. McRobbie, 'Settling accounts with subcultures: a feminist critique', *Screen Education*, no. 34 (May 1980), p. 40.
110   A. McRobbie and J. Garber, 'Girls and subcultures', *Working Papers in Cultural Studies*, nos. 7/8 (Summer 1975), p. 212.
111   S. Frith, *The Sociology of Rock* (Constable 1978), p. 64.
112   McRobbie and Garber, p. 213.
113   Brake, *The Sociology of Youth Culture*, p. 144.
114   N. Dorn and N. South, '*Of males and markets: a critical review of "youth culture" Theory*', Research Paper 1, Centre for Occupational and Community Research (Middlesex Polytechnic 1982).

Chapter 5   The practice of youth control 1: regulation and restraint

1   S. Humphries, *Hooligans or Rebels? An Oral History of Working Class Childhood and Youth, 1889–1939* (Blackwell 1981), p. 31.
2   P. Corrigan, *Schooling the Smash Street Kids* (Macmillan 1979), p. 33.
3   See R. Johnson, 'Really useful knowledge', in J. Clarke, C. Critcher and R. Johnson, (eds.), *Working Class Culture* (Hutchinson 1979); and B. Simon, *Studies in the History of Education 1780–1870* (Lawrence and Wishart 1980).
4   P. Corrigan and S. Frith, 'The politics of youth culture', *Working Papers in Cultural Studies*, nos 7/8 (Summer 1975), p. 234.
5   Humphries, *Hooligans or Rebels?*, p. 88.

6   Corrigan, *Schooling the Smash Street Kids*, p. 44.
7   See Chapter 1.
8   Corrigan, *Schooling the Smash Street Kids*, p. 22.
9   ibid., p. 45.
10   ibid., p. 62.
11   P. Willis, *Learning to Labour* (Gower 1980), p. 68.
12   ibid., pp. 12–13.
13   D. Hargreaves, *Social Relations in a Secondary Modern School* (Routledge and Kegan Paul 1967), chapter 8.
14   M. J. Power *et al.*, 'Delinquent Schools', *New Society*, 19 October 1967, pp. 542–3.
15   D. Reynolds, 'When pupils and teachers refuse a truce: the secondary school and the creation of delinquency' in G. Mungham and G. Pearson (eds.), *Working Class Youth Culture* (Routledge and Kegan Paul 1976), pp. 124–38.
16   ibid., p. 133.
17   R. Ling, 'Special units: a new institutional solution to an old administrative problem', *Youth and Policy*, 1, no. 3 (Winter 1983), p. 32.
18   Willis, *Learning to Labour*, pp. 95–6.
19   ibid., p. 100.
20   ibid., p. 177.
21   ibid., p. 178.
22   S. Frith, *The Sociology of Rock* (Constable 1978), pp. 32–3.
23   *Department of Employment Gazette*, May 1982.
24   T. Forester, 'Young and out of work: a political timebomb', *New Society*, 16 July 1981, p. 95.
25   *The Sunday Times*, 5 September 1982.
26   *Guardian*, 12 November 1982.
27   Youthaid, 'Election briefing: youth unemployment', *Youthaid* (May 1983), p. 1.
28   Forester, 'Young and out of work', p. 96.
29   P. Cohen, 'School for Dole', *New Socialist*, no. 3 (January/February 1982), p. 45.
30   D. Morgan, 'Youth call-up: social policy for the young', *Critical Social Policy*, 1, no. 2, 1981, p. 102.
31   C. Short and D. Taylor, 'Unemployment: causes and palliatives', *Youth and Policy*, 1, no. 2 (Autumn 1982), p. 30.
32   Quoted by Morgan, 'Youth call-up', pp. 105–6.
33   ibid., p. 109.
34   L. Rhodes, 'Young people need incomes too', *Youth and Policy*, 1, no. 2 (Autumn 1982), p. 8.
35   Gordon Oakes, quoted by M. Loney, 'Making myths', *Youth in Society*, June 1981, p. 11.

36   Youthaid, *Annual Report*, (Youthaid 1981), p. 2.
37   S. Box and C. Hale, 'Economic crisis and the rising prisoner population in England and Wales', *Crime and Social Justice*, no. 17 (Summer 1982), p. 28.
38   D. Hirsch and J. Yates, 'Discipline or justice', *Youthaid Bulletin*, no. 9 (April 1983), p. 4.
39   J. Fairley, 'The great training robbery', *Marxism Today*, 25, no. 11 (November 1982), p. 30.
40   D. Finn, 'The youth training scheme: a new deal?', *Youth and Policy*, 1, no. 4 (Spring 1983), p. 22.
41   A. Stafford, 'Learning not to Labour', *Capital and Class* (Autumn 1982), p. 77.
42   Corrigan, *Schooling the Smash Street Kids*, p. 121.
43   ibid., p. 133.
44   ibid., p. 139.
45   P. Cohen, 'Policing the working class city', in NDC/CSE, *Capitalism and the Rule of Law* (Hutchinson 1979), p. 128.
46   B. Roberts, 'The debate on SUS', in E. Cashmore and B. Troyna, *Black Youth in Crisis* (Allen and Unwin 1982), p. 103.
47   M. Kettle and L. Hodges, *Uprising* (Pan 1982), p. 92.
48   A. Brogden, 'From SUS to "Stop and Search" ', *Youth in Society* (March 1981), p. 13.
49   Leicester City Council, Youth in the City: Conference Report, 15 January 1983, unpublished.
50   J. Williams, 'Football Hooligans', *Youth in Society* (March 1981), p. 9.
51   J. Young, *The Drugtakers: The social meaning of drug use* (Paladin 1971).
52   O. Gill, *Luke Street: Housing Policy, Conflict and the Creation of the Delinquent Area* (Macmillan 1977).
53   W. Chambliss, *Crime and the Legal Process* (New York: McGraw Hill 1969), p. 84.

Chapter 6   The practice of youth control 2: correction and confinement

1   A. Bottoms, 'On the decriminalisation of the English juvenile courts', in R. Hood (ed.), *Crime, Criminology and Public Policy* (Heinemann 1974), p. 329.
2   D. Thorpe *et al.*, *Out of care: the community support of juvenile offenders* (Allen and Unwin 1980), p. 8.
3   J. Pitts, 'Policy, delinquency and the practice of youth control 1964–1981', *Youth and Policy*, 1, no. 1 (Summer 1982), p. 8.
4   C. Lupton, 'Courting trouble', *New Society*, 19 August 1982, p. 299

5   DHSS, *Offending by Young People: A Survey of Recent Trends* (DHSS 1981).

6   R. Rohrer, 'Lost in the myths of crime', *New Statesman*, 22 January 1982, p. 6.

7   P. Cavadino, 'Young Offenders and the Criminal Justice Bill', *Youth and Policy*, 1, no. 3 (Winter 1983), p. 31.

8   Pitts, 'Policy, delinquency and the practice of youth control', p. 12.

9   P. Priestley, D. Fears and R. Fuller, *Justice for Juveniles: The 1969 CYPA: A case for Reform?* (Routledge and Kegan Paul 1977).

10   H. Parker, M. Casburn and D. Turnbull, *Receiving Juvenile Justice* (Blackwell 1981).

11   J. A. Ditchfield, *Police Cautioning in England and Wales*, Home Office Research Study, no. 37 (HMSO 1976).

12   Priestley, Fears and Fuller, p. 85.

13   Parker, Casburn and Turnbull, p. 244.

14   ibid., p. 135.

15   J. Thorpe, *Social Inquiry Reports: A Survey*, Home Office Research Study, no. 48 (HMSO 1979).

16   W. E. Cavenagh, *The Juvenile Court* (Barry Rose 1976), p. 8.

17   Parker, Casburn and Turnbull, p. 48.

18   Cavenagh, *The Juvenile Court*, p. 18.

19   Parker, Casburn and Turnbull, p. 116; and A. Morris *et al.*, *Justice for Children* (Macmillan 1980), p. 44.

20   A. Morris and H. Giller, 'The juvenile court: the client's perspective', *Criminal Law Review*, April 1977.

21   Rohrer, 'Lost in the myths', p. 7.

22   See R. Tarling, *Sentencing Practices in Magistrates' Courts* Home Office Research Study, no. 56 (HMSO 1979); and M. Fitzgerald and J. Muncie, *System of Justice* (Blackwell 1983), chapter 2.

23   1969 figures taken from P. Cavadino, 'Custody or community care?', *Youth in Society*, no. 31 (1978), p. 15. 1981 figures from Home Office, *Criminal Statistics for England and Wales* (HMSO 1981), pp. 160–1.

24   L. Taylor, R. Lacey and D. Bracken, *In Whose Best Interests?: The unjust treatment of children in courts and institutions* (Cobden Trust/MIND 1979), p. 46.

25   ibid., p. 48.

26   H. Jones, 'The approved school: a theoretical model', in J. B. Mays (ed.), *The Social Treatment of Young Offenders* (Longman 1975), p. 112.

27   N. Tutt, 'Recommitals of juvenile offenders', *British Journal of Criminology*, 16, no. 4, 1976.

28   D. B. Cornish and R. V. G. Clarke, *Residential Treatment and its effects on Delinquency*, Home Office Research Study, no. 32 (HMSO 1976).

29   D. Thorpe, C. Green and D. Smith, *Punishment and Welfare*, Occasional Papers in Social Administration, no. 4 (University of Lancaster 1980).

30   P. Cawson, *Young Offenders in Care* (DHSS 1981).

31   M. Zander, 'What happens to young offenders in care?', *New Society*, 24 July 1975.

32   Taylor, Lacey and Bracken, *In whose best interests?*, pp. 52–4.

33   *Daily Mirror*, 18 February 1981.

34   Cavadino, 'Custody or community care?', p. 15.

35   NACRO Briefing, *Prison, Some Facts and Figures* (NACRO December 1982), p. 2.

36   I. Jack, 'British Youth', *The Sunday Times*, 1 November 1981, p. 73.

37   S. Millham, R. Bullock and R. Hosie, *Locking up Children*, (Saxon House 1978).

38   N. Murray, 'Dispelling the myths about juvenile crime', *Community Care*, 1 April 1982, p. 13.

39   *The Times*, 24 March 1981.

40   Taylor, Lacey and Bracken, *In whose best interests?*, p. 65.

41   Murray, 'Dispelling the myths', p. 13.

42   Taylor, Lacey and Bracken, pp. 67–71.

43   ibid., p. 71.

44   *Hansard*, 20 May 1982, Column 454.

45   NACRO Briefing, *Juveniles in Custody* (NACRO November 1982), p. 1.

46   ibid., p. 2.

47   C. McCreadie, 'Children we lock away', *New Society*, 14 May 1981, p. 264.

48   Children's Legal Centre, *Locked up in care* (The Children's Legal Centre Ltd 1982), p. 3.

49   Millham, Bullock and Hosie, *Locking up children*.

50   P. Cawson and M. Martell, *Children Referred to Closed Units*, DHSS Research Report, no. 5 (HMSO 1979), p. 213.

51   Children's Legal Centre, p. 4.

52   Home Office, *Juvenile offenders and Juveniles in need of care or control* (HMSO 1975), p. 18.

53   NACRO Briefing, *Alternatives to Imprisonment* (NACRO December 1982), p. 2.

54   A. B. Dunlop, *Junior Attendance Centres*, Home Office Research Study, no. 60 (HMSO 1980).

55   Taylor, Lacey and Bracken, *In whose best interests?*, p. 56.

56   D. Thorpe *et al.*, *Out of Care*, p. 104.

57   Cavadino, *Young Offenders*, p. 30.

58   Thorpe, Green and Smith, *Punishment and Welfare*, p. 16.

59   R. Adams *et al.*, *A Measure of Diversion? Case Studies in Intermediate Treatment* (National Youth Bureau 1981), p. 33.

60   P. Lerman, *Community Treatment and Social Control* (Chicago: University Press 1975).
61   Morris *et al.*, *Justice for Children*; and Taylor, Lacey and Bracken, *In whose best interests?*
62   Taylor, Lacey and Bracken, pp. 22–3.
63   ibid., p. 50.
64   Thorpe *et al.*, *Out of Care*, p. 106.
65   R. Hogg, 'Juvenile justice: some aspects of current debates' (University of Sheffield 1981), unpublished, p. 34.

Bibliography

Abrams, M., *The teenage consumer*, London Press Exchange Ltd 1975

Adams, R., Allard, S., Baldwin, J., and Thomas, J., *A Measure of Diversion*, National Youth Bureau 1981

Aries, P., *Centuries of Childhood*, Jonathan Cape 1962

Barker, P. and Little, A., 'The Margate offenders – a survey', *New Society*, 30 July 1964

Becker, H., *Outsiders: Studies in the Sociology of Deviance*, New York: Free Press 1963

Belson, W. A., *Juvenile Theft: The Causal Factors*, Harper and Row 1975

Benedictus, D., 'Defeated youth', *Sunday Times*, 8 June 1975

Blanch, M., 'Imperialism, nationalism and organised youth', in J. Clarke, C. Critcher, and R. Johnson (eds.), *Working Class Culture*, Hutchinson 1979

Booker, C., *The Neophiliacs*, Fontana 1970

Boss, R., *Social Policy and the Young Delinquent*, Routledge and Kegan Paul 1967

Bottomley, A. K., *Criminology in focus*, Martin Robertson 1979

Bottoms, A., 'On the decriminalisation of the English juvenile courts', in R. Hood (ed.), *Crime, Criminology and Public Policy*, Heinemann 1974

Box, S. and Hale, C., 'Economic crisis and the rising prisoner population in England and Wales', *Crime and Social Justice*, no. 17, July 1982

Brake, M., *The sociology of youth culture and youth subcultures*, Routledge and Kegan Paul 1980

Brogden, A., 'From "SUS" to "Stop and Search" ', *Youth in Society*, March 1981

Brown, J., *Shades of Grey*, Cranfield: Institute of Technology 1977

Burt, C., *The Young Delinquent*, University of London Press, 4th edition 1945

Campbell, A., *Girl Delinquents*, Blackwell 1981

Campbell, H., 'Rastafari: culture of resistance', *Race and Class*, **22**, 1980

Carlebach, J., *Caring for Children in Trouble*, Routledge and Kegan Paul 1970

Carpenter, M., *Reformatory Schools for the Children of the Perishing and Dangerous Classes and for Juvenile Offenders*, Gilpin 1851

Carpenter, M., *Juvenile Delinquents, their condition and treatment*, Cash 1853

Carson, W. G. and Wiles, P., (eds.), *Crime and Delinquency in Britain*, Martin Robertson 1971

Cashmore, E., 'After the Rastas', *New Community*, **9**, no. 2, 1980

Cavadino, P., 'Custody or community care?', *Youth in Society*, no. 31, 1978

Cavadino, P., 'Young Offenders and the Criminal Justice Bill', *Youth and Policy*, **1**, no. 3, (Winter 1983)

Cavenagh, W. E., *The Juvenile Court*, Barry Rosé 1976

Cawson, P., *Young Offenders in Care*, DHSS 1981

Cawson, P. and Martell, M., *Children referred to Closed Units*, DHSS, Research Report, no. 5, 1979

Children's Legal Centre, *Locked up in Care*, Children's Legal Centre Ltd 1982

Chambliss, W., *Crime and the Legal Process*, New York: McGraw Hill 1969

Chibnall, S., *Law and Order News*, Tavistock 1977

Clarke, J., *Football Hooliganism and the Skinheads*, Stencilled Paper, University of Birmingham 1973

Clarke, J., *The three Rs: repression, rescue and rehabilitation. Ideologies of control for working class youth*, University of Birmingham, unpublished, 1975

Clarke, J., 'Style', *Working Papers in Cultural Studies*, nos. 7/8, 1975

Clarke, J., 'The skinheads and the magical recovery of community' *Working Papers in Cultural Studies*, nos. 7/8, 1975

Clarke, J., 'Football and working class fans: tradition and change' in R. Ingham *et al.*, *Football Hooliganism: the wider context*, Inter-Action Inprint 1978

Clarke, J., and Jefferson, T., *The politics of popular culture: cultures and subcultures*, Stencilled Paper, University of Birmingham 1973

Clarke, J., Hall, S., Jefferson, T. and Roberts, B., 'Subcultures, cultures and class', *Working Papers in Cultural Studies*, nos. 7/8, 1975

Clarke, J., and Jefferson T., 'Working class youth cultures', in G. Mungham and G. Pearson (eds.), *Working Class Youth Culture*, Routledge and Kegan Paul 1978

Clarke, R. V. G., (ed.), *Tackling Vandalism*, Home Office Research Study, no. 47, HMSO 1978

Cloward, R. and Ohlin, L., *Delinquency and Opportunity: a theory of delinquent gangs*, New York: Free Press 1960

Cohen, A., *Delinquent Boys: the culture of the gang*, Chicago: Free Press 1955

Cohen, P., 'Subcultural conflict and working class community', *Working Papers in Cultural Studies*, no. 2, 1972

Cohen, P., 'Policing the working class city', in NDC/CSE, *Capitalism and the Rule of Law*, Hutchinson 1979

Cohen, P., 'Sore thumb – knuckle sandwich revisited', *Youth in Society*, August 1980

Cohen, P., 'School for Dole', *New Socialist*, Jan/Feb., no. 3, 1982

Cohen, S., 'The politics of vandalism', *New Society*, 12 December 1968

Cohen, S., 'The failures of criminology', *The Listener*, 8 November 1973

Cohen, S., *Folk devils and moral panics: the creation of mods and rockers*, Paladin 1973

Cohen, S., 'Property destruction: motives and meanings', in C. Ward (ed.), *Vandalism*, Architectural Press 1973

Cohen, S., 'Symbols of trouble', Introduction to new edition of *Folk Devils and Moral Panics*, Martin Robertson 1980

Cohen, S. and Young, J., *The Manufacture of News: Deviance, Social Problems and the Mass Media*, Constable 1973

Collinson, M., 'Questions of juvenile justice', in P. Carlen and M. Collinson (eds.), *Radical Issues in Criminology*, Martin Robertson 1980

Conger, J., *Adolescence and Youth*, Harper and Row 1973

Contemporary Affairs Briefing, *Football and the Fascists*, 1, no. 3, Centre for Contemporary Studies 1981

Cornish, D. B. and Clarke, R. V. G., *Residential Treatment and its effects on Delinquency*, Home Office Research Study, no. 32, HMSO 1976

Corrigan, P., *Schooling the Smash Street Kids*, Macmillan 1979

Corrigan, P. and Frith, S., 'The politics of youth culture', *Working Papers in Cultural Studies*, nos. 7/8, 1975

Davis, J., 'The London garotting panic of 1862', in A. Gatrell, B. Lenman and G. Parker (eds.), *Crime and the Law*, Europa 1980

De Quincy, T., *Confessions of an opium eater*, Penguin 1975

DHSS, *Offending by Young People: a survey of recent trends*, DHSS 1981

Ditchfield, J. A., *Police Cautioning in England and Wales*, Home Office Research Study, no. 37, HMSO 1976

Ditton, J., *Part-time Crime*, Macmillan 1977

Dorn, N., 'The conservatism of the cannabis debate', in NDC (eds.) *Permissiveness and Control*, Macmillan 1980

Dorn, N. and South, N., *Of Males and Markets: A critical review of 'Youth Culture' Theory*. Research Paper, Centre for Occupational and Community Research, Middlesex Polytechnic 1982

Downes, D., *The Delinquent Solution*, Routledge and Kegan Paul 1966

Dunlop, A. B., *Junior Attendance Centres*, Home Office Research Study, no. 60, HMSO 1980

Dunning, E., *Soccer: the social origins of the sport and its development as a spectacle and profession*, Sports Council/SSRC 1979

Fairley, J., 'The great training robbery', *Marxism Today*, 25, no. 11, November 1982

Field, S. and Southgate, P., *Public Disorder*, Home Office Research Study, no. 72, HMSO 1982

Finestone, H., *Victims of Change*, Westport, Connecticut: Greenwood 1976

Finn, D., 'The Youth Training Scheme: a new deal?', *Youth and Policy*, 1, no. 4, Spring 1983

Fitzgerald, M. and Muncie, J., *System of Justice*, Blackwell 1983

Forester, T., 'Young and out of work: a political timebomb', *New Society*, 16 July 1981

Frith, S., 'The punk bohemians', *New Society*, 9 March 1978 no. 805

Frith, S., *The Sociology of Rock*, Constable 1978

Frith S., 'Youth in the eighties: a disposessed generation', *Marxism Today*, November 1981

Frith, S., *Sound effects: Youth, leisure and the politics of rock 'n' roll*, Constable 1983

Gill, O., *Luke Street: Housing Policy, Conflict and the Creation of the Delinquent Area*, Macmillan 1977

Gillis, J. R., *Youth and History*, Academic Press 1974

Gillis, J. R., 'The evolution of juvenile delinquency in England 1890–1914', *Past and Present*, no. 67, 1975

Hall, G. S., *Adolescence: Its psychology and its relations to physiology, anthropology, sociology, sex, crime, religion, and education*, 1, New York: Appleton 1904

Hall, S., 'The hippies: an American moment', in J. Nagel (ed.), *Student Power*, Merlin 1969

Hall, S., 'The determinations of news photographs', in S. Cohen and J. Young, *The Manufacture of News*, Constable 1973

Hall, S., 'Culture, the media and the "Ideological Effect" ' in J. Curran, M. Gurevitch and J. Woolacott (eds.), *Mass Communication and Society*, Arnold 1977

Hall, S., 'The treatment of football hooliganism in the press' in R. Ingham, S. Hall, J. Clarke, P. Marsh and J. Donovan, *Football Hooliganism*, Inter-Action Inprint 1978

Hall, S., *Drifting into a Law and Order Society*, Cobden Trust 1979

Hall, S., 'The Law's out of order', *Guardian*, 5 January 1980

Hall, S. and Jefferson, T., *Resistance through Rituals*, Hutchinson 1976

Hall, S., Clarke, J., Critcher, C., Jefferson, T. and Roberts, B., *Newsmaking and Crime*, Stencilled Paper, University of Birmingham 1975

Hall, S., Critcher, C., Jefferson, T., Clarke J. and Roberts, B., *Policing the Crisis, Mugging, the State, and Law and Order*, Macmillan 1978

Hall, S. and Scraton, P., 'Law, class and control', in M. Fitzgerald, G. McLennan and J. Pawson (eds.), *Crime and Society*, Routledge and Kegan Paul/Open University 1981

Hargreaves, D., *Social Relations in a Secondary Modern School*, Routledge and Kegan Paul 1967

Harrington, J., *Soccer Hooliganism*, John Wright and Sons 1968

Harrison, P., 'Soccer's tribal wars', *New Society*, 5 September 1974

Heathcote, F., 'Social disorganisation theories', in M. Fitzgerald, G. McLennan and J. Pawson, *Crime and Society*, Routledge and Kegan Paul/Open University 1981

Hebdige, D., 'Reggae, Rastas and Rudies', *Working Papers in Cultural Studies*, nos. 7/8, 1975

Hebdige, D., 'The meaning of Mod', *Working Papers in Cultural Studies*, nos. 7/8, 1975

Hebdige, D., *Subculture: the meaning of style*, Methuen 1979

Hebdige, D., 'Skinheads and the search for white working class identity', *New Socialist*, no. 1, September/October 1981

Henry, S., *The Hidden Economy*, Martin Robertson 1978

Hinckle, W., 'The coming of the hippies', in *Ramparts* (eds.), *Conversations with the New Reality*, San Francisco: Canfield 1971

Hoffman, A., *Revolution for the hell of it*, Pocket 1970

Hogg, R., 'Juvenile Justice: Some Aspects of Current Debates', University of Sheffield 1981, unpublished

Home Office, *Juvenile Offenders and Juveniles in need of care or control*, HMSO 1975

Home Office, *Criminal Statistics for England and Wales*, HMSO 1981

Howard League Working Party, *Unruly children in a human context*, Barry Rose 1977

Humphries, S., 'Steal to survive: the social crime of working class children, 1890–1940', *Oral History Journal*, 9, no. 1, 1981

Humphries, S., *Hooligans or Rebels? An oral history of working class childhood and youth 1889–1939*, Blackwell 1981

Huxley, A., *The Doors of Perception*, Penguin 1972

Ingham, R., Hall, S., Clarke, J., Marsh, P. and Donovan, J., *Football Hooliganism: the wider context*, Inter-Action Inprint 1978

Jack, I., 'British Youth', *Sunday Times*, 1 November 1981

Jacques, M., 'Trends in youth culture: some aspects', *Marxism Today*, September 1973

Jefferson, T., 'Cultural responses of the Teds', *Working Papers in Cultural Studies*, nos 7/8, 1975

Jefferson, T., Critcher, C., Hall, S., Roberts, B. and Clarke, J., 'Mugging and Law 'n' Order', Stencilled Paper, University of Birmingham 1975

Johnson, R., 'Really Useful Knowledge', in J. Clarke, C. Critcher and R. Johnson (eds.), *Working Class Culture*, Hutchinson 1979

Jones, H., 'The approved school: a theoretical model', in J. B. Mays (ed.), *The Social Treatment of Young Offenders*, Longman 1975

Kettle, M. and Hodges, L., *Uprising*, Pan 1982

Kiernan, T. and Kiernan, K., 'Punk: self styled politics', *Youth in Society*, March 1981

Leamer, L., *The Paper Revolutionaries*, Simon and Schuster 1972

Leary, T., *The Politics of Ecstacy*, Paladin 1970

Leech, K., *Youthquake*, Sheldon 1973

Leigh, D., 'LSD: the real risks', *New Society*, 16 March 1978

Lemert, E., *Instead of Court*, National Institute of Mental Health, Washington DC 1971

Lemert, E., *Human deviance, social problems and social control*, Englewood Cliffs: Prentice Hall 1967

Lenski, G., *Power and Privilege*, New York: McGraw Hill 1966

Lerman, P., *Community Treatment and Social Control*, Chicago: University Press 1975

Levenson, H., *Children in Prison*, NCCL Report 1976

Ling, R., 'Special units: a new institutional solution to an old administrative problem', *Youth and Policy*, 1, no. 3, Winter 1983

Loney, M., 'Making myths', *Youth in Society*, June 1981

Loney, M., 'The youth opportunities programme: requiem and rebirth' in R. Fiddy (ed.), *In Place of Work*, Falmer 1983

Lupton, C., 'Courting trouble', *New Society*, 19 August 1982

Marcuse, H., *One dimensional man*, Abacus 1972

Marcuse, H., *An Essay on Liberation*, Penguin 1972

Marr, J., 'Solvent abuse', *Youth in Society*, July 1982

Marsh, P., 'Understanding aggro', *New Society*, 3 April 1975

Marsh, P., 'Dole queue rock', *New Society*, 20 January 1977

Marsh, P., Rosser, E. and Harre, R., *The Rules of Disorder*, Routledge and Kegan Paul 1978

Marshall, R., 'Vandalism: the seeds of destruction', *New Society*, 17 June 1976

Matza, D., *Delinquency and Drift*, New York: John Wiley 1964

Matza, D. and Sykes, G., 'Techniques of neutralisation: a theory of delinquency', *American Sociological Review*, 22, 1957

Matza, D. and Sykes, G., 'Juvenile delinquency and subterranean values', *American Sociological Review*, 26, 1961

Mays, J. B., *Growing up in the City*, Liverpool University Press 1954

May, M., 'Innocence and experience: the evolution of the concept of juvenile delinquency in the mid-nineteenth century', *Victorian Studies*, 17, no. 1, 1973

Mayhew, H., *London Labour and London Poor*, 1, Griffin Bohn and Co 1861

McCreadie, C., 'Children we lock away', *New Society*, 14 May 1981

McRobbie, A. and Garber, J., 'Girls and subcultures', *Working Papers in Cultural Studies*, nos. 7/8, 1975

McRobbie, A., 'Settling accounts with subcultures: a feminist critique', *Screen Education*, no. 34, 1980

Melly, G., *Revolt into Style*, Penguin 1972

Merton, R., 'Social structure and anomie', *American Sociological Review*, 3, 1938

Miller, W., 'Lower class culture as a generating milieu of gang delinquency', *Journal of Social Issues*, 14, 1958

Millham, S. Bullock, R. and Hosie, R., *Locking up Children*, Saxon House 1978

Morgan, D., 'Youth call-up: social policy for the young', *Critical Social Policy*, 1, no. 2, 1981

Morgan, P., *Delinquent Fantasies*, Temple-Smith 1978

Morris, A. and Giller, H., 'The juvenile court – the client's perspective', *Criminal Law Review*, April 1977

Morris, A. and McIsaac, M., *Juvenile Justice?*, Heinemann 1978

Morris, A., Giller, H., Szwed, E. and Geach, H., *Justice for Children*, Macmillan 1980

Mungham, G. and Pearson, G., (eds.), *Working Class Youth Culture*, Routledge and Kegan Paul 1976

Muncie, J., *Pop culture, pop music and post-war youth*, Units 19/20, Open University Course, U203, Open University 1982

Muncie, J. and Fitzgerald, M., 'Humanising the Deviant', in M. Fitzgerald, G. McLennan and J. Pawson (eds.), *Crime and Society*, Routledge and Kegan Paul/Open University 1981

Murdock, G., 'Mass communication and social violence', in P. Marsh and A. Campbell (eds.), *Aggression and Violence*, Blackwell 1982

Murdock, G. and McCron, R. 'Youth and class: the career of a confusion', in G. Mungham and G. Pearson (eds.), *Working Class Youth Culture*, Routledge and Kegan Paul 1976

Murdock, G. and Troyna, B., 'Recruiting racists', *Youth in Society*, November 1981

Murphy, P. and Williams, J., *Football Hooliganism: An illusion of violence?*, University of Leicester, 1981, unpublished

Murray, N., 'Dispelling the myths about juvenile crime', *Community Care*, 1 April 1982

NACRO Briefing, *Alternatives to Imprisonment*, NACRO, December 1982

NACRO Briefing, *Juveniles in Custody*, NACRO, November 1982

NACRO Briefing, *Prison, some Facts and Figures*, NACRO, December 1982

Neville, R., *Play Power*, Paladin 1971

New Approaches to Juvenile Crime, 'Some facts about Juvenile Crime', Briefing Paper, no. 3, 1980

New Society, 'The law 'n' order vote', *New society*, 12 June 1980

Nuttall, J., *Bomb Culture*, Paladin 1969

Palmer, T., *The Trials of OZ*, Blond and Briggs 1971

Parker, H., *View from the Boys*, David and Charles 1974

Parker, H., 'Boys will be men: brief adolescence in a down-town neighbourhood', in G. Mungham and G. Pearson (eds.), *Working Class Youth Culture*, Routledge and Kegan Paul 1976

Parker, H. and Giller, H., 'British delinquency research since the sixties', *British Journal of Criminology*, **21**, no. 3, July 1981

Parker, H., Casburn, M. and Turnbull, D., *Receiving Juvenile Justice*, Blackwell 1981

Parkin, F., *Middle Class Radicalism*, Manchester University Press 1968

Patrick, J., *A Glasgow Gang Observed*, Methuen 1973

Pearson, G., 'Vandals in the park', *New Society*, 9 October 1975

Pearson, G., 'Does hooliganism make sense?', *Community Care*, 20 August 1975

Pearson, G., *The Deviant Imagination*, Macmillan 1975

Pearson, G., 'Paki-bashing in a North East Lancashire cotton town', in G. Mungham and G. Pearson (eds.), *Working Class Youth Culture*, Routledge and Kegan Paul 1976

Pearson, G., *Hooligan. A History of Respectable Fears*, Macmillan 1983

Pierce, G., 'Unleashing an uncritical press', *Guardian*, 15 March 1982

Pinchbeck, I. and Hewitt, M., *Children in English Society*, 2, Routledge and Kegan Paul 1973

Pitts, J., *Thatcherism and Young Offenders*, Middlesex Polytechnic 1981

Pitts, J., 'Policy, delinquency and the practice of youth control 1964–1981', *Youth and Policy*, 1, 1982

Porteous, M. A. and Colston, N. J., 'How adolescents are reported in the British press', *Journal of Adolescence*, no. 3, 1980

Platt, A., *The Child Savers*, Chicago: University of Chicago Press 1969

Power, M. J., Alderson, M., Philipson, C., Schoenberg, E. and Morris, J., 'Delinquent Schools', *New Society*, 19 October 1967

Pratt, J. D. 'Intermediate treatment and the normalisation crisis', *Howard Journal*, 22, 1983

Pratt, M., *Mugging as a social problem*, Routledge and Kegan Paul 1980

Priestley, P., Fears, D. and Fuller, R., *Justice for Juveniles: The 1969 CYPA: A case for Reform?*, Routledge and Kegan Paul 1977

Race and Class Editorial Committee, 'Notes and Documents', *Race and Class*, 23, nos. 2/3, 1981–2

Radzinowicz, L., 'The criminal in society', *Journal of Royal Society of Arts*, 112, 1964

Rees, T. L. and Atkinson, P., (eds.), *Youth Unemployment and State Intervention*, Routledge and Kegan Paul 1982

Reynolds, D., 'When pupils and teachers refuse a truce: the secondary school and the creation of delinquency', in G. Mungham and G. Pearson (eds.), *Working Class Youth Culture*, Routledge and Kegan Paul 1976

Rhodes, L., 'Young people need incomes too', *Youth and Policy*, 1, no. 2, 1982

Roberts, B. 'The debate on SUS', in E. Cashmore and B. Troyna, *Black Youth in Crisis*, Allen and Unwin 1982

Robins, R. and Cohen, P., *Knuckle Sandwich*, Penguin 1978

Rock, P., 'Rioting', *London Review of Books*, 17–30 September 1981

Rock, P. and Cohen, S., 'The Teddy boys' in V. Bogdanor and R. Skidelsky (eds.), *The age of affluence*, Macmillan 1970

Rohrer, R., 'Lost in the myths of crime', *New Statesman*, 22 January 1982

Roshier, B., 'The selection of crime news by the press', in S. Cohen and J. Young (eds.), *The Manufacture of News*, Constable 1973

Roszak, T., *The Making of a Counterculture*, Doubleday 1971

Rubin, J., *Do it!*, Simon and Schuster 1970

Rudé, G., *The Crowd in History*, New York: Wiley 1967

The Scarman Report, Penguin 1982

Shaw, C. and McKay, H., *Juvenile delinquency and urban areas*, Chicago: University of Chicago Press 1929

Short, C. and Taylor, D., 'Unemployment: causes and palliatives', *Youth and Policy*, 1, no. 2, 1982

Simon, B., *Studies in the History of Education 1780–1870*, Lawrence and Wishart 1960

Sivanandan, A., 'Race, class and the state', *Race and Class*, 18, Spring 1976

Sivanandan, A., 'From resistance to rebellion: Asian and Afro-Carribbean struggles in Britain', *Race and Class*, 23, Autumn 1981

Sparks, C., 'A class riot not a race riot', *Socialist Review*, 16 May 1981

Sports Council/SSRC, *Public disorder and sporting events*, Sports Council 1978

Stafford, A., 'Learning not to Labour', *Capital and Class*, Autumn 1982

Sutherland, E. and Cressey, D., *Principles of Criminology*, 4th edition, Philadelphia: Lippincott 1947

Taylor, I., 'Football mad', in E. Dunning (ed.), *The Sociology of Sport*, Cass 1970

Taylor, I., 'Soccer conciousness and soccer hooliganism', in S. Cohen (ed.), *Images of Deviance*, Penguin 1971

Taylor, I., *Juvenile Justice System*, Unit 22, Open University Course, DE206, 1978

Taylor, I., 'On the sports violence question: soccer hooliganism revisited' in J. Hargreaves (ed.), *Sport, Culture and Ideology*, Routledge and Kegan Paul 1982

Taylor, I. and Walton, P., 'Hey mister this is what we really do', *Social Work Today*, 2, no. 10, 1971

Taylor, L., *Deviance and Society*, Michael Joseph 1971

Taylor, L., Morris, M. and Downes, D., *Signs of Trouble*, BBC 1976

Taylor, L., Lacey, R. and Bracken, D., *In Whose Best Interests?: The unjust treatment of children in courts and institutions*, Cobden Trust/Mind 1979

Taylor, R., 'The born-again CND', *New Society*, 10 September 1981

Thane, P., 'Childhood in History', in M. King (ed.), *Childhood Welfare and Justice*, Batsford 1981

Thomas, C., 'High Society', *Youth in Society*, July 1982

Thompson, E. P., *The Making of the English Working Class*, Penguin 1963

Thorpe, D., Smith, D., Green, C. J. and Paley, J. H., *Out of Care: The Community Support of Juvenile Offenders*, Allen and Unwin 1980

Thorpe, D., Green, C. and Smith, D., *Punishment and Welfare*, Occasional Papers in Social Administration, no. 4, University of Lancaster 1980

Thorpe, J., *Social Enquiry Reports: A Survey*, Home Office Research Study, no. 48, HMSO 1979

Thrasher, F. M., *The Gang*, Chicago: University of Chicago Press 1927

Tickell, P., 'Mass culture and rock', *Socialist Challenge*, 12 October 1978

Tiernay, J., 'Political deviance: a critical commentary on a case study', *Sociological Review*, 28, no. 4, 1980

Trivizas, E., 'Offences and offenders in football crowd disorders', *British Journal of Criminology*, 20, no. 3, 1980

Tutt, N., 'Recommittals of juvenile offenders', *British Journal of Criminology*, 16, no. 4, 1976

Walker, I., 'Skinheads: the cult of trouble', *New Society*, 26 June 1980

Walker, I., 'The delicious escape', *New Society*, 8 January 1981

Walter, J. A., *Sent Away: A study of young offenders in care*, Saxon House 1978

Ward, C., 'Vandalism. Don't panic', *New Society*, 19 October 1978

Warth, M. J., 'The story of the acid profiteers', *Village Voice*, 19, no. 32, 1974

Whannel, G., 'Football crowd behaviour and the press', *Media, Culture and Society*, 2, no. 4, 1979

White, J., 'The summer riots of 1919', *New Society*, 13 August 1981

Wiles, P., 'Criminal statistics and sociological explanations of crime', in W. Carson and P. Wiles (eds.), *Crime and Delinquency in Britain*, Martin Robertson 1971

Wiles, P., (ed.), *The Sociology of Crime and Delinquency in Britain, Vol. 2: The New Criminologies*, Martin Robertson 1976

Wilkins, L., *Social Deviance*, Tavistock 1964

Williams, J., 'Football hooligans', *Youth in Society*, March 1981

Willis, P. E., *Profane Culture*, Routledge and Kegan Paul 1978

Willis, P. E., *Learning to Labour*, Gower 1980

Willmott, P., *Adolescent Boys of East London*, Routledge and Kegan Paul 1966

Wolfe, T., *The Electric Kool-Aid Acid Test*, Bantam 1969

Young, J., *The Drugtakers*, Paladin 1971

Young, J., 'Mass media, drugs and deviance', in P. Rock and M. McIntosh (eds.), *Deviance and Social Control*, Tavistock 1974

Young, J., 'Working class criminology' in I. Taylor, P. Walton and J. Young (eds.), *Critical Criminology*, Routledge and Kegan Paul 1975

Young, J., 'Left idealism, reformism and beyond: from new criminology to Marxism', in NDC/CSE, *Capitalism and the Rule of Law*, Hutchinson 1979

Young, J., 'Thinking seriously about crime' in M. Fitzgerald, G. McLennan and J. Pawson (eds.), *Crime and Society*, Routledge and Kegan Paul/Open University 1981

Young, J. and Critchley, J. B., 'Student drug use', *Drugs and Society*, 2, Part 1, 1972

Zander, M., 'What happens to young offenders in care', *New Society*, 24 July 1975

Index